Indo-US Trade : Recent Scenario

INDO-US TRADE
Recent Scenario

Dr. Bhawna Pandey

PRASHANT PUBLISHING HOUSE
DELHI-110094

Published by :
Prashant Publishing House
C-34, 28 Foota Road, Gali-3,
West Karwal Nagar, Delhi-110094
Phone : 011-22963970, Mob. : 9810396373
e-mail.: prashantpublishinghouse@gmail.com

Indo-US Trade : Recent Scenario

Reserved
First Published 2020

ISBN 978-93-88526-28-9

PRINTED IN INDIA
Published by Mr. R.K. Jha M/s Prashant Publishing House and Published at H.S. Offset House Press, Delhi.

Preface

India continues to emerge as one of the most important markets in the developing world and an important trading partner for the US. The United States and India view one another as important strategic partners to advance common interests regionally and globally. Bilateral trade in goods and services is 2% of US world trade, and has grown in recent years.

India-US bilateral relations today not only encompass the major pillars of our strategic partnership - including security, energy and technology - but have deepened with greater bilateral economic engagement and ever increasing people-to-people contacts. In the last few years, the bilateral relationship also has expanded into a global partnership with greater convergence of views on a number of issues such as international terrorism and shared approach to rules-based order in the Indo-Pacific region.

India US Trade Relations is the significant aspect of the global and strategic partnership existing between the two countries, United States and India. India's export of goods to the US is about $50-billion. Not all products are under GSP and most of the products that top India's exports to US are not under GSP, for example- precious stones (diamonds), jewellery, Motor vehicles, fuel (refined crude), Pharmaceuticals, many apparel products etc. Of the major export products, some chemical products, machinery and parts, automobile parts are covered under GSP and their exports will be impacted.

India and the United States cooperate closely at multilateral organizations, including the United Nations, G-20, Association of Southeast Asian Nations (ASEAN) Regional Forum, International Monetary Fund, World Bank, and World Trade Organization. The United States supports a reformed UN Security Council that includes India as a permanent member. India is an ASEAN dialogue partner, an Organization for Economic Cooperation and Development partner, and an observer to the Organization of American States. India is also a member of the Indian Ocean Rim Association (IORA), at which the United States is a dialogue partner.

India and the US are an odd couple. Even as Prime Minister Narendra Modi and Chinese President Xi Jinping conduct their two-day 'informal summit' in Mamallapuram in Tamil Nadu, and despite the fact that the two democracies can't stop bickering under their breath, they do keep professing their love for each quite loudly.

This is a reference book. All the matter is just compiled and edited in nature, taken from the various sources which are in public domain.

With trade one of the primary calling cards of Donald Trump's presidency so far and his election campaign before that, it should perhaps not be surprising that it is now a bone of contention in the US-India relationship. Yet many observers have been surprised by the speed of the gear shift.

—*Editor*

Contents

1

Introduction

INDIA–US RELATIONS

The foreign policy of the United States is the way in which it interacts with foreign nations and sets standards of interaction for its organizations, corporations and individual citizens. The U.S. is highly influential in the world. The global reach of the United States is backed by a $15 trillion economy, approximately a quarter of global GDP, and a defence budget of $711 billion, which accounts for approximately 43% of global military spending. The U.S. Secretary of State is analogous to the foreign minister of other nations and is the official charged with state-to-state diplomacy, although the president has ultimate authority over foreign policy; that policy includes defining the national interest, as well as the strategies chosen both to safeguard that and to achieve its policy goals. The current Secretary of State is Hillary Clinton.

The officially stated goals of the foreign policy of the United States, as mentioned in the Foreign Policy Agenda of the U.S. Department of State, are "to create a more secure, democratic, and prosperous world for the benefit of the American people and the international community." In addition, the United States House Committee on Foreign Affairs states as some of its jurisdictional goals: "export controls, including nonproliferation of nuclear technology and nuclear hardware; measures to foster commercial intercourse with foreign nations and to safeguard American business abroad; international commodity agreements; international education; and protection of American citizens abroad and expatriation." U.S. foreign policy and foreign aid have been the subject of much debate, praise and criticism both domestically and abroad.

When asked if the WikiLeaks of 2010 would damage American relations with other countries, Secretary of Defence Robert Gates noted that "governments deal with the United States because it's in their interest, not because they like us, not because they trust us, and not because they believe we can keep secrets."

Long considered a "strategic backwater" from Washington's perspective, South Asia has emerged in the 21st century as increasingly vital to core U.S. foreign policy interests. India, the region's dominant actor with more than one billion citizens, is often characterized as a nascent major power and "natural partner" of the United States, one that many analysts view as a potential counterweight to China's growing clout.

Washington and New Delhi have since 2004 been pursuing a "strategic partnership" based on shared values such as democracy, pluralism, and rule of law. Numerous economic, security, and global initiatives, including plans for "full civilian nuclear energy cooperation," are underway. This latter initiative, launched by President Bush in July 2005 and provisionally endorsed by the 109th Congress in 2006 (P.L. 109-401, the "Hyde Act"), would reverse three decades of U.S. nonproliferation policy. It requires, among other steps, a Joint Resolution of Approval by Congress. Also in 2005, the United States and India signed a ten-year defence framework agreement that calls for expanding bilateral security cooperation. Since 2002, the two countries have engaged in numerous and unprecedented combined military exercises. Major U.S. arms sales to India are planned. The influence of a growing and relatively wealthy Indian-American community of more than two million is reflected in Congress's largest countryspecific caucus.

Both leading U.S. presidential candidates express full-throated support for a deepened and expanded U.S.-India partnership. Senator Barak Obama would like to see U.S.-India ties strengthened "across the board," with a particular focus on energy issues. Senator John McCain claims the United States has a "vested interest in India's success" and he calls for improved military and counterterrorism cooperation, along with mutual efforts to strengthen democracy and energy security. Both Senators are explicit supporters of U.S.-India civil nuclear cooperation as proposed by the Bush Administration.

Cold War Era

India played a key role in establishing the Non-Aligned Movement in 1961. Though India pursued close relations with both USA and USSR, it decided not to join any major power bloc and refrained from joining military alliances. India, however began establishing close military relationship with the Soviet Union.

After the Sino-Indian War and the Indo-Pakistani War of 1965, India made considerable changes to its foreign policy. It developed a close relationship with the Soviet Union and started receiving massive military equipment and financial assistance from the USSR. This had an adverse effect on the Indo-USA relationship. The United States saw Pakistan as a counter-weight to pro-Soviet India and started giving the former military assistance. This created an atmosphere of suspicion between India and USA. The USA-India relationship suffered a considerable setback during the Soviet invasion of Afghanistan when India openly supported the Soviet Union.

Relations between India and the United States came to an all-time low during the early 1970s. Despite reports of atrocities in East Pakistan, and being told, most notably in the *Blood telegram*, of genocidal activities being perpetrated by Pakistani forces, U.S. Secretary of State Henry Kissinger and U.S. President Richard Nixon did nothing to discourage then Pakistani President Yahya Khan and the Pakistan Army. Kissinger was particularly concerned about Soviet expansion into South Asia as a result of a treaty of friendship that had recently been signed between India and the Soviet Union, and sought to demonstrate to the People's Republic of China the value of a tacit alliance with the United States. During the Indo-Pakistani War of 1971, Indian Armed Forces, along with the Mukti Bahini, succeeded in liberating East Pakistan which soon declared independence. Richard Nixon, then USA President, feared that an Indian invasion of West Pakistan would mean total Soviet domination of the region, and that it would seriously undermine the global position of the United States and the regional position of America's new tacit ally, China. In order to demonstrate to China the *bona fides* of the United States as an ally, and in direct violation of the USA Congress-imposed sanctions on Pakistan, Nixon sent military supplies to Pakistan, routing them through Jordan and Iran, while also encouraging China to increase its arms supplies to Pakistan.

When Pakistan's defeat in the eastern sector seemed certain, Nixon sent the USS *Enterprise* to the Bay of Bengal, a move deemed by the Indians as a nuclear threat. The *Enterprise* arrived on station on December 11, 1971. On 6 December and 13 December, the Soviet Navy dispatched two groups of ships, armed with nuclear missiles, from Vladivostok; they trailed U.S. Task Force 74 into the Indian Ocean from 18 December 1971 until 7 January 1972. The Soviets also sent a nuclear submarine to ward off the threat posed by USS *Enterprise* in the Indian Ocean.

Though American efforts had no effect in turning the tide of the war, the incident involving USS *Enterprise* is viewed as the trigger for India's subsequent nuclear program. American policy towards the end of the war was dictated primarily by a need to restrict the escalation of war on the western sector to prevent the 'dismemberment' of West Pakistan. Years after the war, many American writers criticized the White House policies during the war as being badly flawed and ill-serving the interests of the United States. India carried out nuclear tests a few years later resulting in sanctions being imposed by United States, further drifting the two countries apart. In recent years, Kissinger came under fire for comments made during the Indo-Pakistan War in which he described Indians as "bastards." Kissinger has since expressed his regret over the comments. Until 1971 nonalignment had a dual effect on United States policies in South Asia. On the one hand, Washington considered Indian economic and political stability necessary to prevent that important regional player from succumbing to communism and Soviet influence; hence the United States gave economic assistance and support to India during its 1962 war with China.

On the other hand, India's nonalignment had led the United States in 1954 to ally itself with Pakistan, which appeared to support Western security interests. The United States-Pakistan alliance was renewed in 1959, with accompanying assurances from President Dwight D. Eisenhower to Nehru that the arms supplied to Pakistan would not be used in any aggressive war. When Pakistan and India went to war in 1965, the United States government refused to support India and suspended military transfers to both countries.

In 1971 the intertwining of the United States-Soviet, Chinese-Soviet, and Indian-Pakistani conflicts dragged India-United States relations to the nadir. That year, while Washington initiated a new relationship with Beijing, New Delhi signed a friendship treaty with Moscow to counteract United States and Chinese influence in South Asia. As the situation in East Pakistan deteriorated, India was unable to convince the United States to cease arms deliveries to Pakistan and persuade Pakistan's leaders to reach a political settlement with East Pakistan's elected representatives. Indira Gandhi's November 1971 visit to Washington failed to alter President Richard M. Nixon's pro-Pakistan stance. When war formally began after Pakistani strikes on Indian airfields in early December 1971, the United States and China voted for a cease-fire in the UN Security Council, but the Soviet Union's veto prevented any resolution from coming into effect. Washington's subsequent deployment of a naval task force to the Bay of Bengal left many in India convinced that the United States was a major security threat.

Relations between India and the United States verged on the antagonistic throughout the 1970s. After Nixon abruptly terminated US$82 million in economic assistance, India closed down a large United States Agency for International Development program. The Indian government also restricted the flow of American scholars and students to India. India's criticisms of United States policies in Vietnam and Cambodia increased, and it upgraded its representation in Hanoi.

When the United States expanded its naval base on the island of Diego Garcia and engaged in naval exercises with Pakistan in the Indian Ocean in 1974, India saw its security further threatened. Both governments, however, attempted to limit the damage to bilateral relations. A 1973 agreement defused a dispute over United States rupee holdings by writing off more than 50 percent of the debt and directing use of the remainder to mutually acceptable programs. In 1974 the Indo-United States Joint Commission was established to insulate bilateral dealings in education and culture, economics, and science and technology from political controversy and to provide mechanisms for regular exchanges at high levels of public life.

Hopes for improved relations were expressed in 1977 when Jimmy Carter became president of the United States and the Janata Party government led by Morarji Desai took over in India. These expectations came to an abrupt end two years later when the Soviet Union invaded Afghanistan. The promulgation of the Carter Doctrine, establishment of the Rapid Deployment Force (later called the United States Central Command) and an Indian Ocean fleet, planned expansion of the naval base at Diego Garcia, and arrangements to supply Pakistan with US$3.2 billion in military and economic aid over five years all appeared as direct United States intervention in the countries of the Persian Gulf and Indian Ocean. These actions fueled instability in the region and, in India's view, threatened India's security.

The personal rapport between Indira Gandhi and United States president Ronald Reagan, established during a series of meetings in the early 1980s, enabled the two countries gradually to begin improving bilateral relations. The Reagan administration reassessed its policy toward India and decided to expand areas of cooperation, particularly in the economic and scientific realms, as a means of counteracting Soviet influence in the region. Washington also regarded New Delhi's status as the major regional power in South Asia in a more favourable light. For her part, Gandhi realized that India was unable to block United States arms sales to Pakistan, but that improved dialogue with the United States could open other areas of interaction that could benefit Indian interests. Indira Gandhi's highly successful 1982 state visit to the United States was followed by a series of high-level exchanges, including the visits of Vice President George Bush and Secretary of State George Shultz to India. In addition, in 1982 the two sides resolved their dispute concerning supplies of fuel and spare parts for the nuclear power plant at Tarapur. In 1984 the United States decided to expand technology transfers to India.

The warming trend in relations between New Delhi and Washington continued with the 1985 and 1987 visits by Prime Minister Rajiv Gandhi to Washington. Furthermore, as the United States appreciation of India's role as a force for stability in South Asia grew, Washington supported New Delhi's moves in Sri Lanka in 1987 and in Maldives in 1988. In the mid-and late 1980s, visits exchanged by the United States secretary of defence and the Indian minister of defence symbolized a modest but growing program of cooperation in military technology and other defence matters. In 1988 Washington and New Delhi finalized an accord to provide United States technology for India's light combat aircraft program and also agreed to transfer technology for the F-5 fighter. Cooperation between India and the United States in a variety of scientific fields followed the signing of a bilateral agreement on scientific and technological exchanges in 1985. Nonmilitary technology transfers also accelerated, and in 1987 India purchased a Cray supercomputer for agricultural research and weather forecasting and accepted stringent United States safeguards to preclude military uses. Furthermore, economic liberalization measures paved the way for increased trade and United States investment in India. In 1988 the improved economic climate resulted in the conclusion of a deal for a Pepsi-Cola plant and the signing of a bilateral tax treaty. In 1989 United States investment in India reached US$1 billion.

In the 1980s, the Indian and United States governments had divergent views on a wide range of international issues, including Afghanistan, Cambodia, the Middle East, and Central America. Serious differences also remained over United States policy toward Pakistan and the issue of nuclear proliferation. India was repeatedly incensed in the 1980s when the United States provided advanced military technology and other assistance to Pakistan. New Delhi also found objectionable Washington's unwillingness to cut off military assistance to Islamabad despite United States concerns about Pakistan's covert nuclear program.

For its part, Washington continued to urge New Delhi to sign the Treaty on the Non-Proliferation of Nuclear Weapons and, after the successful test launch of the Indian Agni intermediate-range ballistic missile in May 1989, called on New Delhi to refrain from developing a ballistic missile capability by adhering to the restrictions of the Missile Technology Control Regime. India rejected these appeals on the grounds that it had a right to develop such technology and that the Treaty on the Non-Proliferation of Nuclear Weapons and the United States-sponsored Missile Technology Control Regime discriminated against nonnuclear states.

Bureaucratic and private-sector resistance to foreign participation in the economy, infrastructure problems, bureaucratic red tape, and legal problems remained formidable obstacles to significant Indian-United States economic cooperation. In the late 1980s, India had differences with the United States over improving its legal protection of intellectual property rights, opening its markets to American service industries, and liberalizing its foreign investment regulations. In April 1991, the Office of the United States Trade Representative placed India on Washington's watch list over intellectual property rights issues. Six months later, the United States gave India a three-month grace period before imposing retaliatory sanctions against India's pharmaceutical industry for inadequate patent protection. India resisted United States pressure to adopt a less protectionist stance in the Uruguay Round of negotiations to renew the General Agreement on Tariffs and Trade (GATT).

In the early 1990s, economic reforms permitted a qualitative breakthrough in relations between India and the United States. Washington was instrumental in speeding a US$1.8 billion IMF credit that New Delhi obtained in January 1991 to deal with a severe external-debt-payments crisis. In 1990 India and the United States signed a double taxation pact designed to facilitate American investment in India, further breaking a thirty-year deadlock in economic relations. The United States provided only modest bilateral economic assistance in the form of food aid but was India's largest trading partner and an important source of investments and technology. In December 1990, the United States approved the export of a second Cray supercomputer for the Indian Institute of Science in Bangalore, Karnataka, although the deal fell through two years later because of India's unwillingness to accept safeguards to prevent the computer's diversion to military uses.

The Soviet withdrawal from Afghanistan in 1989 had led Washington to reassess its relationship with Pakistan, with positive ramifications for New Delhi. Without containment of the Soviet Union as the driving factor behind close Pakistani-United States ties, and concerns mounting about Pakistan's nuclear weapons program, the United States suspended military and economic assistance to that country in October 1990. New Delhi appreciated this action and was relieved in summer 1991 when the United States Congress voted not to include India in the Pressler Amendment, which forbade United States assistance to Pakistan if it violated nuclear nonproliferation criteria. Washington also took a more evenhanded approach to the Kashmir problem in 1990, urging both antagonists to resolve their dispute peacefully under the terms of the Simla Accord. Furthermore, the United States began pressuring Pakistan to end its support for Kashmiri and Punjabi Sikh separatists. This pressure was in addition to efforts initiated in the 1980s to prevent assistance to Sikh terrorists from the Sikh expatriate community in the United States. In the wake of terrorist bombings in Bombay in March 1993—widely believed in India to have been instigated by Pakistanis—and stepped-up activities among Kashmiri militants, Indian politicians and the media reveled in the possibility that the United States might declare Pakistan a practitioner of state-sponsored terrorism. Washington's decision in July 1993 not to declare Pakistan a terrorist-supporting state displeased many prominent Indians, and Indian political analysts accused the United States of having a "double standard" in regard to specific states sponsoring terrorism.

Military cooperation also grew. Exchanges of senior military officials became frequent, a high-level bilateral conference on regional security affairs was held, and Minister of Defence Sharad Pawar journeyed to Washington in April 1992 to discuss arms supplies and military technology. Not only did United States navy ships make occasional ports calls in India, but the two navies conducted their first-ever joint exercise in May 1992. Indian officials came to have a greater appreciation of United States interests in maintaining a military presence on Diego Garcia and in the Persian Gulf.

In 1993, India and the United States appeared committed to improve relations and bilateral cooperation despite differences over India's refusal to sign the Treaty on the Non-Proliferation of Nuclear Weapons and to participate in discussions with the United States, Russia, China, and Pakistan on establishing a South Asian nuclear-free zone.

Nevertheless, Washington directed its efforts to creating a climate of restraint between New Delhi and Islamabad in order to freeze or roll back their nuclear weapons programs. However, India and the United States remained wary of each other's long-term strategy regionally and globally. Some Indian political analysts criticize the United States for following a "two-track policy." On the one hand, Washington has supported New Delhi's economic reform and has facilitated international loans to India, but, on the other, it has relentlessly pursued an agenda to force India's accession to United States nonproliferation goals and has used human rights issues to try to force India to meet Washington's political objections.

Moreover, many Indians have expressed worries that, with the emergence of the United States as the sole superpower, and as the leader of a Western-dominated coalition after the Persian Gulf War, Washington might attempt to impose its own standards for democratic values, human rights, and free markets. India fears that a United States vision of a new world order not only would hurt the interests of Third World countries economically and politically, but also would damage India's drive to become a leading power in a multipolar system. Washington's decision not to place Pakistan on its list of nations that sponsor terrorism and its successful efforts in getting Russia to cancel the sale of cryogenic engines to India are seen as detrimental to good Indian-United States relations.

In the midst of increasing anti-United States political rhetoric and newspaper headlines, Indian and United States officials have seemed to agree on only one thing, that bilateral relations had reached their lowest point in two decades. Observers in both countries believe that the administration of President William Clinton places a low priority on relations with India despite the fact that the United States has become India's prime trade partner. Against this backdrop, Prime Minister Rao visited the United States in May 1994 for an uneventful round of talks with President Clinton, who encouraged India's economic reforms. Six memorandums of understanding were signed with the intent of expanding official contacts, reviewing and updating a 1984 understanding on high-technology transfer, enhancing defence cooperation, stimulating bilateral ties, and establishing a business partnership initiative.

High-level visits to India in early 1995 portended greater stability in India-United States relations. Secretary of Defence William J. Perry visited New Delhi in January to sign a "landmark agreement" on military cooperation that was seen by some local observers as a convergence in India-United States security perceptions after nearly fifty years of divergent viewpoints. Following the Perry visit was a commercial mission led by Secretary of Commerce Ronald H. Brown that also occurred in January. Agreements signed by Indian and United States businesses during the visit resulted in US$7 billion in contracts and investments in the communications, health care, insurance, finance, and automotive sectors. Some of the deals consummated were intended to build the infrastructure needed by foreign firms to do business in India. In March 1995, Hilary Rodham Clinton, the wife of the United States president, toured India as part of an extensive South Asian goodwill tour. In April, Secretary of the Treasury Robert E. Rubin visited New Delhi to sign a bilateral investment protection treaty reflecting the substantial increases in United States investment in India since 1991 and Washington's encouragement to India to apply for Agency for International Development loans.

U.S.-INDIA BILATERAL TRADE AND INVESTMENT

In 2018, India GDP was an estimated $2.7 trillion (current market exchange rates); real GDP was up by an estimated 7.1%; and the population was 1.3 billion. U.S. goods and services trade with India totaled an estimated $142.6 billion in 2018. Exports were $58.7 billion; imports were $83.9 billion. The U.S. goods and services trade deficit with India was $25.2 billion in 2018.

India is currently our 9th largest goods trading partner with $87.9 billion in total (two way) goods trade during 2018. Goods exports totaled $33.5 billion; goods imports totaled $54.3 billion. The U.S. goods trade deficit with India was $20.8 billion in 2018.

Trade in services with India (exports and imports) totaled an estimated $54.8 billion in 2018. Services exports were $25.2 billion; services imports were $29.6 billion. The U.S. services trade deficit with India was $4.4 billion in 2018.

According to the Department of Commerce, U.S. exports of Goods and Services to India supported an estimated 197 thousand jobs in 2015 (latest data available) (82 thousand supported by goods exports and 116 thousand supported by services exports).

Exports

- India was the United States' 12th largest goods export market in 2018.
- U.S. goods exports to India in 2018 were $33.5 billion, up 30.6% ($7.9 billion) from 2017 and up 89.5% from 2008. U.S. exports to India account for 2.0% of overall U.S. exports in 2018.
- The top export categories (2-digit HS) in 2018 were: precious metal and stone (diamonds) ($7.9 billion), mineral fuels ($6.7 billion), aircraft ($2.9 billion), machinery ($2.2 billion), and organic chemicals ($1.6 billion).
- U.S. total exports of agricultural products to India totaled $1.5 billion in 2018. Leading domestic export categories include: tree nuts ($663 million), cotton ($333 million), fresh fruit ($163 million), dairy products ($48 million), and prepared food ($33 million).
- U.S. exports of services to India were an estimated $25.2 billion in 2018, 6.6% ($1.6 billion) more than 2017, and 151% greater than 2008 levels. Leading services exports from the U.S. to India were in the travel, intellectual property (computer software, audio and visual related products), and transport sectors.

Imports

- India was the United States' 10th largest supplier of goods imports in 2018.
- U.S. goods imports from India totaled $54.3 billion in 2018, up 11.9% ($5.8 billion) from 2017, and up 111.4% from

2008. U.S. imports from India account for 2.1% of overall U.S. imports in 2018.

- The top import categories (2-digit HS) in 2018 were: precious metal and stone (diamonds) ($11 billion), pharmaceuticals ($6.3 billion), machinery ($3.3 billion), mineral fuels ($3.2 billion), and vehicles ($2.8 billion).
- U.S. total imports of agricultural products from India totaled $2.7 billion in 2018. Leading categories include: spices ($261 million), rice ($216 million), essential oils ($193 million), processed fruit & vegetables ($141 million), and other vegetable oils ($127 million).
- U.S. imports of services from India were an estimated $29.6 billion in 2018, 4.9% ($1.4 billion) more than 2017, and 134% greater than 2008 levels. Leading services imports from India to the U.S. were in the telecommunications, computer, and information services, research and development, and travel sectors.

Trade Balance

- The U.S. goods trade deficit with India was $20.8 billion in 2018, a 9.0% decrease ($2.1 billion) over 2017.
- The United States has a services trade deficit of an estimated $4.4 billion with India in 2018, down 3.7% from 2017.

Investment

- U.S. foreign direct investment (FDI) in India (stock) was $46.0 billion in 2018, a 3.4% increase from 2017. U.S. direct investment in India is led by professional, scientific, and technical services, manufacturing, and finance and insurance.
- India's FDI in the United States (stock) was $9.6 billion in 2018, down 2.0% from 2017. India's direct investment in the U.S. is led by professional, scientific, and technical services, manufacturing, and depository institutions.
- Sales of services in India by majority U.S.-owned affiliates were $27.0 billion in 2016 (latest data available), while

sales of services in the United States by majority India-owned firms were $17.0 billion.

U.S. Goods and Services Trade with India (in billions of dollars)

	1995	2000	2008	2013	2014	2015	2016	2017	2018
Total	11.2	19.1	66.1	97.3	104.6	109.4	114.4	126.0	142.6
Exports	4.6	6.5	27.7	35.1	36.8	40.0	42.2	49.3	58.7
Imports	6.6	12.6	38.4	62.2	67.8	69.4	72.2	76.8	83.9
Balance	-2.0	-6.1	-10.6	-27.1	-31.0	-29.4	-30.0	-27.5	-25.2

U.S. Goods Trade with India (in billions of dollars)

	1995	2000	2008	2013	2014	2015	2016	2017	2018
Total	9.0	14.4	43.4	63.6	66.9	66.2	67.7	74.2	87.9
Exports	3.3	3.7	17.7	21.8	21.5	21.5	21.6	25.6	33.5
Imports	5.7	10.7	25.7	41.8	45.4	44.8	46.0	48.5	54.3
Balance	-2.4	-7.0	-8.0	-20.0	-23.9	-23.3	-24.4	-22.9	-20.8

U.S. Agricultural Trade with India (in billions of dollars)

	1995	2000	2008	2013	2014	2015	2016	2017	2018
Total	0.7	1.0	2.1	4.4	4.2	3.9	3.4	4.2	4.2
Exports	0.2	0.2	0.5	0.9	1.1	1.2	1.3	1.6	1.5
Imports	0.5	0.8	1.6	3.5	3.2	2.7	2.1	2.6	2.7
Balance	-0.3	-0.6	-1.1	-2.6	-2.1	-1.5	-0.8	-1.0	-1.2

U.S. Manufacturing Trade with India (in billions of dollars)

	1995	2000	2008	2013	2014	2015	2016	2017	2018
Total	NA	13.0	40.3	58.8	61.4	60.5	61.8	65.6	74.8
Exports	NA	3.2	15.8	19.5	18.9	18.5	18.8	21.1	24.5
Imports	NA	9.7	24.5	39.4	42.5	41.9	43.1	44.4	50.1
Balance	NA	-6.5	-8.7	-19.9	-23.6	-23.4	-24.3	-23.3	-25.6

U.S. Services Trade with India (in billions of dollars)

	1995	2000	2008	2013	2014	2015	2016	2017	2018
Total	2.2	4.7	22.7	33.7	37.8	43.2	46.7	51.8	54.8
Exports	1.3	2.8	10.0	13.3	15.3	18.5	20.6	23.6	25.2
Imports	0.9	1.9	12.7	20.4	22.4	24.7	26.2	28.2	29.6
Balance	0.5	0.9	-2.6	-7.1	-7.1	-6.1	-5.6	-4.6	-4.4

Last updated: August 15, 2019

A NEW US-INDIA TRADE DEAL

With exports doing poorly for months and the Indian economy requiring a speedy revival, it is a welcome move that the India-US trade talks have resumed again after a stalemate in September 2019. In September, US President Donald Trump had announced: "I think very soon we'll have a trade deal." This was after talks began between top trade officials of the two countries which later fell through. Again, in November, India's Commerce Minister began talks with his counterpart while visiting the US. There is some hope of a trade deal before the end of the year.

There is much scope for enhancing the bilateral trade, and India can try to persuade the US to revoke the removal of GSP on Indian exports imposed since June. The removal of GSP will cost India dearly as it allows $6.3 billion of goods to enter US duty free.

The India-US trade relations, however, have been gaining momentum over the years, especially in merchandise trade. India has a trade surplus of $31 billion with the US – a bone of contention for President Trump. The bilateral trade in goods and services grew at an average rate of 7.59 per cent from $68.4 billion to $142 billion. The US is India's second biggest trade partner and the bonhomie between President Trump and Prime Minister Modi in Houston indicated that the time was ripe for striking a trade deal between the two countries. Yet, Trump has remained acerbic and unhappy about India's high duties, calling India the "tariff king" specially regarding the high duties on Harley Davidson motorcycles from the US. Trump has been insisting on greater access to Indian markets for its various exports.

According to a report published by the Atlantic Council and India US strategic Partnership Forum by Mark Linscott, a former trade official of the Trump administration, the two countries should be able to manage current challenges and address those that are likely to surface in the future. Otherwise the two countries are at a crossroads, with one direction leading to an initial bilateral agreement, but the other to outright conflict. They need to cultivate trust and achieve confidence building measures as both countries are showing signs of growing protectionism which is only exacerbating tensions.

The new trade deal, however, will have to resolve the sticky points and there seem to be a near solution as Piyush Goyal announced at the US-India Strategic Forum in Washington DC that US Trade Representative Ambassador Robert Lighthizer and he have almost "resolved the broad contours of what was going to be announced." Recently the two parties have come down to discussing duty cuts on 40 goods, including apples, almonds and mobile phones, smart watches and engineering goods.

US specifically has sought duty cut on pulses and has complained to the WTO, along with Australia and Canada, as to why India has banned the import of certain pulses. The US thinks this is because India wants to control fall in prices of its own domestic produce.

US has also demanded unconditional market access for dairy products which India has not been able to grant because of religious and cultural reasons. The US cows are fed with animal feeds or blood meal made of blood from cattle and pigs in order to give them a high protein dietary supplement which increases milk output. This practice is not acceptable to Indians. For protecting religious sensitivities, now dairy is out of India-US talks.

India requires certification that animals have never been fed blood meal. If India provided market access to dairy exports, US exports would rise by $100 million. Yet, it is an avenue which is likely to remain closed. India also wants easier certification for its fruit exports like grapes and pomegranates for better market access to the US market.

The US is insisting on duty cuts on certain US imports like medical devices into India and that India should have no price control on them. The growth in the imports of medical devices from the US has been quite impressive – the US being the main supplier. Imports of such devices rose by 24 per cent to Rs 38, 837 crore in FY 19. The government slashed the prices of medical devices by 85 per cent and capped the trade margins for coronary stents in 2017. This is because the Indian government equated high trade margins to 'illegal profiteering.' It capped the prices of high-end heart stents (small wire mesh structures used to treat blocked arteries) at around $450 compared to $3,000 charged earlier. This was followed up with a round of price controls on knee implants. The government defended its move, saying it had imposed price control to rein in unethical practices and trade distortionary measures in the industry. Many US companies were hit like Boston Scientific, Stryker and Johnson and Johnson.

The government can relent a bit on the price controls, but it is unlikely to give it up entirely because it has been seen to benefit the common person whose extra medical expenses come from his/her own pocket. India has one of the highest Out of Pocket expenditures and patients pay up to 61 per cent of the medical expenses from their own savings, leading many to penury in case of diseases like cancer and heart problems. The National Pharmaceutical Pricing Authority has been pushing for more controls.

On the whole, it seems that the bilateral relationship is at an important juncture. If the deal goes through, it will help to expand India's exports, especially if the GSP withdrawal is revoked. Otherwise, there can be a tit-for-tat retaliatory war like the one US is currently engaged in with China. The US is also an important investor and highest source of FDI ($3.13 billion in 2018-19). If the trade deal is concluded, then an investment deal can follow. India needs to increase employment which only manufacturing can provide and rise in exports is imperative for it.

Both countries have to review their priorities, and the US should not treat India based on the size of its GDP alone. The per capita income of India is one seventeenth of the US's per capita income – and the 'affordability' question is important.

INDIA US TRADE RELATIONS

India US Trade Relations is the significant aspect of the global and strategic partnership existing between the two countries, United States and India. The India US Trade Relations over the years have grown to reach US $ 31.917 billion in 2006.

Features of India US Trade Relations

The premiers of both the nations believe that the cordial India US Trade Relations will have a long lasting and positive influence on the future international system, promoting stability, democracy, prosperity and peace across the world. The significant features of the India US Trade Relations are as follows:

- The Next Steps in Strategic Partnership provides a more transparent U.S. licensing arrangements for Indian imports of sensitive items and technology. This in turn have lead to an enhancement in the high-tech trade between the two countries.
- The India US Trade Relations was further boosted with the conclusion of an Open Skies Agreement between the two nations in the year 2005. This agreement is supposed to increase the air connectivity between the two countries, thereby improving the commercial and trade relations.
- The visits of US Commerce Secretary Gutierrez and USTR Susan Schwab in this year has been a great impetus for the India US Trade Relations highlighting the multilateral issues including those on the Doha Round of Multilateral Trade Negotiations.
- The US-India Agricultural Alliance agreed upon on 2005, between the two countries concentrates on promoting teaching, research, service and commercial linkages. In the following year under the bilateral Knowledge Initiative on Agriculture there was an agreement to link universities, technical institutions and businesses to support agriculture education, joint research and capacity building projects specially in biotechnology.

- Outsourcing of knowledge work to India by the US based companies is a significant feature of the India US Trade Relations as producing goods and services in India makes them cheaper in the US.
- The India US Trade Relations is also characterized by the inter-dependence in terms of financial markets as US institutional investors are increasingly investing in India and on the other hand Indian multinational corporations are going on buying companies in the US and establishing operations in the US.
- Areas like infrastructure, IT, Telecom sector, energy and other knowledge industries such as pharmaceuticals and biotechnology, are the favorite areas for economic cooperation between India and the US. Some of the major multi national corporations of USA doing a profitable business in India are- General Electric, Whirlpool Ford (India), 3M, Tecumseh Products (India) Limited, Pepsi, Proctor and Gamble (India), Microsoft, Intel, and IBM Corporation.

Export from India to US

The main export items from India to US are like precious gems and jewelry, textiles, organic chemicals and engineering goods, IT and agricultural products. In 2006, it is found that the total amount of Indian exports to the US increased by 16.07%.

US Export to India

The main items of US exports to India. are machinery, precious stones and metals, organic chemicals, optical and medical instruments, aircraft and aviation machinery with the total amount increased by 26.31% in 2006.

Impediments in the India-US Trade relations There are some obstacles that have an adverse effect on the India-US Trade relations as US criticizes India for certain reasons like:

- High tariff rates on imports
- High surcharges and taxes on a variety of imports

- Non-tariff barriers on US exports to India

Higher education in US for Indian Students is made a bit easier and convenient by the American institutions who have successfully reached out to international students via scholarships, exchange programs, the Fulbright Program, other grants and loans, and cost-sharing with the government.

Among the most prized institutions for higher Education in US for Indian Students, the University of Southern California is the leading host institution for all international students. Other favorite destinations for Higher Education in US for Indian Students are University of Texas, Arlington, Purdue, and Arizona State University. The most popular fields of study for Higher Education in US for Indian Students are Business Management, Engineering, Mathematics, and Computer Sciences, Physical and Life Sciences, Health care related programs, Intensive English Language programs, and Agriculture.

The United States Educational Foundation in India or the USEFI, is one of the most important institutions which promotes academic and cultural exchanges between India and USA. It has a significant role in developing partnerships between Indian and American institutions, and facilitates the entry and establishment of accredited US schools in India and vice versa.

MAJOR STREAMS OF THOUGHT IN INDIAN FOREIGN POLICY

In the assessment of one former U.S. diplomat and longtime South Asia expert, there are two major schools of thought in India's current foreign policy approach: "21st century Nehruvian" and "great power advocates." The former is notable for its essential continuation of Jawaharlal Nehru's emphasis on developing world unity and an attendant skepticism regarding U.S. power, which, from this view, may require taking action to balance against. The latter, energized by India's rapid economic growth and higher visibility on the world stage, concentrates on New Delhi's triangular relations with Washington and Beijing with an eye toward increasing India's relative power, mainly through economic growth and innovation. Yet both schools share several important basic characteristics, including a view of India as a more-or-less natural regional hegemon; limited attention to global governance issues; a commitment to maintaining India's "strategic autonomy"; and a preference for hedging strategies, be they balancing against a more aggressive China by welcoming a continued major U.S. presence in the region, or by working with China and Russia to preclude an excessively dominant American presence.

In an informal but extensive survey of Indian elite opinion about the United States, this same expert found broad areas of consensus and concluded that Washington has now supplanted Moscow as New Delhi's most important external partner. As is reflected in opinion surveys of the Indian public more broadly, views of the United States, its varied power capabilities, and its continued substantive presence as a player in Asia are widely welcomed by Indian decision makers.

The United States is seen to possess a unique ability to turn innovation into wealth and military power, both coveted by aspiring global powers such as India. America's national will and soft power tend to be admired by Indians, and the leading U.S. role in international institutions may serve as a model for New Delhi. Moreover—40 years after the Nixon Administration was seen to "tilt" toward Pakistan by sending the *USS Enterprise* carrier task force into the Bay of Bengal—American military capabilities and ability to project significant power into the Indian Ocean Region are no longer viewed as threatening to most in New Delhi, where there is a widely held view of the United States as the only viable hedge against the rise of a potentially adversarial or revisionist China.

The above-noted schools of thought correspond closely to what two other senior observers identify as India's "traditional nationalist" and "pragmatist" strains of foreign policy visions. These analysts see policy makers tending to "split the difference" by mouthing traditional nationalist rhetoric while pursuing a largely pragmatic course. While nationalists are inherently opposed to any international alliance that would constrict India's autonomy and tend toward legal-moral rather than political arguments, pragmatists are accepting of a balance of power approach emphasizing a flexible pursuit of Indian national interests over ideological positioning.

One result is that pragmatists are less averse to alliance-making and international treaties. Their rising influence thus opens greater possibilities for closer and more meaningful U.S.-India ties, perhaps especially in the area of nonproliferation (New Delhi's Iran policy has become a bellwether issue of contention between nationalists and pragmatists).

Rivalry and Conflict With Pakistan

Three full-scale wars—in 1947-1948, 1965, and 1971—and a constant state of military preparedness on both sides of their mutual border have marked more than six decades of bitter rivalry between India and its western neighbor, Pakistan. The acrimonious partition of British India into two successor states in 1947 and the unresolved issue of Kashmiri sovereignty have been major sources of tension. Both countries have built large defence establishments at significant cost to economic and social development, and the bilateral conflict has precluded the development of meaningful regional organizations.

A major factor in U.S. interest in South Asia is ongoing tension between India and Pakistan rooted largely in competing territorial claims and in "cross-border terrorism" in both Kashmir and major Indian cities. In the interests of regional stability, the United States strongly endorses a recently revived India-Pakistan peace initiative, and it remains concerned about the potential for India-Pakistan to cause open hostilities between these two nuclear-armed countries. Senior Indian officials continue to press the U.S. government to convince Islamabad to take stronger action against anti-India terrorist groups operating inside Pakistan. The effects of this bilateral conflict are seen to negatively affect U.S.-led efforts to stabilize Afghanistan. Most observers assert that U.S. success in Afghanistan is to a significant degree dependent on improved India-Pakistan relations, the logic being that Pakistan will need to feel more secure vis-à-vis a perceived existential threat on its eastern front in order to shift its attention and military resources more toward the west. Some in Pakistan believe that, by feeding their country's insecurities, the increasingly warm U.S.-India relationship actually foments regional instability. In 2010, Indian decision makers became discomfited by signs that the United States and its allies are preparing to leave Afghanistan in such a way that would provide a central role for Pakistan in mediating between Kabul and Taliban elements, perhaps even to include a role for the latter in Afghanistan's governance. Such an outcome would be anathema to Indian leaders, who wish to limit Islamabad's influence in a post-war Afghanistan. During his 2010 confirmation hearing, the U.S. military commander in Afghanistan (and current Director of Central Intelligence), Gen. David Petraeus, said India "without question" has a legitimate interests in Afghanistan.

Also in 2010, conflict over water resources emerged as another major exacerbating factor in the bilateral relationship. Some in Pakistan accuse India of violating international law, bilateral agreements, and ethical principles of peaceful coexistence through the allegedly illicit manipulation of water flows into Pakistan. Of particular concern for Indian and Western observers has been the fact that some of these complaints are emanating from the leaders of militant Pakistani Islamist groups such as Lashkar-e-Taiba. Pakistan's then-foreign minister said water was "emerging as a very serious source of [bilateral] tension," but a senior Indian official denied that India is in violation of the Indus Waters Treaty and called Pakistani rhetoric a "political gimmick" meant to distract from Islamabad's own poor water management.

The Indian government suspended the bilateral peace process following the late 2008 terrorist attack on Mumbai that was traced to a Pakistan-based terrorist group. In early 2011, New Delhi chose to reengage dialogue with Islamabad despite the fact that many of the alleged planners of that attack have not been brought to justice. A panel of experts of security and terrorism brought together by *India Today* magazine in 2010 outlined ten strategies for India-Pakistan dialogue. Each of the top three involved actions to be taken by Pakistan: (1) firmer and more rapid action the perpetrators of the 11/08 Mumbai attack; (2) extradition of the fugitives most wanted in India; and (3) action against the "terrorist infrastructure" on Pakistani soil. The experts also called for establishment of a regular dialogue between the two countries' intelligence chiefs. These remain among New Delhi's key concerns.

The immense pressures now faced by Islamabad—ongoing and widespread Islamist militancy and extremism, the unprecedented embarrassments of bin Laden's discovery and an attack on a naval base in May, and deteriorating relations with the United States foremost among them—may have the effect of shifting the focus of Pakistan's military decision makers away from conflict with New Delhi. This may in turn open a window of opportunity for India to pursue improved relations with Pakistan.

INDIA AND THE TRUMP ADMINISTRATION'S AGENDA

February 7, 2017: Indians are optimistic about how their bilateral relationship with the United States will fare under the Trump administration. They expect important changes in the U.S. geopolitical outlook. The resulting disruption may bring dangers but also opportunities for India. In assessing its policies for a world of much greater uncertainty, the basic foreign policy goals we wrote about in *India at the High Table* will largely survive, though India, as we anticipated, may need to tweak how it thinks about strategic autonomy. Some aspects of the new administration's approach to the U.S. domestic economy may wind up having an impact on international trade as well - and hence on India.

US-India relations look promising: A recent visit to Delhi found Indians - both official and unofficial - decisively upbeat about the effect of a Trump presidency on bilateral relations with the United States. Most expect that President Trump and Indian prime minister Narendra Modi will quickly develop a strong personal relationship. Both are politicians who beat the odds to become national leaders; both had promised to shake up the political systems in their countries; both like direct and sometimes provocative communications. Especially after a buoyant phone conversation praised in both countries, observers expected the security and economic ties that have built up over the past two decades to carry on.

Trump's strong anti-immigration stance, and word of his dislike for the H-1B visa program that brings many Indian tech workers to the United States, is recognized as a potential problem. It has generated a great deal of excitement, especially as legislation changing the program has been considered once again in the U.S. Congress. A delegation from the Indian tech industry is expected to visit Washington in February to advocate for retaining the program. However, this issue was generally not expected to disrupt the upward trajectory of U.S.-India relations.

The Global Order at an Inflection Point: Trump's campaign said relatively little about foreign policy, but what it did say felt revolutionary. This tone has continued since the election, with Trump publicly calling NATO "obsolete," questioning the viability of the European Union, and threatening trade wars. Observers outside the Indian government expressed uneasiness about unpredictable U.S. behavior which could lead to global uncertainty.

Indian government officials seem to be watching three issues in particular. The first and most important is what will happen to U.S.-China relations. Ideally, India would like the U.S. and China to keep their relations reasonably stable, but not so close as to cut India out of the role it seeks in Asia and on the world stage. China has a big economic relationship with India as well as a profound influence on the security outlook in the Indian Ocean and Southeast Asia – areas critical to Indian security. India's ability to expand its trade and its influence to its East has benefited from the U.S. economic and security profile in Southeast Asia. Now, the watchword is uncertainty.

The second important issue for India is U.S.-Russian relations. Trump's warm words about Putin suggested that U.S.-Russian relations might improve. This would be widely welcomed in India. Finally, Indian officials are closely watching the perennial question of U.S. relations with Pakistan. The effusive reports of a December phone conversation between Trump and Pakistan Prime Minister Nawaz Sharif inevitably left many Indians wondering whether the old U.S.-Pakistan attraction would resume. Those who follow events in the U.S. recognized that Trump and senior figures in his administration are also deeply suspicious of Muslims, and Modi is expected to try to build on this common view. There was remarkably little speculation on whether the U.S. administration was likely to try to broker a Kashmir settlement - an effort we regard as most unlikely, which would be welcomed in Pakistan and rejected in India.

We were particularly impressed with one experienced observer's comments on the strategic implications for India of Trump's global outlook and the nationalist rise in Europe. He noted that the liberal international order that prevailed for the past seventy years might be morphing, perhaps into a Hobbesian "war of all against all." This might not take military form. It could mean that countries that had relied on a predictable set of international relationships might find themselves without support that they could count on. If China's economy went through serious difficulties, this would add a strong element of economic disruption to the geopolitical shifts.

If the basic underpinnings of the world order are shifting for the United States and China, this observer argued, the resulting uncertainty might offer opportunities as well as risks for India. He offered little explanation of what these newly open "doors" might be. Three seemed to us implicit in the rest of his discussion. India might have new opportunities for multilateral leadership. Fluid relations among the United States, China and Russia might offer

India opportunities to use its ties with those three major powers to shape the global balance of power.

More broadly, this observer noted, if the United States is fundamentally reevaluating its approach to the world, perhaps India might need to do the same. Looking back over the seventy years since modern India became independent, three foreign policy drivers have been extraordinarily durable. India has consistently sought to maintain regional preeminence. This is likely to become, if anything, even more important in an era marked by uncertainty, fluid international relationships, and a Chinese powerhouse competing with the United States.

A second driver, the commitment to nonalignment and more recently to its intellectual descendant, "strategic autonomy," could come in for some redefinition in a world of more changeable international relationships. India's greater power is unlikely to relieve it of the need to work with other countries to achieve its goals. What is unclear is how complicated it may be to develop sustained friendships in a more Hobbesian international order, should that materialize.

The Economic Dimension: The third major Indian foreign policy driver, nurturing India's expanding economy as an instrument of national power, only achieved its present prominence in the last quarter century. This objective will, if anything, become even more important in Indian foreign policy if early projections of the emerging international order are correct.

India's economic surge and greater openness to the global economy developed as global trade was expanding. The Indian government remains highly cautious, however, in considering further market opening. Trump's decision to withdraw the United States from the Trans Pacific Partnership (TPP) was greeted with relief in Delhi. India had not joined the TPP talks, which it felt would open the doors faster than its economy and its democratic politics could manage. It feared U.S. pressure to join the TPP, but was uneasy about the impact on its export markets of an agreement that gave competitors like Vietnam preferential access to the US market. The background of President Trump's appointees to senior U.S. government positions, their public statements, and what Trump himself said on the campaign trail, point to a sharp departure from seven decades of U.S. trade policy. India now faces a more inward-looking global economic environment - and a more inward-looking United States, one of its key economic partners. Consider the priorities that top Trump administration officials have articulated so far:

- Export access was the key U.S. objective during most of the world's trade negotiations since 1947; the accent has now shifted to penalizing imports.
- The U.S. objective is job creation - but not just any jobs: Trump and his appointees are focused chiefly on manufacturing, and specifically on heavy industry: steel, aluminum, automobiles. Services and tech jobs are mentioned much less frequently. One doesn't hear much about encouraging innovation, or about small business.
- Local supply is in. Global supply chains are out. The border tax that has been floated would take direct aim at them.
- Multilateral negotiations are out - too diffuse, too complicated. Even "plurilateral" negotiations with a handful of countries are suspect. Bilateral negotiations are in, with a specific transactional focus. Powerful countries often prefer bilateral encounters, which magnify their power differential (this has generally been true of India as well). But a world of bilateral agreements makes trade rules more diverse, and hence makes trade more complicated.
- The administration, and Trump in particular, want to short-circuit the way businesses made decisions during the globalizing years. They want CEOs to decide on the future of their production facilities based on citizenship, not global efficiency.
- Short term action is in. Trump seems to favor coercive negotiations with business leaders, leading to company-

> specific deals. Long term planning is out: remedies involving education and training are not immediate enough. Trade adjustment for displaced U.S. workers is seen as too far off to be a solution.

The Trump Administration is nothing if not impatient, but it may take some months - or more - to get a clear fix on the effect of its changed emphasis. Its top trade priorities are likely to be NAFTA and China. India is large enough to be noticeable in U.S. trade, but not weighty enough to have a decisive influence. It may find some of its export markets under pressure. India's successful auto parts exports could be a case in point, especially if they come from U.S.-owned corporations operating in India.

India is unlikely to get much support in the U.S. government for retaining short term work visas (the H-1B category, for example); finding an alternative business model may be a more viable strategy. Finding an argument that connects trade growth between India and the United States with job growth in both countries will be key to avoiding nasty surprises.

What kind of partnership? India and the United States have been working toward a partnership since 2000, but both have historical baggage which has made it hard to define what that should mean.

As the Trump administration settles in, two basic concepts are in play. One is strategic collaboration resting on some core common interests, including anti-terrorism and similar goals for Asian security.

With India, this would not involve agreement on the full range of either country's interests. The other model is a succession of transactional deals, involving trade and investment, but potentially also more specific security issues. These would be agreements in which both parties know with great specificity what they are offering and receiving. These are not incompatible; ideally, a solid and enduring partnership would draw on both models.

The challenge for President Trump and Prime Minister Modi is to keep their eyes on the strategic ball. This should not rule out more specific deals - far from it.

But India is not yet a big enough player for a trade agreement here and an anti-terrorism cooperation understanding there to carry the rest of their relationship. President Trump has thus far showed much more enthusiasm for specific deals than for broad strategic partnerships. Prime Minister Modi has built his foreign policy success on larger understandings between leaders. A lot is riding on their ability to find a common "sweet spot."

2

U.S.-India Bilateral Trade

BILATERAL TRADE

Rapidly expanding trade and commercial linkages between India and U.S. form an important component of the multi-faceted partnership between the two countries. Total bilateral trade (goods and services) between India and US increased at a CAGR of 15% from $20 BN in the year 2000 to over $132 BN in the year 2015 (Services trade data available only till 2013). In this period, the growth in bilateral trade was accelerated by services trade, which grew at a CAGR of 20%. Goods trade grew at a CAGR of 11% in the same period. Based on the most recent figures, both goods and services contributed almost equally to the total bilateral trade with goods accounting for 49% and services accounting for 51% of the total trade value.

Goods Trade: Starting from a modest $ 14 BN in 2000, the bilateral trade in goods has increased to $66 BN in 2015 (CAGR of 11%), making U.S. our second largest trading partner. Of this, India exported $44.7 BN to US and imported $21.5 BN from US. Trade in goods during Jan-May 2016 was $27.37 billion as compared to $27.97 billion during Jan-May 2015; which is a 2.1% drop in trade.

A PATH FORWARD FOR US-INDIA ECONOMIC TIES

The last few months have witnessed a rising tide of bipartisan support for US-India relations. The Howdy Modi summit in

Houston, featuring President Trump and Prime Minister Modi, was attended by a number of top US lawmakers. House Speaker Nancy Pelosi, in her remarks on Mahatma Gandhi's 150th anniversary, categorised US-India relationship as "a shining example of mutual cooperation, prosperity, and respect." Beyond just optics, these reaffirm a new era of greater strategic and economic convergence.

However, since 2018, the Trump administration has criticised India as a "tariff king", increased duties on 14 per cent of India's exports, and withdrawn India from the Generalised System of Preferences (GSP) programme. India retaliated by slapping tariffs on about 6 per cent of US exports. On the strategic side, too, our "natural alliance" cannot be taken for granted.

At a recent hearing on Capitol Hill, Democratic lawmakers questioned India's democratic credentials. None of these differences is new, but they show the cracks in the relationship and tell us that it cannot claim automatic support – even from the people who have built it.

The US needs a richer and more powerful India to drive economic opportunity for the US private sector across the region. For its part, India needs the US in its fight against terrorism, counter a hegemonic China, and sustaining economic conditions and technology investments for growth.

Areas of convergence

It is time we set a geo-economic direction to the bilateral relationship, with economic cooperation as the bedrock of the relationship. The first step is to build on our areas of economic convergence that can ultimately work in the national interest of both countries.

For instance, US energy exports to India have grown rapidly in the past few years. This helps both to meet India's growing energy demands, and to shrink the US trade deficit with India – a major concern for the Trump administration. The US can support

India's shift towards alternative energy source through exports of natural gas and bio-fuels, and investments in renewable energy technologies. Healthcare also stands to benefit from the US and India collaborating on innovative solutions to patient costs, regulatory, and access issues.

On defence cooperation, the US can help India meet its military modernisation goals. India has the world's fifth largest defence budget, and the US has become India's second largest defence supplier, following Russia. As US companies expand manufacturing operations in India, this should create additional opportunities for US Tier 2 and Tier 3 suppliers, allowing India to grow its manufacturing capacity and reduce trade deficit with the US.

On the other side, US remains one of the top destinations for India's services exports. The US is still supply-constrained when it comes to technology, and India is helping to fix the gap. Indian companies provide world-class IT services to global companies, and are now deeply entrenched in the American ecosystem through local hiring, innovation centres, and facilitating STEM education opportunities for the communities they work in.

Second, it is necessary to set the foundation for growing bilateral trade by securing at least a partial trade deal in the near-term. Remarkably, even without any formal arrangements, US-India trade has been on the upswing. According to a USISPF study, US-India trade is projected to grow to $238 billion in 2025 from the current $143 billion if the 7.5 per cent average annual growth rate is maintained.

A partial deal would be a great start to lay the groundwork for a future free trade agreement, providing policymakers a platform for binding our economies more purposefully. A US-India trade deal could also secure a political win for the Trump administration in an election year – especially if India's GSP benefits are reinstated, providing relief to American farmers and manufacturers to the tune of $250 million.

Trade matters

Finally, both Prime Minister Modi and President Trump need to "walk the talk" on free and fair trade. India needs to move forward on some much-needed market reforms, such as eliminating preferential market access and instilling regulatory coherence in the business environment. On the US side, actions like the Section 301 review of India's e-commerce policies or leaning hard on India to ban Chinese telecom giant Huawei from supplying equipment for 5G wireless technology deflects attention from current and future areas of economic collaboration.

The commitment to build a strong US-India bilateral economic relationship with an eye towards the future needs to start now. The stakes for this relationship are way too high — businesses and governments on both sides cannot afford complacency to set in.

BILATERAL TRADE RELATIONS

31. US is India's largest trading partner in goods and services. The overall India-US bilateral trade in goods and services has increased from US$126 billion in 2017 to US$142 billion in 2018. This growing trend continues in the first four months of 2019, which has seen an increase in bilateral merchandise trade of 14% compared to the same period in 2018. A snapshot of bilateral trade from January 2017 to April 2019 is as follows:

(US $ Billions)	Jan - Dec 2017	Jan - Dec 2018	% Change
Merchandise	74.33	87.53	17.75%
Services	51.88	54.56	5.16%
Total Trade	126.21	142.09	12.58%

Merchandise Trade (Jan-Apr 2019)

(US $ Billions)	Jan Apr 2018	Jan-Apr 2019	% Change
India's Exports to US	17..53	19.71	12.44%
US Exports to India	10.23	12.01	17.45%
Total Trade	27.76	31.72	14.29%

Investment

As per data release by US Department of Commerce, Bureau of Economic Analysis, FDI from US to India as on year 2017 amounted to $44.46 billion whereas Indian FDI into the US amounted to $13.12 billion.

As per a report released in November 2017 by Confederation of Indian Industries (CII) titled "Indian Roots, American Soil", Indian investment in US amounts to $18 billion, based on a survey of 100 Indian companies across 50 states in US for this report.

India and the United States held the India-U.S. Bilateral Trade meeting in New Delhi on 6 May 2019. Shri Suresh Prabhu, Minister of Commerce & Industry and Civil Aviation, Government of India and Mr. Wilbur Ross, Secretary of Commerce, co-chaired. Both appreciated the strong, robust and growing bilateral ties between India and the U.S. across the entire spectrum of trade and commerce. Both sides expressed satisfaction over the progress during the year 2018, with bilateral trade in Goods and Services registering a growth of 12.6% from $ 126 billion in 2017 to $142 billion in 2018. Both sides agreed to deepen economic cooperation and bilateral trade by ensuring greater cooperation amongst stakeholders, including Government, businesses and entrepreneurs. US Trade Winds Indo-Pacific Business Forum and Mission initiative 2019, was held at New Delhi from 8-10thMay, 2019.

USIBC's India Ideas Summit: The US-India Business Council (USIBC) held its annual "India Ideas Summit" on 12-13 June 2019 in Washington, D.C. The summit was inaugurated by Ambassador of India, and it featured a robust selection of speakers from senior levels of the U.S. government, U.S. Congress, and the India-US business community, including Secretary of State Mike Pompeo, Secretary of Commerce Wilbur Ross, Co-Chair of the Senate India Caucus Mark Warner (D-VA), and US Ambassador to India Kenneth Juster, among others. Dignitaries from both India and the U.S. recognized the progress made in the bilateral relationship and laid out the framework for this relationship to expand even further.

Investment

USA is one of the top 5 investment destinations for FDI from India. A survey done by CII in November 2017 found that 100 Indian companies have invested $ 17.9 billion in the United States creating 113,000 jobs in all 50 states of US. India's top companies, including Wipro, Infosys, L&T and Mahindra have recently made announcements for increasing their investments in the US. Mahindra became the first company in over 25 years to invest in Detroit investing $230 Million. The first vehicle rolled out from the plant on March 2, 2018. US direct investment in India amounts to about $ 33 Billion across several sectors such as manufacturing, services, pharmaceuticals etc.

Trade Policy Forum (TPF)

The 11thTrade Policy Forum (TPF) Meeting was held in Washington DC on 26 October 2017. The meeting was co-chaired by Commerce and Industry Minister (CIM) Mr. Suresh Prabhu and U.S. Trade Representative Ambassador Robert Lighthizer. Discussions were held on issues related to bilateral trade between the two countries, areas of mutual cooperation, market access in agriculture, non-agricultural goods and services and Intellectual Property Rights (IPR). At the conclusion of TPF, both Ministers decided that the two countries will continue to work towards building strong trade and investment ties to realize mutual gains from the partnership. Both sides also expressed the desire to reduce the existing gaps and work towards resolution of the outstanding issues before the next round of the TPF. The next round is expected to be held in India.

An important trend in bilateral trade has been the reduction in trade deficit, which has come down by about US$ 1.4 billion in 2017 and with oil and gas purchases along with commencement of delivery of civilian aircrafts, this trend is expected to continue. Significant exports of oil and gas from US to India have begun in the last one year. There is expectation that India will import about US$ 2 billion each of oil and gas from the US every year. If the prices are found to be competitive, this amount may increase significantly in coming years. Indian air carriers have placed orders for more than 300 civilian aircrafts from Boeing which will be delivered over the next 6-7 years. The estimated value of this order is about US$ 39 billion.

Commercial Dialogue

The Commercial Dialogue was created out of the Security and Commercial dialogue in 2017. The first session of the U.S.-India Commercial Dialogue under this new structure was held in Washington DC on 27 October 2017. The Dialogue, co-chaired by Secretary of Commerce Mr. Wilbur Ross and Commerce and Industry Minister (CIM) Mr. Suresh Prabhu focused on promoting joint economic growth, job creation, and prosperity. In the joint statement following the Dialogue, it was stated "During their meeting, Secretary Ross and Minister Prabhu reviewed progress to date under the U.S.-India commercial relationship, including cooperation in the areas of standards, ease of doing business, and travel and tourism. In standards, they noted positive outcomes from holding best practices exchanges between the National Institute of Standards and Technology (NIST), the Bureau of Indian Standards (BIS), and India's National Physical Laboratory (NPL)." Both sides also committed to strive for meaningful progress in areas such as Standards, Business Climate and Investment, and Travel and Tourism. A MoU on Standards was signed between CII and American National Standards Institute (ANSI) on the side-lines of the Commercial dialogue and another MoU between EXIM bank of US with Export Credit Guarantee Corporation of India (ECGC). The next round is expected to be held in India.

Global Entrepreneurship Summit (GES)

India and the US successfully co-hosted the Global Entrepreneurship Summit in Hyderabad on November 28-30, 2017. The theme of GES 2017 was "Women First, Prosperity for All". Ms. Ivanka Trump, Advisor to the US President attended the Summit. The Summit brought together leading investors, entrepreneurs, academicians, think tanks and other stake holders from India and the US.

Energy Cooperation/Strategic Energy Partnership

India and US have established a Strategic Energy Partnership (SEP) replacing the erstwhile Energy Dialogue. This was done during the last meeting held in New Delhi on 17 April 2018 between Minister of Petroleum and Natural Gas Shri Dharmendra Pradhan and US Secretary for Energy, Mr. Rick Perry. The SEP has four primary pillars of cooperation: (i) Oil and Gas; (ii) Power and Energy Efficiency; (iii) Renewable Energy and Sustainable Growth; and (iv) Coal. As a first step, they also announced the establishment of US-India Natural Gas Task Force to support India's vision for natural gas. The two sides also reaffirmed their strong commitment to early and full implementation of our civil nuclear energy partnership, including the Westinghouse civil nuclear project in Kovvada.

Diaspora and People-to-People Contacts

The 3-million strong Indian American community is an important ethnic group in the U.S., accounting for about 1% of the total population in the country. It is the 3rd largest Asian ethnic group in the US after the Chinese and the Filipinos. The Indian American community enjoys great reputation and significant influence on the American society and polity with its large number of professionals, business entrepreneurs and educationalists marking their positive presence on the national scene. Almost 40% of all Indians in the United States have a master's, doctorate or other professional degree, which is about five times the national average. With two nationwide well-known Indian Americans having occupied posts of the Governor and several representatives in the Congress and state legislatures, the Indian Diaspora has been a catalyst in cementing closer ties between India and the U.S. In addition, about 1.28 million Indians reside in the United States as Green Card holders, temporary workers, students, etc.

U.S.-INDIA CIVIL NUCLEAR DEAL

For many observers, however, the challenge of managing this Chinese initiative has been complicated by the U.S. decision to renew civilian nuclear cooperation with India, which like Pakistan is also a non–nuclear-weapon state under the NPT and does not accept full-scope safeguards as a matter of national policy. The fact that the United States has treated India differently from the rest of the NPT outliers—creating a unique "carve out" that enables New Delhi to engage in peaceful nuclear cooperation internationally despite its refusal to sign the NPT—is often viewed as weakening Washington's ability to oppose the current Chinese transgression. As one reporter summarized the situation, "China wants to sell two nuclear reactors to Pakistan. The Obama administration thinks that's a bad idea—but how to oppose that plan while dodging charges of hypocrisy, given [that] the administration only last year sealed a U.S. deal to supply India with civilian nuclear equipment?"

Others, such as Brad Glosserman, executive director of the Pacific Forum Centre for Strategic and International Studies, have gone further, arguing that the U.S.-India deal has in fact opened the floodgates for exactly such transactions as are now proposed by China toward Pakistan: "We all knew at the time that an agreement such as the India-U.S. one would have consequences for the nonproliferation regime and that's what you are seeing now.... The India-U.S. deal was a bad, troubling example to set, for proliferators, however justified the desire in Washington to improve ties with India." In other words, if the U.S.-India agreement had not been consummated, the currently proposed Chinese sale of new nuclear rectors to Pakistan would likely not have occurred. These claims, however, are not persuasive.

Whatever one's views of the U.S.-India civilian nuclear cooperation agreement, the accord reached between President George W. Bush and Prime Minister Manmohan Singh is fundamentally different from the proposed Chinese effort to export additional power reactors to Pakistan. *Pace* the recent claims of Maleeha Lodhi, the U.S.-Indian agreement is not "a fundamental violation of the [Nuclear Non-Proliferation] Treaty" 3 because nothing in the treaty forbids agreements for peaceful nuclear cooperation—to include the export of reactors, other nuclear technologies, and nuclear materials—with states that are not signatories to it. All that the NPT requires is that every nuclear transaction with any non-signatory state be solely for peaceful uses and that all transferred items be fully safeguarded by the International Atomic Energy Agency (IAEA). The U.S.-India civilian nuclear cooperation agreement meets both these conditions and, therefore, cannot be considered a violation of the NPT by any stretch of the imagination.

The bilateral agreement between Washington and New Delhi, however, was clearly in conflict with the full-scope safeguards criterion encoded in the 1978 U.S. Nuclear Nonproliferation Act (NNPA) and adopted by the NSG at its Warsaw meeting in 1992 (which enjoined its members to refrain from any significant nuclear exports to non–nuclear-weapon states that had not adopted comprehensive safeguards). Consequently, the Bush administration expended enormous political capital in the U.S. Congress to amend the relevant components of American law, primarily of the Atomic Energy Act, which previously had permitted nuclear cooperation agreements with non– nuclear-weapon states only after they had accepted full-scope safeguards.

Thereafter, the administration, working in concert with the government of India, committed significant diplomatic resources to convince the NSG to accord India an exceptional waiver from the full-scope safeguards criterion that would have otherwise stymied international nuclear cooperation with New Delhi. From the very beginning, President Bush always had the option of pursuing nuclear cooperation with India in the manner now pursued by China toward Pakistan.

That is, the United States—after amending its own national laws— could have unilaterally begun nuclear trade with India, disregarding the sentiments of its NSG partners and abusing the normative character of the NSG's guidelines. Because maintaining the integrity of the global nonproliferation regime, however, was always important to the United States— and was perhaps even more important because of the exceptional treatment contemplated for India—the Bush administration spent considerable energy from October 2005 until the final extraordinary plenary in September 2008— consulting with its NSG partners *during eight meetings over four years,* not to mention the bilateral discussions that occurred in national capitals—to finally secure the special waiver for India that exempted it from the constraining condition of fullscope safeguards.

The current Sino-Pakistani nuclear transaction could not be more different. For starters, the interstate agreement governing the potential export of the two Chinese reactors to Pakistan is a secret covenant, secretly concluded. Unlike the U.S.-India nuclear initiative, whose terms were public and vociferously debated in both countries starting with the initial announcement in July 2005, the conditions regulating the proposed Chinese sale (and any potential future transfers) are unknown to the international community.

Furthermore, the Chinese have sought to advance this transaction with Pakistan by subterfuge. By insinuating privately, but without any accompanying formal declaration, that the prospective sale of two nuclear rectors to Pakistan is grandfathered, in Maleeha Lodhi's masterfully equivocal formulation, "under the [Sino-Pakistani] agreement dating back to the 1980s that provided for an understanding in 2003 for further long-term collaboration," Beijing has sought to convey that all Chinese sales to Pakistan are *ipso facto* exempted from its obligation to uphold the NSG's requirement of full-scope safeguards because China joined the NSG only in 2004, well after the latest "understanding" reached with Pakistan.

This minor detail, however, eluded Chinese diplomats when they provided the NSG with a rendition of their outstanding commitments upon joining the organization. As Mark Hibbs has described it, "China then explained to the NSG that a longstanding framework agreement with Pakistan committed China to provide a second reactor, Chashma-2, more research reactors, plus supply of all the fuel in perpetuity for these units."

Notice there is not a word about additional power reactors beyond the already contracted Chashma-2, which began construction in 2005, the year after Beijing joined the NSG. Finally, and most conspicuously, unlike the U.S.-Indian civilian nuclear initiative, China has made no effort thus far—and is unlikely to make any in the future—to seek a specific NSG exemption for its nuclear trade with Pakistan. The Bush administration campaigned for a waiver from the NSG's full-scope condition for India on two defensible grounds: first, India's nonproliferation record justified its progressive integration into the international nuclear regime and, second, its growing technological mastery over different nuclear fuel cycles made the international regime stronger through its inclusion rather than its continued exclusion. After long and arduous diplomatic efforts, these arguments finally carried the day—but not before the NSG wrested from New Delhi a strong reiteration of its disarmament obligations.

What is most pertinent, however, is that the United States made the investment over several years to persuade the NSG and, further, that the NSG's members took their time to consider the American proposal in all its complexity. To be sure, many were torn by the nature of the U.S. initiative; some were frustrated by what was perceived as strong American pressure; others had to balance their long-standing commitment to nonproliferation with their strong ties to India and/or the United States; and all had to struggle to figure out how best to integrate India into the global nuclear regime.

When the consensus finally came, it did only after all the competing interests were weighed and adjudicated in 44 national capitals—which is exactly what the process was meant to do. China, in contrast, has chosen a different route: seeking to short-circuit the NSG rather than appeal to its judgment. Knowing full well that Pakistan's poor nonproliferation record and its continuing reluctance to come clean on the activities of A. Q. Khan and his cohort will prevent the NSG from granting Pakistan any waiver from the full-scope safeguards requirement, Beijing appears committed to persisting with the course of action it has adopted thus far: namely, to attempt consummating various nuclear trades with Pakistan secretly if it believes it can get away with such dealings because of either diffidence or contrivance on the part of the international community.

The glaring differences between the U.S.-Indian agreement and the proposed Chinese-Pakistani transaction thus say more about, in Hibbs' apt phrase, "China's growing nuclear assertiveness" 7 than they do about any purported similarity between these two initiatives.

Consequently, the United States can— and should—oppose China's current effort to sell new reactors to Pakistan without fear of "charges of hypocrisy." If duplicity is at issue on this question, it emanates only from Beijing and not Washington.

3

Global Trade Scenario and Realignment of India's Exports

From an investment perspective, it's easy to adopt a sanguine view of Asia. The region's growth rate—expected to hit 5.1% this year[1]—continues to incite envy from its peers in the developed world. Equally significant is the fact that the continent occupies the quality end of the emerging-market (EM) universe, making it more appealing to investors. However, that's not to say that the region is immune from the global economic slowdown.

In our view, the economic downturn in Asia has yet to hit a bottom. Although global risk sentiment has improved in recent weeks, stubbornly low economic growth and low inflation leave markets vulnerable to a reversal in sentiment. We expect a prolonged bottoming-out process and believe subsequent growth will be "L-shaped."

As the world's growth engine, the shape of Asia's recovery has enormous relevance to investors. There are two key reasons why we believe that an L-shaped growth path looks most likely: first, there are numerous headwinds to growth; and second, the region's governments' ability to revive growth—from a policy perspective—is somewhat constrained.

Headwinds to growth

Asia's economic growth is typically tied to the global industrial cycle, which has been dampened as a result of deteriorating business investment, itself a consequence of the uncertainty brought about by the U.S.-China trade war. Fixed asset investment growth in the region has already slowed significantly on a year-on-year basis from 5.1% at the start of 2018 to just half a percent in mid-2019.[2] Notably, given that the cumulative impact of the trade dispute has yet to be fully reflected in the economic data so far,[3] it's fair to surmise that Asian exports are likely to remain sluggish through 2020.

Global growth and Asian exports

China isn't coming to the rescue: Over the past decade, the global economy has grown accustomed to relying on Chinese stimulus to rekindle growth. Previous slowdowns, most notably in 2008/09 and 2016, saw China unleash huge lending programs to spur construction, reviving the domestic economy and giving the global economy a nice lift along the way. Interestingly, although growth in China has slowed to its lowest level in nearly three decades, policy response to the current downtown has been limited to measures such as tax reforms, cuts to bank reserve requirements, and tweaks to local government bond issuance.

We believe Beijing will have to accept that it might miss its 6% GDP growth target for 2020—a development that would mark a critical turning point in the global growth cycle. Of note, we believe the Chinese government's restraint can be traced back to how previous rounds of credit-fueled stimulus aggravated problems in the financials sector. Given the authorities' stated preference to avoid fueling financial instability, the scale of any forthcoming stimulus will likely be limited in scope and insufficient to reflate the global economy.

China credit impulse and global growth

Weakness in manufacturing sectors as a result of trade uncertainty is weighing on domestic demand: On a year-on-year basis, growth in private consumption demand growth has slowed significantly in the last 18 months—from 5.8% in January 2018 to

4.1% in June 2019. On balance, we're inclined to believe that the risk is for more pronounced weakness in the months ahead.

Asia investment slowdown and private consumption (%)

Inventories are at risk of deeper correction cycle: Manufacturing inventory ratios in Thailand, Taiwan, and South Korea remain at multi-year highst—where we're concerned this is a sign that the inventory correction cycle could have further to run.

Idiosyncratic risk factors are surfacing: Geography-specific factors are weighing on domestic demand. The ongoing social unrest in Hong Kong, which contributed to tipping the territory into a technical recession in the third quarter, is one such example. Similarly, financial stability concerns in India stemming from the prolonged financial stress among rural households are also on the rise—a credit crunch among nonbank financial institutions have also increased the probability of a more entrenched slowdown in India. These are all issues that investors should monitor in the year ahead.

Policy space is relatively constrained

In our view, the policy space within which global central banks can maneuver to support growth is constrained by the already low level of interest rates. As monetary policy reaches its natural limits, the focus is shifting increasingly toward fiscal policy. Asian central banks are in a similar position given that policy rates in many countries are already at, or near, record lows. This perhaps explains why we've seen a flurry of announcements on the fiscal front in recent months—corporate tax cuts in India and Thailand, labor law reforms in Indonesia that are aimed at boosting investment, and China's decision to bring forward special purpose bonds for infrastructure spending. Crucially, while the room to ease fiscal policy varies widely across Asia, it's important to note that much of the region still has fiscal space to implement such measures. However, as budget deficits widen, deficit financing, liquidity, and the government budget constraint become important considerations.

U.S.-China: implications of a "strategic decoupling"

From a long-term perspective, we believe that the United States and China are engaged in a prolonged strategic decoupling. Consequently, although the current détente appears to be supporting risk appetite, we don't expect this to be sustainable. In other words, a breakdown in the phased U.S.-China trade talks continues to be a key risk in the year ahead, particularly as the focus of negotiations broadens to include more complex topics.

Issues where both sides aren't likely to come to an agreement easily come to mind:

- Intellectual property rights protection (specifically in the technology space)
- China's response to the U.S.-led Blue Dot Network, which is widely seen as a project devised to rival China's Belt and Road Initiative
- The recent inclusion of nearly 30 Chinese companies on the U.S. Commerce Department's "entity list"

These issues are likely to make already difficult negotiations even more delicate. Where markets are concerned, this could mean further weakness in the Chinese yuan and a risk-off environment—particularly in light of slowing Chinese growth. In our view, investors will need to be more discriminating and selective in 2020.

That said, we continue to view Asia as a relatively attractive region from an asset allocation perspective—especially within the EM complex given the region's narrower output gap, low and steady inflation, and low market volatility. Nonetheless, given the unpredictable nature of U.S.-China trade discussions, quick reversals in risk appetite are unlikely to disappear.

Within Asia, we prefer markets that are less exposed to trade tensions. As U.S. firms scramble to identify alternative products to replace Chinese imports, Malaysia's likely to feature—in our view—near the top of their list in the short run, with Thailand and the Philippines not far behind. However, if the global manufacturing and supply chain were to shift away from China in a more permanent fashion, then Vietnam is likely to be the main beneficiary over the longer term, followed by Malaysia, Singapore, and India.

Key risks to our view

Economic forecasting, although quantitative in nature, isn't an exact science. As the late professor Rudi Dornbusch once said, "In economics, things take longer to happen than you think they will, then they happen faster than you thought they could." In this instance, our analysis could be undermined by a much sharper than expected depreciation in the U.S. dollar (USD), which could loosen global financial conditions and reboot the global business cycle, and a stimulus package from Beijing that's large enough to rekindle growth. In our view, these two factors will play an outsized role in determining the shape of the coming Asian recovery.

FOREIGN TRADE OF INDIA

Foreign trade in India includes all imports and exports to and from India. At the level of Central Government it is administered by the Ministry of Commerce and Industry. Foreign trade accounted for 48.8% of India's GDP in 2017.

History

Even before independence, the Government of India maintained semi-autonomous diplomatic relations. It had colonies (such as the Aden Settlement), who sent and received full missions, and was a founder member of both the League of Nations and the United Nations. After India gained independence from the United Kingdom in 1947, it soon joined the Commonwealth of Nations and strongly supported independence movements in other colonies, like the Indonesian National Revolution. The partition and various territorial disputes, particularly that over Kashmir, would strain its relations with Pakistan for years to come. During the Cold War, India adopted a foreign policy of non-alignment policy itself with any major power bloc. However, India developed close ties with the Soviet Union and received extensive military support from it.

Around 100CE

The Periplus of the Erythraean Sea is a document written by an anonymous sailor from Alexandria about 100CE describing trade between countries, including India.

Around 1500

In 1498 Portuguese explorer Vasco da Gama landed in Calicut (modern day Kozhikode in Kerala) as the first European to ever sail to India. The tremendous profit made during this trip made the Portuguese eager for more trade with India and attracted other European navigators and tradesmen.

Pedro Álvares Cabral left for India in 1500 and established Portuguese trading posts at Calicut and Cochin (modern day Kochi), returning to Portugal in 1501 with pepper, ginger, cinnamon, cardamom, nutmeg, mace, and cloves. The profits made from this trip were huge.

1991 economic reform

Prior to the 1991 economic liberalisation, India was a closed economy due to the average tariffs exceeding 200 percent and the extensive quantitative restrictions on imports. Foreign investment was strictly restricted to only allow Indian ownership of businesses. Since the liberalisation, India's economy has improved mainly due to increased foreign trade.

Trade in services

India was the eighth largest exporter of commercial services in the world in 2016, accounting for 3.4% of global trade in services. India recorded a 5.7% growth in services trade in 2016-17.

Exports and imports

India exports approximately 7500 commodities to about 190 countries, and imports around 6000 commodities from 140 countries. India exported US$318.2 billion and imported $462.9 billion worth of commodities in 2014.

The Government of India's Economic Survey 2017–18 noted that five states – Maharashtra, Gujarat, Karnataka, Tamil Nadu and Telangana – accounted for 70% of India's total exports. It was the first time that the survey included international export data for states. The survey found a high correlation between a state's Gross State Domestic Product (GSDP) per capita and its share of total exports. With a high GSDP per capita but low export share, Kerala was the only major outlier because the state's GSDP per capita was heavily influenced by remittances.

The survey also found that the largest firms in India contributed to a smaller percentage of exports when compared to countries like Brazil, Germany, Mexico, and the United States. The top 1% of India's companies accounted for 38% of total exports.

Trade statistics

Summary table of recent India Foreign Trade(in billion $):

Year	Export	Import	Trade Deficit
1999	36.3	50.2	-13.9
2000	43.1	60.8	-17.7
2001	42.5	54.5	-12.0
2002	44.5	53.8	-9.3
2003	48.3	61.6	-13.3
2004	57.24	74.15	-16.91
2005	69.18	89.33	-20.15
2006	76.23	113.1	-36.87
2007	112.0	100.9	11.1
2008	176.4	305.5	-129.1
2009	168.2	274.3	-106.1
2010	201.1	327.0	-125.9
2011	299.4	461.4	-162.0

2012	298.4	500.4	-202.0
2013	313.2	467.5	-154.3
2014	318.2	462.9	-144.7
2015	310.3	447.9	-137.6
2016	262.3	381	-118.7
2017	275.8	384.3	-108.5

The top 10 commodity exports in 2007 were as follows:

Rank	Commodity	HS Code	Value (US$ billion)	Share (%)
1	Refined Petroleum	27	61.2	19.2
2	Gems, precious metals, coins	71	41.2	13
3	Vehicles	87	14.5	4.6
4	Machines, engines, pumps	85	13.6	4.3
5	Organic chemicals	29	12.1	3.8
6	Pharmaceuticals	30	11.7	3.7
7	Cereals	10	10.1	3.2
8	Iron and steel	72	9.1	2.9
9	Clothing (not knit or crotchet)	58	9.1	2.9
10	Electronics	85	9.1	2.8

The top 10 commodity imports in 2007 were as follows:

Rank	Commodity	HS Code	Value (US$ billion)	Share (%)
1	Oil	27	177.5	38.3
2	Gems, precious metals, coins	71	60	13
3	Electronics	85	32	6.9
4	Machines, engines, pumps	85	31.2	6.7
5	Organic chemicals	29	18.3	4
6	Plastics	39	11.8	2.6
7	Iron and steel	72	11.4	2.5
8	Animal/vegetable fats and oils	15	10.7	2.3
9	Ores, slag and ash	26	7.4	1.6
10	Medical and technical equipment	90	7.1	1.5

Trading partners

India's largest trading partners in descending order of value of total trade are the United Arab Emirates, China, United States, Saudi Arabia, Switzerland, Singapore, Germany, Hong Kong, Indonesia, Iraq, Russia and Japan.

INTERNATIONAL TRADE SCENARIO AND REALIGNMENT OF INDIA'S EXPORTS

The global economy has been on a subdued growth path since the advent of 'Financial Crisis' of 2008, and has now started to show signs of global recovery. In October 2017, the IMF projected world GDP growth to pick up from 3.2% in 2016 to 3.6% in 2017, and further to 3.7% in 2018. Economic activity has also picked up in developed market economies such as the US, UK, and Europe. There is a rise in global demand, which is expected to remain buoyant. The developing and emerging market economies have seen mixed economic performance. The pickup in momentum of global demand has been led by investment demand. More specifically, production of both consumer durables and capital goods have rebounded since the second half of 2016. Some factors that have contributed to these developments include global recovery in investments, led by infrastructure and real estate investment in China; firming global commodity prices; and end of an inventory cycle in US.

On the back of this global recovery, the world is witnessing a pickup in global trade. The Asian Development Bank, in its recent update1, noted that most of the emerging economies (excluding China) are witnessing a rebound in manufacturing exports, "particularly in electronics, where foreign direct investment has been strengthening". The economies of south-east Asia are also gaining from increased activity along cross-border manufacturing supply chains. The World Trade Organisation (WTO), has recently in its September 2017 press release upgraded the growth forecast for global trade in the year 2017, from 2.4% to 3.6%. Particularly, in the first half of 2017, world trade rose by a robust 4.2% (year on year), driven by exports of developing economies which grew by 5.9 percent as compared to a growth of 3.1 percent witnessed in exports of developed economies. Imports by developed and developing economies also increased by 2.1% and 6.9%, respectively. Moreover, the ratio of trade growth to world GDP growth is also set to recover and reach around 1.3, which will be at a highest level in last 5 years.

This pickup in global growth which has boosted demand for imports, spurred intra-Asia-trade as demand was transmitted through global value chains. In this current scenario, even though India is witnessing a mild rebound in its exports, there are concerns that merchandise exports in Asia's second largest economy are lagging behind other major Asian economies. Today global attention is riveted on emerging and developing economies and especially Asia, driven by the continent's growing appetite for industrial investment, burgeoning infrastructural requirements and its quest for expanding trade.

Indian economy and its trade scenario

India's growth story, especially since the start of the 21st century has been remarkable. The Indian economy has come a long way since its economic liberalisation, and is amongst the fastest growing major economies of the world today. While India witnessed a relatively moderate growth during the period 2011-12 to 2013-14, on account of the global economic slowdown, the economy recorded a robust growth averaging 7.5 percent during the period 2014-15 to 2016-17, much above the growth rate of other emerging and developing economies. In the last one year, it has seen major economic policy developments with the introduction of Goods and Services Tax (GST) and demonetisation of higher currency notes.

Even though the GDP growth in the first quarter of current fiscal has fallen down to a low of 5.7%, its lowest since March 2014, it is widely believed that the economy has bottomed out and it can only rise from here. According to the IMF, India is expected to grow at 7.2% in this fiscal year, aided by higher government spending and a pickup in the service sector performance.

Fueling India's growth through international trade

In recent years, India's robust growth has been driven by the dynamic private sector. An encouraging phenomenon that has been witnessed has been the emergence of a large number of investment driven small and medium enterprises with immense potential for growth. A large number of such enterprises have also endeavoured to expand their business operations overseas. The Indian economy is more globalised than we could imagine. As a result, India's foreign trade has seen a multi-fold increase, since liberalisation of the economy.

Accordingly, there have been significant structural shifts not only in the product basket, but also in the geographical composition of India's foreign trade. The opening up of Indian economy led to a massive increase in the foreign trade, which aided in sustained GDP growth over last two decades. During the last 25 years Indian exports have increased by 17 times and imports by 19 times. India's share in global merchandise exports has risen from 0.6 percent in early 1990s to 1.7 percent in 2016, and similarly the share of imports has risen from 0.6 percent to 2.4 percent during the same period. India's trade to GDP ratio, a measure of an economy's openness and integration into the global economy, has witnessed a phenomenal increase over the last few decades. Foreign trade which constituted around 13-15 percent of India's GDP in the early nineties, peaked at 55 percent in 2012- 13 and today accounts for around 40 percent in 2016-17. India also, ranked as the 20th largest exporter and 14th largest importer in the world in 2016.

Concomitantly, India's engagement with Global Value Chains (GVCs), which have become dominant feature of world trade, has increased significantly since 1990s. In manufacturing sector, especially for electrical and optical equipment, India is more integrated with the south east Asian region, while for services the integration in GVCs is with western countries like the US and UK. According to an OECD estimate, developing economies with fastest growing GVC participation have experienced a GDP per capita growth rate percent above average.

India has set an ambitious target of achieving exports worth US $ 900 billion by 2020, while accounting for a share of 3.5 percent of global exports4. In the current global macroeconomic scenario, while it seems like a challenging task, concerted efforts would need to be made for India to be able to achieve its trade target and realign its foreign trade policy with the new global trading system.

While the global economic scenario is crucial, the domestic factors are no less important, when it comes to trade. India's overall trade policy faces certain challenges viz. inadequate export diversification in terms of products and geographical distribution; insignificant involvement of a majority of states in exports; rationalisation of the tariff regime and export promotion schemes; and factor market reforms which are critically linked with export performance. These challenges not only affect the productivity and competitiveness of domestic firms but also restrict them from participating in global production networks.

What needs to be done?

Integrating into and moving up the value chain. Most manufactured products, often high technology manufactured products, that are part of GVCs are infrastructure critical products whose parts are manufactured in several countries. A robust transport and connectivity network supported by fast entry/exit through port/customs is a precondition to making such products as delay may disrupt the entire value chain. There is a need for India to focus on expanding production capacity along with value addition, and moving up the value chain,while creating an enabling environment to account for a sizeable share in major leading global exports. This gain seven more significance given that India's labour force is projected to swell by about 110 mn by 2020. The biggest challenge is to employ the surplus labour coming out of agriculture into industry and services.

Upscaling Manufacturing

The Make in India initiative is an important initiative of the Government of India, which envisages to promote India as a manufacturing hub and investment destination. There is need for highlighting the potential and stimulating the manufacturing sector through supporting mechanisms and conducive policy measures, including support for R&D, technology orientation and investment incentives. A Higher expenditure on R&D generally correlates with increase in high-technology exports, and increased local value addition. R&D expenditure as a percentage share of GDP in India has remained extremely low at less than1 percent, much lower even in comparison to other developing economies. Also, while we lay emphasis on the manufacturing sector and thereby on manufactured exports, it is also important to ensure an enabling environment and improving our competitiveness by investing in infrastructure such as better connectivity through roads and ports, coal availability, labour reforms and flexibility in factor markets.

Aligning India's Export Capability in-Line with Global Import Demand

With regard to India's exports, while merchandise exports have more than doubled over the period 2006-07 to 2016-17 from US$ 126 billion to more than US$276 billion, there remains huge potential for exports of select products to select countries in line with India's export capability and import demand. There is need for identifying and aligning India's export capability vis-à-vis global import demand. Such in-depth analysis has been the focus of research studies in Exim Bank. Comparative analyses of global trends in trade, undertaken in such studies have yielded interesting results.

To Sum Up

All in all, a pick-up in global growth is expected to contribute to the revival of international trade, but the downside risks such as the possible adoption of protectionist trade policies by especially developed market economies, around the world weigh on the recovery of trade. As a result, there is an increasing need for India and other emerging market economies, relying on export led economic growth, to take a proactive stand for globalisation and international trade.

There is a need to shift our focus from exporting what we can (or supply based), to items that are globally demanded. A demand-based export basket diversification approach could give a big push to exports. While India has made remarkable progress in the recent past, it facesan even more challenging global environment today. Itis certainly a daunting, yet possible, task to ensure that India repositions itself as an important driver of global economic growth.

4

India US Trade Relations

India-US bilateral relations today not only encompass the major pillars of our strategic partnership - including security, energy and technology - but have deepened with greater bilateral economic engagement and ever increasing people-to-people contacts. In the last few years, the bilateral relationship also has expanded into a global partnership with greater convergence of views on a number of issues such as international terrorism and shared approach to rules-based order in the Indo-Pacific region.

Visit of Prime Minister

Following the assumption of office by President Trump, PM visited Washington DC on 26-27 June 2017. This was the first opportunity for the two leaders to meet and exchange views. PM also had a meeting with Vice President Pence. The then Secretary of State Rex Tillerson and then Secretary of Defence Jim Mattis separately called on PM. PM's programme included an interaction with US CEOs and address to the Indian community.

Among the important outcomes of the visit were the decision to initiate 2+2 meeting of the External Affairs and Defence Ministers with their US counterparts, agreement on principles for the Indo-Pacific region and a decision to further advance our security and defence relationship. It was also decided to establish a new consultation mechanism on domestic and international terrorist designation i.e. a Terrorist Designation Dialogue.

Meetings/Interactions of PM with President Trump

PM met with President Trump again in Manila, Philippines in November 2017 on the margins of the 31st ASEAN Meeting. Both the leaders have also been in contact with each other, holding telephone conversations to discuss issues relating to bilateral cooperation and international developments. More recently, Prime Minister Shri Narendra Modi also met with President Donald J. Trump and Prime Minister Shinzo Abe of Japan on 30 November 2018 in Buenos Aires, Argentina, which was also the first trilateral leaders' meeting of the three countries. The trilateral meeting was held on the side-lines of the 2018 G20 Leaders' Summit.

Ministerial 2 Plus 2 Dialogue

Secretary of State Michael R. Pompeo and then Secretary of Defence James N. Mattis visited India on 6 September 2018 for the inaugural India-U.S. Ministerial 2+2 Dialogue with Minister of External Affairs [EAM] Sushma Swaraj and Minister of Defence/ Raksha Mantri [RM] Nirmala Sitharaman. During the visit, Secretary Pompeo and Secretary Mattis jointly called on the Prime Minister. They also held separate bilateral meetings with EAM and RM, respectively. The launch of the 2+2 Dialogue is a reflection of the shared commitment by Prime Minister Modi and President Trump to provide a positive, forward-looking vision for the India-U.S. strategic partnership and to promote synergy in their diplomatic and security efforts. During the visit, the Communications Compatibility and Security Agreement (COMCASA) was signed that will facilitate access to advanced defence systems and enable India to optimally utilize its existing U.S.-origin platforms. The two sides agreed to the creation of a new, tri-services exercise and to further increase personnel exchanges between the two militaries and defence organizations. It was also agreed to start exchanges between the U.S. Naval Forces Central Command (NAVCENT) and the Indian Navy, underscoring the importance of deepening their maritime cooperation in the western Indian Ocean. A Memorandum of

Intent [MoI] between the U.S. Defence Innovation Unit (DIU) and the Indian Defence Innovation Organization – Innovation for Defence Excellence (DIO-iDEX) was also concluded on the eve of the Dialogue.

Further, at the Dialogue, it was agreed to increase information-sharing efforts on known or suspected terrorists and to implement UN Security Council Resolution 2396 on returning foreign terrorist fighters. Both sides also agreed to enhance their ongoing cooperation in multilateral fora such as the UN and FATF. Further, both sides reaffirmed their support for a UN Comprehensive Convention on International Terrorism that will advance and strengthen the framework for global cooperation and reinforce the message that no cause or grievance justifies terrorism.

High Level Exchanges

Hon'ble Vice President of India Shri Venkaiah Naidu visited the United States of America on 8-9 September 2018 to deliver an address at the 2nd World Hindu Conference held in Chicago. During his visit, he also interacted with members of the Indian community in the United States.

As part of worldwide implementation of Passport Seva Project, the Hon'ble Minister of State for External Affairs Gen. V.K. Singh (Retd.) inaugurated the launch of this project at the Embassy of India in Washington, DC on 24 November 2018. The Passport Seva Project is part of the flagship Passport Seva Programme of Ministry of External Affairs. The event was attended by members of Indian community as well as several passport applicants, who received their passports issued under the new project directly from the Hon'ble MOS. Speaking on the occasion, MOS highlighted the efforts of the government in making passport services more accessible and user friendly. MOS pointed out that with the implementation of the Passport Seva Project in the USA, there would be a further improvement and streamlining of the passport services rendered to Indian citizens living abroad. In addition to inaugurating the Passport Seva Project in Washington DC, Hon'ble

MOS had earlier launched the project at the Consulate General of India in New York on 21 November 2018 and launched the project at the Consulate General of India in Atlanta on 25 November 2018. During the visit, he also held separate interactions with members of the Indian community in New York, Baltimore and Washington, DC.

National Security Advisor Shri Ajit Doval paid an official visit to the United States on 14 September 2018. During the visit, he held separate meetings with US National Security Advisor Mr. John Bolton and Secretary of Defence Mr. James N. Mattis. A wide range of bilateral and regional issues of mutual interest were discussed in the meetings.

Foreign Secretary and Defence Secretary together visited USA on 14-16 March 2018 and held discussions with a number of senior US Administration officials. Both Foreign Secretary and Defence Secretary jointly met with the then National Security Advisor Mr. H.R. McMaster, Deputy National Security Advisor Ms. Nadia Schadlow, Under Secretary of State for Political Affairs Mr. Thomas Shannon and Under Secretary of Defence for Policy John Rood, and Under Secretary of Commerce for Export Administration Mira Ricardel. Foreign Secretary also held a separate meeting with the United States Trade Representative Mr. Robert Lighthizer and the Defence Secretary met with Under Secretary of Defence for Acquisition, Technology and Logistics, Ms. Ellen Lord.

Foreign Secretary again visited the United States on 8-10 August 2018 to hold preparatory discussions for the Ministerial 2 Plus 2 Meeting. During the visit, Foreign Secretary held separate meetings with Under Secretary of State for Arms Control and International Security Affairs Ms. Andrea Thomson, Under Secretary of Defence for Policy Mr. John Rood and Deputy National Security Advisor Ms. Mira Ricardel.

Extensive interactions at the level of State Governments, cities and business organisations are also a regular feature. These are marked by the visits of Chief Ministers, Governors, Ministers, business delegations, etc., from both sides which take forward and deepen the engagement between the two countries.

Foreign Secretary visited the United States on 10-13 March 2019 and held discussion with senior US Administration officials. During the visit, he held separate meetings with US National Security Advisor Mr. John Bolton and Secretary of State Mr. Micheal Pompeo. He also meet Senator and Congressmen at the Hill.

Defence Cooperation

India-US defence cooperation is based on New Framework for India-US Defence Cooperation, which was renewed for a period of ten years in 2015. Bilateral dialogue mechanisms in the field of defence include Defence Policy Group (DPG), Defence Joint Working Group (DJWG), Defence Procurement and Production Group (DPPG), Senior Technology Security Group (STSG), Joint Technical Group (JTG), Military Cooperation Group (MCG), and Service-to-Service Executive Steering Groups (ESGs).

India US defence cooperation is marked by high level exchanges at Ministerial and official levels. Raksha Mantri Smt. Nirmala Sitharaman met with Secretary of Defence James N. Mattis on the margins of the 5th ASEAN Defence Ministers Plus Meeting [ADMM Plus] on 19 October 2018 in Singapore. Both the leaders reviewed the progress in the bilateral defence cooperation and discussed a wide range of bilateral and regional issues of mutual interest.

Raksha Mantri Smt. Nirmala Sitharaman paid an official visit to the United States of America from 02-07 December 2018, at the invitation of Secretary of Defence James N Mattis. In Washington DC, she had a meeting with Secretary Mattis where discussions were held on the growing partnership between India and US in the defence sphere. Views were also exchanged on a broad range of bilateral and international issues of mutual interest. Both sides agreed to further strengthen bilateral defence cooperation, building on the discussions and outcomes of the '2 + 2 Dialogue' held in September 2018. Raksha Mantri highlighted the steps taken by

Government of India to promote defence sector manufacturing, under Prime Minister Shri Narendra Modi's 'Make in India' flag-ship programme. Following her engagements in Washington DC, Raksha Mantri visited Reno, Nevada on 4 December where she held interactions with select leaders of Indian community in the US. On 5 December, she visited the Defence Innovation Unit (DIU) of the US Department of Defence in San Francisco and interacted with start-ups and venture capitalists associated with this unit. From 5-7 December 2018 Raksha Mantri visited Honolulu, which is the headquarters of the US Pacific Command (PACOM), recently renamed as INDO-PACOM. During the visit, she held meetings with Commander of INDO-PACOM, Admiral Philip S. Davidson. She also visited Joint Base Pearl Harbour Hickam, where she boarded a US Guided Missile Destroyer and was briefed on the INDO-PACOM activities.

Defence Trade and Technology Initiative

In 2012, with a view to increase the pace and quality of defence cooperation, the Defence Technology and Trade Initiative [DTTI] was launched. The DTTI is led at the level of US Under Secretary for Acquisition and Secretary Defence Production. It includes a DTTI Task Force and seven Working Groups, including those on ISR(development/ production of ISTAR aircraft); Air Systems; Other System Mobile Electric Hybrid Power Source (MEHPS) anNext Generation Protective Ensemble (NGPE) The last meeting of DTTI was held in New Delhi on 18 July 2018.

Defence Trade

Defence procurements from the US has been an area of remarkable growth in the last decade. India has procured around $ 18 billion worth of defence items from the US since 2008. India already has several US military platforms and equipment and many such proposals for new acquisitions are in the pipeline. The defence procurement activities are monitored through the Defence Production and Procurement Group (DPPG), the last meeting of which took place in Washington DC on 7-9 June 2018.

Defence Agreements

Apart from the agreements signed during the inaugural 2+2 Dialogue, other agreements signed in the recent past include Logistics Exchange Memorandum of Association (LEMOA) (August 2016); Fuel Exchange Agreement (November 2015); Technical Agreement (TA) on information sharing on White (merchant) Shipping (May 2016) and the Information Exchange Annexe (IEA) on Aircraft Carrier Technologies (June 2016). The most significant of these is the Logistics Exchange Memorandum of Agreement (LEMOA). LEMOA is a facilitating agreement that establishes basic terms, conditions, and procedures for reciprocal provision of logistic support, supplies, and services between the armed forces of India and the U.S. As mentioned above, the Communications Compatibility and Security Agreement (COMCASA) was signed during the inaugural Ministerial 2 Plus 2 Dialogue held on 06 September 2018 in New Delhi. A Memorandum of Intent [MoI] between the U.S. Defence Innovation Unit (DIU) and the Indian Defence Innovation Organization – Innovation for Defence Excellence (DIO-iDEX) was also concluded on the eve of the Dialogue.

Mil-to-Mil cooperation

The two countries now conduct more bilateral exercises with each other than they do with any other country. Bilateral exercises held annually include Malabar (between the two Navies and also include Japan; the last Malabar exercises were held in June 2018 in Guam), Cope-India (Air Force), Yudh Abhyas (Army) and Vajra Prahar (Special Forces). India also participates in annual RIMPAC exercises as well as in Red Flag exercises which are US led multinational exercises. It was agreed to add a new bilateral tri-service exercise during the Ministerial 2 Plus 2 Dialogue held in September 2018 in New Delhi.

Major Defence Partner [MDP]: During the visit of the then US Secretary of Defence Ashton Carter to India in December 2016 an understanding was reached regarding US export control policy towards India and on recognition of India as a "Major Defence Partner" of the US. This US government designation, a status unique to India, is intended to elevate defence trade and technology sharing with India to a level to similar to its closest allies and partners. The most important element of MDP was also implemented on 30 July 2018 when US Commerce Secretary Wilbur Ross announced the US Government's decision to move India into Tier-1 of the US Department of Commerce's Strategic Trade Authorisation license exception.

Maritime Security Dialogue: The third round of the India-US Maritime Security Dialogue was held on 30 April-01 May 2018 in Goa. The Indian delegation was led jointly by Dr. Pankaj Sharma, Joint Secretary (D&ISA), Shri Munu Mahawar, Joint Secretary (AMS), Ministry of External Affairs and Smt. Richa Misra, Joint Secretary (Navy), Ministry of Defence. Mr. David Helvey, Principal Deputy Assistant Secretary of Defence for Asian and Pacific Security Affairs and Mr. Daniel Rosenblum, Deputy Assistant Secretary, Bureau of South and Central Asian Affairs led the US side. During the Dialogue, the two sides discussed developments in the maritime domain in the Indo-Pacific Region and exchanged views on ways to further strengthen bilateral maritime security cooperation. They also reviewed the implementation of the decisions taken during the previous Maritime Security Dialogues.

Counter Terrorism Cooperation

Cooperation in counter-terrorism has seen considerable progress with intelligence sharing, information exchange, operational cooperation and sharing of counter-terrorism technology and equipment. India-U.S. Counter-Terrorism Cooperation is carried out through the India-U.S. Joint Working Group on Counter-Terrorism which held its 15th meeting in March 2018 in New Delhi.

Terrorist Designation Dialogue: To take this process of CT cooperation forward, it was agreed during PM's visit to the US in June 2017 to launch a new consultation mechanism on domestic and international terrorist designations listing proposals [Terrorist Designation Dialogue]. The first Terrorist Designation Dialogue between India and US was held on 18-19 December 2017 in Delhi. There was an understanding to designate terrorists based on each other's requests and on which detailed dossiers had already been exchanged.

During the last one year, US has designated Hizbul Mujahideen as a Foreign Terrorist Organization on 16 August 2017 following the designation of its leader Syed Salahuddin as Specially Designated Global Terrorist (SDGT) on 26 June 2017. Subsequently on 4 April 2018, it also designated Milli Muslim League and Tehreek-e-Azadi Kashmir as aliases of LeT and its seven leaders as SDGT. US has also worked closely with India in the Financial Action Task Force (FATF) for the grey listing of Pakistan.

Home Land Security Dialogue

The Homeland Security Dialogue [HSD], at the Home Minister/Homeland Secretary level that began in May 2011 has six [06] Joint Working Groups on megacity policing, global supply chain of trans-national crime, countering illicit financing and counterfeiting, cyber security, capacity building and application of S&T in homeland/internal security. The Second HSD was held in May 2013. The third meeting, scheduled twice in 2016, had to be postponed due to unrelated circumstances and efforts are on to reschedule them at the earliest. In a significant development, India and the US signed the Homeland Security Presidential Directive-6 (HSPD-6) understanding on 2 June 2016. A Senior Officials Meeting [SOM] of the Department of Homeland Security and MHA was held on 18 July 2018 in New Delhi.

Trilateral Dialogue and QUAD

Cooperation on Indo-Pacific issues is carried out in the trilateral format between India, USA and Japan and in the QUAD format, where Australia also joins. Sharing perspectives on security threats ranging from maritime challenges to counter terrorism and non-proliferation are part of these dialogues. Yet another focus area is building consensus on basic principles for the Indo-Pacific and working jointly in ensuring greater acceptance of these by the countries in the region. More recently, a new facet of cooperation on infrastructure and connectivity has been added to the trilateral mechanism. The QUAD format has met only twice at the DG level in November 2017 and in June 2018. The trilateral has met twice at Ministerial level in 2015 and 2017 in New York on the sidelines of UNGA and holds regular meetings at the DG level.

India, Japan and the United States held the 9th Trilateral Meeting at Joint Secretary/Director General/Assistant Secretary level in New Delhi on 4 April 2018 to hold consultations on regional and global issues of mutual interest. In accordance with the directions received from their Foreign Ministers, who met in New York on 18 September 2017 on the margins of UNGA, the officials explored practical steps to enhance cooperation in the areas of connectivity and infrastructure development; counter-proliferation; counter-terrorism; maritime security, maritime domain awareness and HADR. The officials reviewed the outcomes of the Trilateral Infrastructure Working Group that met in Washington in February 2018 and agreed to continue to collaborate to promote increased connectivity in the Indo-Pacific.

First Trilateral Summit

Prime Minister Shri Narendra Modi met with President Donald J. Trump and Prime Minister Shinzo Abe of Japan on 30 November 2018in Buenos Aires, Argentina, which was the first trilateral leaders' meeting of the three countries. The trilateral meeting was held on the side-lines of the 2018 G20 Leaders' Summit. The three leaders exchanged views on the Indo-Pacific and agreed that a free, open, inclusive and rules based order is essential for the region's peace and prosperity. The leaders also agreed on the central role of ASEAN and agreed to work on maritime and connectivity issues and to synergize efforts in this regard.

QUAD: Senior Officials from Ministry of External Affairs of India, Department of Foreign Affairs and Trade of Australia, Ministry of Foreign Affairs of Japan and Department of State of the United States of America met in Singapore on 15 November 2018 for consultations on regional and global issues of common interest.

The senior official meet in Bangkok on May 31, 2019 for consultations on regional and global issues of common interest and discussed cooperation in the areas of connectivity and infrastructure development; regional security, including counterterrorism, Humanitarian Assistance and Disaster Relief; maritime cooperation; and cyber security issues, with a view to promoting peace, stability and prosperity in the Indo-Pacific region. They reaffirmed their commitment towards a free, open, prosperous and inclusive Indo-Pacific Region based on shared values and principles. The participants reiterated their strong support for ASEAN-Centrality and ASEAN-led mechanisms in the regional architecture for the Indo-Pacific and in this regard welcomed the initiative of ASEAN towards a common vision for the Indo-Pacific.

Cyber Security Dialogue

The fourth India-US Cyber Security Dialogue was held in Washington in February 2018. The Indian delegation was led by Deputy NSA and included National Cyber Security Coordinator and Additional Secretary (Cyber Diplomacy) from MEA. This dialogue was held after a long hiatus and resulted in reviving our earlier agreement to set up four sub-groups under the dialogue to promote law enforcement cooperation, capacity building, CERT to CERT cooperation and testing and standards. The US and India have also worked closely in multilateral and UN platforms on issues such as norms of state behavior, confidence building measures and capacity building. The basis of our cooperation in cyber is the India-US Cyber Framework signed in September 2016, which was the first agreement of its type for both India and US to sign.

INDIA-US TRADE TENSIONS THREATEN THE TIES THAT BIND

The US and India are long-standing allies, and trade is an important part of the relationship. However, a row over market access and tariffs has escalated, leading to fears of a protracted dispute.

The US is already mired in a deepening trade conflict with China, the world's most populous nation. Now it appears to be on course for one with the world's second most populous – India.

While the US-China trade conflict dominated headlines for the last year, trade tensions between New Delhi and Washington have been quietly simmering in the background.

They have come to the boil in recent weeks. Earlier this month, the US suspended Indian trade privileges from its Generalized System of Preferences (GSP), a 43-year-old program which gives US market access to less developed economies. India had been the biggest beneficiary of the scheme.

India said that it would hit back with tariff hikes and those levies duly took effect at the weekend – 28 specified US imports to India, including agricultural products such as lentils, chickpeas, apples and walnuts, are now subject to significantly higher rates than previously.

Much emphasis is being put on a meeting due to take place in New Delhi toward the end of the month between US Secretary of State Mike Pompeo and his Indian counterpart, Subrahmanyam Jaishankar, ahead of the G20 summit in Japan which takes place from June 28-29.

More than almonds and shrimp to this relationship

The US-India relationship is very important on several levels. The deepening security partnership between India and the US has been complemented in recent years by a growing trade relationship. The US buys more Indian exports than any other country.

According to the US state department, US-India bilateral trade reached $142 billion (€126 billion) in 2018, amounting to a massive sevenfold increase since 2001. Just last month, the Indo-American Chamber of Commerce said that figure could jump to $500 billion annually within five years.

However, the US has long taken issue with what it sees as unfair protectionist measures by the Indian government, including high tariffs and other trade barriers, which Washington says contributes to the huge trade deficit between the countries. India exports far more to the US than it imports from the country. According to the MIT Observatory of Economic Complexity, the deficit stood at almost $20 billion in 2017.

With trade one of the primary calling cards of Donald Trump's presidency so far and his election campaign before that, it should perhaps not be surprising that it is now a bone of contention in the US-India relationship. Yet many observers have been surprised by the speed of the gear shift.

Within a year, the countries were increasing tariffs on each other – the US refused to exempt India from the wide-ranging tariffs it levied on steel and aluminum imports, while India targeted US food products such as almonds and shrimp. Trump had also started to loudly question the benefits Indian exporters were receiving through the GSP.

Flipping out over Flipkart

Now Indian exporters of around $6 billion worth of goods ranging from chemical products to diamonds, textiles to crustaceans face reduced access in their biggest foreign market while US farmers will face tariffs of around 100% on several food products for which India is one of the main customers.

Yet how damaging it will ultimately be to US-India trade volumes remains to be seen. The Indian tariffs, in effect since Sunday morning, cover around $1.4 billion of goods, which is not a monumental amount in the overall US-India trading relationship.

How other aspects of the countries' economic relationship play out may prove just as significant. Washington was irked earlier this year when India announced a regulatory clampdown on US e-commerce giants like Amazon and Flipkart (Indian-founded but now owned by Walmart).

Huawei is another potential sore point. The Chinese tech giant has plans for expansion in India and hopes to play a role in building the country's 5G network, something Washington is unlikely to take too kindly.

For its part, India is less than impressed by US threats to impose sanctions if the country buys oil from Iran and if it proceeds with plans to purchase Russian anti-aircraft missiles.

Let's be friends again?

Yet, while recent developments have put a strain on US-India relations, it is still a world away from the enmity which has come to define the US-China trade relationship. The tariff volumes also pale in comparison.

The meeting slated for later this month may yet produce a "deal" of some kind, which could go some way to cooling tensions.

Pompeo recently said the US was open to restoring India's preferential trade treatment, offering a chink of light that a resolution could be reached. "We'll probably discuss the recent decision on the GSP program," he said.

However he added that he hoped "India will drop their trade barriers and trust in the competitiveness of their own companies, their own businesses, their own people and private sector companies," a nod to the kind of gestures the US will be seeking in return.

ECONOMIC RELATIONS

The United States seeks an expanded trade relationship that is reciprocal and fair. Bilateral trade in 2018 was $142 billion, a 12.6 percent increase from 2017. U.S. energy exports are an important area of growth in the trade relationship. In 2018 India purchased 48.2 million barrels of U.S. crude oil, a significant increase from 9.6 million in 2017. Last year, Indian students enrolled at U.S. colleges and universities contributed over $7 billion to the U.S. economy. The total number of Indian students in the United States has more than doubled over the last decade, from 81,000 in 2008 to a record high of 196,000 in 2018.

International Cooperation

India and the United States cooperate closely at multilateral organizations, including the United Nations, G-20, Association of Southeast Asian Nations (ASEAN) Regional Forum, International Monetary Fund, World Bank, and World Trade Organization. The United States supports a reformed UN Security Council that includes India as a permanent member. India is an ASEAN dialogue partner, an Organization for Economic Cooperation and Development partner, and an observer to the Organization of American States. India is also a member of the Indian Ocean Rim Association (IORA), at which the United States is a dialogue partner.

5

Preferential Trade Agreement

US PRESIDENT DONALD TRUMP TERMINATES PREFERENTIAL TRADE STATUS FOR INDIA

Washington accuses New Delhi of deploying a wide range of trade barriers that negatively affect US commerce. Media reports say that India could impose higher import duties on US goods in response to Trump's latest move.

"I have determined that India has not assured the United States that it will provide equitable and reasonable access to its markets," Trump said.

"Accordingly, it is appropriate to terminate India's designation as a beneficiary developing country effective June 5, 2019," the statement added.

The GSP program was introduced more than 40 years ago, in 1976, to promote economic growth in developing countries, allowing the export of certain products from these nations to the US duty free.

The Indian government dubbed Trump's move "unfortunate" but said that it will continue to seek to build strong economic ties with Washington.

"India, like the US and other nations, shall always uphold its national interest in these matters," the government said in a statement on Saturday. New Delhi said that it viewed the issue as part of its ongoing economic relationship with the US and "will continue to build on our strong ties with the US, both economic and people-to-people."

"We are confident that the two nations will continue to work together intensively for further growing these ties in a mutually beneficial manner," it added.

Scheduled since March

In a letter to leaders of the US Congress on March 4, the White House said that India and Turkey were set to lose their preferential trade treatment with the US. Last month, 24 members of the US Congress sent a letter to Trump, urging him not to end India's GSP status.

Removing a country from the GSP requires 60 days' notice, and it appears that President Trump waited until after India's mammoth elections before completing the move.

Indian media reports said New Delhi was considering higher import duties on more than 20 US goods, including agricultural produce and chemicals, in response.

Indian 'protectionism'

Washington's GSP program allows $5.6 billion (€4.94 billion) worth of Indian exports to enter the US duty free.

An Indian official cited by Reuters in March said that the "actual benefit" from the program to the Indian economy was only $250 million per year.

"GSP is more symbolic of the strategic relationship, not in value terms," the official said.

US trade officials, however, accuse New Delhi of deploying "a wide array of trade barriers that create serious negative effects on US commerce." US authorities said their country's trade deficit with India reached $27.3 billion in 2017.

In February, India started enforcing new rules on e-commerce in an attempt to shield domestic traders from foreign-based business giants. The rules caused severe disruption for Amazon and Flipkart, which is majority-owned by the US retail giant Walmart.

Last year, New Delhi ordered Visa and Mastercard to store their data on transactions involving users in India solely on Indian servers. US firms have opposed such legislation in various parts of the world. India also increased tariffs on electronics and smartphones. Previously, the Trump administration imposed tariffs of 25% on steel and 10% on aluminum imported from India.

Oil imports and Iran conflict

New Delhi and Washington are also at odds over Iranian oil imports. In April, the US announced it would not extend sanction exemptions to countries importing oil from Iran when they expired in early May. It meant countries and companies trading with Iran without Washington's consent would risk US sanctions and getting cut off from the American financial system.

India is one of the countries likely to be the hardest hit by the US decision. India is the world's third-biggest oil consumer, but its energy needs are primarily met through imports. The South Asian nation imports almost 80% of its oil requirements and Iran is its third-largest supplier, contributing over 11% of its crude oil demand. In the fiscal year 2018-19, India imported about 23.5 million tons of Iranian oil.

Following the US decision, India may try to increase its supplies of oil from countries like Saudi Arabia and the United Arab Emirates. Indian refiners are increasing their planned purchases from the nations of the Organization of the Petroleum Exporting Countries (OPEC), Mexico and the United States, to hedge against the loss of Iranian oil.

Official figures released on Friday showed that India's growth slowed for the third straight quarter, to 5.8% in January-March, while unemployment hit a 45-year high last year.

INDIA-US: WHAT IS PREFERENTIAL TRADE STATUS AND HOW WILL ITS REMOVAL AFFECT TIES?

With US President Donald Trump on Wednesday announcing plans to end preferential trade treatment for India under the Generalised System of Preferences (GSP) post a 60-day notice period, speculation is rife about how hard India will be impacted and its response to the move. Here's a look at exactly what is at stake:

What are Preferential Trade Agreements (PTAs)?

These agreements give signing nations special or preferential access to each other's markets, giving a boost to overall trade. In the US, the GSP programme - designed to promote economic growth in the beneficiary developing countries - provides duty-free entry for up to 4,800 products from 129 designated beneficiary countries and territories.

The criteria for inclusion in the GSP programme include factors such as providing the US with equitable and reasonable market access, respecting arbitral awards in favour of US citizens or corporations, combating child labour, providing adequate and effective intellectual property protection, and respecting internationally recognised worker rights, among others.

India was the largest beneficiary of the programme in 2017 with $5.6 billion worth of exports to the US being given duty-free status, according to a Congressional Research Service report issued in January. According to The Washington Post, while the US remains India's top export partner, receiving more than $48 billion in goods from the country in 2017, just over 10% of imports from India benefit from the programme, which was to expire in December 2020. Turkey, the other new target in Trump's trade wars, was the fifth largest beneficiary with $1.7 billion in covered imports.

In his letter to Speaker of the US House of Representatives Nancy Pelosi signalling his "intent to terminate" trade benefits,

Trump said he was determined that New Delhi had "not assured" the US that it would "provide equitable and reasonable access" to the markets of India.

The move is the latest push by the Trump administration to reduce US trade deficits and redress what it considers to be unfair trading relationships with other countries, starting with China. In addition, Trump has repeatedly called out India for high tariffs. In April 2018, the US launched an eligibility review of India's compliance with the GSP market access criterion.

What will be the impact on India?

The bilateral trade between India and the US stood at $74.5 billion in 2017-18, up 15.5 per cent from $64.5 billion in the previous fiscal. However, the numbers are skewed in India's favour. For instance, India reportedly imported items worth $26.3 billion from the US in FY19 (April-December) but posted total export of $38.8 billion. According to Commerce Secretary Anup Wadhawan, "GSP withdrawal will not have a significant impact on India's exports to the US" since the duty benefit, or savings on import tariffs, amounts to only $190 million annually.

Moreover, Monideepa M Mukherjee, a spokeswoman for India's commerce ministry, told Associated Press that GSP was in any case "meant for least-developed countries, and India has graduated out of that". In January, the International Monetary Fund had reconfirmed India's 'fastest-growing major economy' tag and predicted GDP growth at 7.5 per cent in FY20.

The Federation of Indian Export Organisations (FIEO) also believes that India's exports to the US will remain unaffected by Trump's latest move since it will only have a marginal impact on a few domestic sectors such as processed food, leather, plastic, building material and tiles, engineering goods, and hand tools, among others.

"India was getting tariff preference on 5,111 tariff lines [or products] out of 18,770 tariff lines in the US. However, on only 2,165 tariff lines, the tariff advantage was 4 per cent or more," said

Ganesh Kumar Gupta, the president of the exporters' body. "While we hope that the exporters would be able to absorb the duty loss where it is 2-3 per cent, we need to provide fiscal support to those products where GSP tariff advantage was significant [higher] particularly in the labour-intensive sector."

According to him, the removal of these duty concessions would make the above products relatively uncompetitive in terms of prices in the US market compared to exports from other developing countries. For example, the import price of most of the chemical products, which constituted a large chunk of India's exports, is expected to increase by about 5 per cent. Industry body FICCI concurs that GSP withdrawal will make the Indian industry less competitive.

What will be India's next move?

The buzz is that India may take a firm stance by imposing retaliatory tariffs on the US from the next month. If this comes to pass, a total of 29 items imported from the US, including walnuts, lentils, boric acid and diagnostic reagents, will face higher duties, cutting benefits to the US exporters. The move will put extra burden of $290 million per year on US items exported to India.

According to Wadhawan, the Trump administration decided to go ahead with tariff cut despite the fact that India was working on an "extensive and reasonable" trade package that covered all concerns related to bilateral trade with the US on sectors such as medical devices, dairy products and agricultural goods. Incidentally, the review of GSP benefits in the US was initiated on account of representations by dairy and medical industries.

He also refuted US' claims of "high tariffs" in India, adding, "Our tariffs are very consistent with the bound rates that we are entitled too in the World Trade Organisation".

AN INDIA-US FREE-TRADE AGREEMENT

India and the US are an odd couple. Even as Prime Minister Narendra Modi and Chinese President Xi Jinping conduct their two-day 'informal summit' in Mamallapuram in Tamil Nadu, and despite the fact that the two democracies can't stop bickering under their breath, they do keep professing their love for each quite loudly.

India and the US accuse each other of unfair trade practices and are among the most active litigants at the World Trade Organisation (WTO). And, yet, they are each other's anchor in their geopolitical strategy in the Asia Pacific — a region now significantly renamed Indo-Pacific according to the US' redrawn strategic map.

The public display of affection between Prime Minister Modi and US President Donald Trump is hard to ignore. Yet, progress on bilateral trade, investment and immigration issues has remained disjointed.

The trade ministers and officials of the two countries argued, while Modi and Trump hugged and sang paeans to each other. India and the US need to deepen both the economic and the strategic aspects of their relationship. Mutual strategic interest alone cannot sustain a meaningful relationship.

The governments of both countries need to settle on a framework of doing business with each other as soon as possible. Essentially, they need a free-trade agreement (FTA).

It does help that both Modi and Trump wear their nationalism on their sleeves, and can also see each other's point of view. A mutual agreement would be more meaningful to them than reliance on any multilateral arbitrator.

The US has been pushing India for an FTA for some time now, and Trump is keen to announce a trade deal with India — even an interim one — as soon as possible. He is on a mission to erase the US' trade deficit with every country, and he may like a quick feather in his cap by neutralising the $24 billion goods and services trade deficit with India.

Trump promised to bring 'Made-in-America' products to Indian consumers at Modi's recent rally in Houston. The US has offered to make India an alternative business hub in the Indo-Pacific, if it signs an FTA.

Trading Emotions

Business leaders of the two countries are quite eager to see the trade niggle between them sorted out as quickly as possible, and that a clear, fair and stable agreement that assures policy and tariff certainty is established.

A delegation of Indian CEOs attending the All India Management Association's (AIMA) US-India Conference at University of California Berkeley on September 27 voiced the need for the two countries to invest in each other's strengths.

Even though India may not gain much in terms of tariff reductions from the US, since its tariffs are already very low, it can gain a lot by bargaining for an easier access to the US' high-paying market, plentiful capital and latest technologies.

However, a common ground will have to be found between 'America First' and 'Make in India'. India would struggle to lower its tariffs, which average about 13%, without hurting local producers and its tax revenues. It will have to be innovative in creating trade-offs that deliver positive net returns.

Agriculture and dairy would be particularly contentious areas because of subsidy and phytosanitary issues. The digital economy has to be central to any FTA, given the rapid shift to digital technologies in both countries.

An FTA will have to reconcile data nationalism with the internet's innate globalism. India's linking of its sovereignty with possession of data, and the US' linking of its national security with origin of vendors, will pose significant challenges to FTA negotiators.

Bilateral trade in professional services would grow along with the growth in economic and strategic integration. It is always tricky to open up markets for licence-dependent professional services, such as audit, law and medicine. But associated services such as accounting, para-legal work and diagnostics can be traded aplenty.

However, free mobility of professionals and data is a fundamental requirement. The two countries will have to work out ways to ensure that.

Intellectual property (IP) has always been a big issue for the US. India will need to strengthen its patent and trademark regime to satisfy the Americans. India would want similar guarantees from the US for its IP, especially in the software, entertainment and pharmaceutical industries.

Done Deal

The FTA will have to cover for non-tariff barriers to trade. Often, exporters are frustrated by harassment by customs, despite compliance. Recently, US companies have complained of Chinese officials dismantling built-up vehicles in the name of inspection.

Achieving an FTA that makes everybody happy is unlikely. But having an FTA would be a huge improvement on not having one. Time has come to replace ad-hoc policies and tariffs with clear, long-term framework for trade and investment between the two countries.

TRUMP TERMINATES PREFERENTIAL TRADE STATUS FOR INDIA UNDER GSP

President Donald Trump has terminated India's designation as a beneficiary developing nation under the key GSP trade programme after determining that it has not assured the US that it will provide "equitable and reasonable access" to its markets.

The Generalized System of Preference (GSP) is the largest and oldest US trade preference programme and is designed to promote economic development by allowing duty-free entry for thousands of products from designated beneficiary countries.

"I have determined that India has not assured the US that it will provide equitable and reasonable access to its markets.

Accordingly, it is appropriate to terminate India's designation as a beneficiary developing country effective June 5, 2019," Trump said in a proclamation on Friday ignoring the plea made by several top American lawmakers.

On March 4, Trump announced that the US intends to terminate India's designations as a beneficiary developing country under the GSP programme. The 60-day notice period ended on May 3.

The Trump administration has prioritised working with the Government of India to ensure that US companies have a level-playing field, a senior State Department official told reporters on Thursday, hours after Narendra Modi was sworn in as Prime Minister for a second time following his spectacular electoral victory in the general elections.

GSP criteria

Under the GSP programme, nearly 2,000 products including auto components and textile materials can enter the US duty-free if the beneficiary developing countries meet the eligibility criteria established by Congress.

India was the largest beneficiary of the programme in 2017 with USD 5.7 billion in imports to the US given duty-free status and Turkey the fifth largest with USD 1.7 billion in covered imports, according to a Congressional Research Service report issued in January.

The GSP criteria includes, among others, respecting arbitral awards in favour of the US citizens or corporations, combating child labour, respecting internationally recognised worker rights, providing adequate and effective intellectual property protection, and providing the US with equitable and reasonable market access. Countries can also be graduated from the GSP programme depending on factors related to economic development.

Impact on US economy

In a statement, Coalition for GSP executive director Dan Anthony said Trump's decision will cost American businesses over USD 300 million in additional tariffs every year. "Without GSP benefits American small businesses face a new tax that will mean job losses, cancelled investments and cost increases for consumers. Only a year after the Senate and House passed a three year reauthorisation of the GSP by a near unanimous margin, the Trump administration has kicked out the GSP country that saves American companies more money than any other," he said.

Anthony said the Trump administration made the decision in the face of opposition from members of the Congress and hundreds of American businesses that have called for continued GSP eligibility for India. "They also acted despite India's willingness to negotiate new market access for American exports. Thus, there are no winners from today's decision. American importers will pay more, while some American exporters will continue to face current market access barriers in India and others, including farmers, are very likely to be subject to new retaliatory tariff, Anthony said.

The Trump administration argues that New Delhi has failed to assure America that it will provide equitable and reasonable access to its markets in numerous sectors. Meanwhile, India had said that the US government's move to withdraw duty concessions on certain products under the GSP programme will not have a significant impact on exports to America as the benefits were only about USD 190 million annually.

Commerce Secretary Anup Wadhawan in March said despite the fact that India was working on an "extensive and reasonable" trade package, the US decided to go ahead with its decision to scrap the preferential trade benefit. The package was covering all concerns related to bilateral trade with the US on sectors including medical devices, dairy products and agricultural goods, he said adding that India could not negotiate issues concerning interests of public healthcare.

In a statement in March, the US Trade Representative (USTR) said that India has failed to provide the US with assurances that it will provide equitable and reasonable access to its markets in numerous sectors. The Trump administration had launched an eligibility review of India's compliance with the GSP market access criterion in April 2018. "India has implemented a wide array of trade barriers that create serious negative effects on United States commerce. Despite intensive engagement, India has failed to take the necessary steps to meet the GSP criterion," the USTR said.

INDIA-US FREE TRADE AGREEMENT WOULD REQUIRE NEW DELHI TO REORIENT KEY POLICIES

For some years now, there have been discussions on the sidelines that India and the US would enter into negotiations for a free trade agreement (FTA).

In the last few weeks, there has also been some speculation that such an augury is in the offing, which has been strengthened by President Donald Trump's statement that a "key announcement" would be made during his meeting with Prime Minister Narendra Modi.

While nothing was announced on Sunday night at the NRG Stadium in Houston, it appears more than likely that something is in the offing.

An FTA between some of the world's largest economies arouses considerable interest, especially because of the nature of these agreements are in the realm of comprehensive economic partnership agreements, which usually cover every possible area of economic, social and environmental policies.

However, India and the US seems to have had considerable differences on a wide gamut of trade and related economic policies, which must be addressed before any move towards a possible FTA is taken.

Deteriorating trade relations

Trade relations between India and the US have been deteriorating since the spring of 2018. This was after the US unilaterally increased tariffs on steel and aluminium, by 25% and 10% respectively, on its imports from several countries including India. The argument used was that imports from these countries threatened US's domestic industries and that higher tariffs could protect them for "national defence" and "national security". Such unilateral measures were adopted despite these being against the rules of the World Trade Organization (WTO).

Like most affected countries, India initiated bilateral negotiations with the US to resolve the issue. This move having failed, India raised its tariffs on select US products using WTO rules, and then approached the dispute settlement mechanism to initiate consultations prior to the initiation of a formal dispute. When almost six months of consultations bore no fruit, India sought the establishment of a dispute settlement panel for resolving its dispute with the US.

A few months ago, the US took yet another unilateral measure to restrict the entry of Indian products into its market, by denying concessional market access under the generalised system of preferences (GSP). A presidential proclamation announced the list of 94 products from the developing countries which would not receive duty-free access into the US, of which 50 were those being imported from India.

Under the GSP, which has been in place since 1971, products exported by developing countries are granted duty-free access in the markets of developed countries. In other words, developed countries granted unilateral concessions to the developing countries for increasing their exports.

The GSP row got worse this year in June when the US withdrew the GSP preferences enjoyed by 3,600 products exported by India. The United States Trade Representative (USTR) announced the termination of India's designation as a beneficiary developing country under its GSP programme for its failure to provide the US with "assurances that it will provide equitable and reasonable access to its markets in numerous sectors".

The US decision was based on an eligibility review conducted by the USTR on "concerns" related to India's compliance with the GSP market access criterion, but more importantly, on two petitions related to the same criterion. The petitions were filed by the US dairy industry and the US medical device industry requesting the USTR to withdraw India as a beneficiary country, given India's "trade barriers" affecting US exports in those sectors. The latter petition was regarding the price controls that the government of India had introduced for coronary stents and knee implants aimed at making these devices affordable in the country.

Linking GSP benefits to market access opportunities provided by India was a violation of the GSP rules, since developed countries grant these preferences unilaterally to developing countries.

To be developed or not?

Denial of GSP preferences should be seen as a part of a larger design of the US administration to get India de-recognised as a "developing country" in the WTO. In a substantial paper submitted to the WTO in February, the US argued that since countries like India and China have climbed up the development ladder, they should not be designated as developing countries.

More recently, President Trump issued a memorandum on Reforming Developing-Country Status in the WTO, the key point of which was that "China and too many other countries have continued to style themselves as developing countries, allowing them to enjoy the benefits that come with that status ...".

As a developing country, India enjoys a number of benefits, including the space to grant higher levels of agricultural subsidies and to maintain higher levels of protection as compared to the developed countries. For instance, developed countries can subsidise their agriculture up to 5% of their value of agricultural production, while the corresponding figure for developing countries is 10%.

Equally importantly, India, as a developing country, has a food subsidy programme like the one that the National Food

Security Act has put in place. This programme would have to be discontinued if India loses its developing-country status.

Over the years, the US has sought plenty of changes in India's trade and investment policies for it found that they were not serving American commercial interests. India has frequently been probed by federal agencies, the last of the major investigations by the US International Trade Commission (USITC): 'Trade, Investment, and Industrial Policies in India: Effects on the U.S. Economy'. This report published in 2014 examined "trade, investment, and industrial policies in India that restrict US exports and investment, and estimates the effects these policies have on US companies, US workers, and the US economy".

One of the more extensive commentaries on India's policies was on its Patents Act, which, according to this report "limits patents for incremental innovation, compulsory license provisions, and onerous patent processes are a deterrent to US companies, especially in IP intensive industries". For exactly two decades, the USTR has been "investigating" India's Patents Act using Section 301 provisions of its Trade Acts of 1974 and 1988. This "investigation" has continued even after India had enacted a patent regime compatible with the WTO Agreement on Trade-Related Aspects of Intellectual Property Rights (TRIPS).

The USITC report was alluding to several public policy provisions that the country's lawmakers had included in the Indian Patents Act to keep the prices of medicines affordable. India denies patents on mere formulations or new uses for existing products and can issue compulsory licences when the patented drugs are sold at prices way beyond the means of the common people. These are important provisions for a country that has substantial income inequalities.

As mentioned earlier, India had imposed price caps on coronary stents and knee implants, resulting in the lowering of prices by 85% and 65% respectively. The US administration has consistently argued that the Indian government must abandon these policies, which are providing affordable healthcare solutions to its citizens

The other critical area in which the US is seeking substantial changes in India's policies is agricultural subsidies, in particular, those granted to the two principal cereals: rice and wheat. The US has argued in the WTO's Committee on Agriculture that India has been giving market price support to these crops way above the level that it is committed to providing. Thus, Washington DC's stance is not exactly supportive of India's critical interests in agriculture, namely, food security and rural livelihoods.

It is clear that the US wants a comprehensive re-orientation of Indian policies; seeking to shift the focus of India's laws away from serving the interests of its citizens. Interestingly, while engaging international processes, the US administration's sole aim has been to serve the interests of its workers, farmers, ranchers and businesses: The Trump-Modi summit could possibly help the US understand that its partner country aims to do similarly.

INDIA-CHILE SET TO EXPAND PREFERENTIAL TRADE, EXPLORE POSSIBILITY OF A FREE TRADE PACT

India hopes to export more generic drugs and textiles to Chile while the South American country wants to increase its exports of fish, oats, fruits, industrial products and chemicals, as the two have formally exchanged the terms of reference for expanding the bilateral preferential trade agreement (PTA).

New Delhi has also sought cooperation in sourcing of Lithium from Chile to support its drive to popularise the use of e-vehicles in the country, in a recent meeting between Commerce Secretary Anup Wadhawan and Special Envoy of Chile for Asia Pacific Eduardo Frez Ruiz-Tagle, a government official told *BusinessLine*.

"India-Chile bilateral trade has a huge potential to expand as it is currently at a low level mostly because of the distance separating the countries. Both governments are hopeful that once the expansion of the existing PTA takes place, there will be greater incentive for exporters in both countries to explore the markets," the official said. Ways to increase investments between the two countries was also discussed. "Once the expanded PTA is in place, the two countries will also explore a possible full-fledged Comprehensive Economic Partnership Agreement including goods, services and investments," the official added. India-Chile bilateral trade is around $2.5 billion annually.

Under the expanded PTA, Chile has offered concessions to India on 1,798 tariff lines (products) with margin of preference (MoP) ranging from 30-100 per cent. This means that once the expanded PTA is implemented, Chile will impose lower duties on 1,798 products imported from India compared to what it imposes on its other trading partners under normal trade. The duties will be lower by 30-100 per cent (margin of preference) depending on the item.

India, on its part has offered concessions to Chile on 1,031 tariff lines with the margin of preference ranging from 10-100 per cent.

Although India's concessions cover a number of farm and food items including meat and meat products, fish and fishery products and vegetable oils, it has not agreed to reduce import duties on Chilean wine as it is a sensitive sector, the official added.

Chile has offered concessions to India in sectors such as agricultural products, organic and inorganic chemicals, pharmaceuticals, plastic and rubber articles, textiles, apparel, articles of iron/steel and copper, machinery and equipments.

India hopes that once the PTA is expanded, the export of pharmaceuticals will increase significantly especially in the light of a recent MoU signed between India's STC and Chilean agency CENABAST for sourcing of high standard generics.

New Delhi's increased engagement with Chile is part of its broader approach of increasing engagement with Latin America so as to expand the countries trade interests beyond the traditional markets of the EU and the US.

6

Growing the India-U.S. Trade and Investment Relationship

Indian barriers to trade and investment, including lack of intellectual property protection and enforcement, continue to undermine the potential of the economic relationship. U.S. policy, such as limits on access to work visas, can also affect growth in economic ties.

Another complication: India is a WTO member but is not a party to the large regional trade negotiations involving the U.S., namely the Trans-Pacific Partnership (TPP) and the Trade in Services Agreement (TiSA). India, in turn, is negotiating the Regional Comprehensive Economic Partnership Agreement—the ASEAN+6 agreement—which does not include the U.S.

OVERVIEW OF INDIA-U.S. TRADE AND INVESTMENT

In 2013, India was the 18th largest goods market for the U.S. That year, total India-U.S. trade was $96.7 billion, up over 400 percent from $23.9 billion in 2003. Of this total, U.S. exports to India were $35.7 billion and imports were $61 billion, producing a bilateral trade deficit of $25.4 billion in 2013, up from a deficit of $6.3 billion in 2003.

A key feature of growth in bilateral trade has been in services, which grew 600 percent since 2003, from $5.8 billion to $32.5 billion in 2013. This includes an increase in India's services exports to the U.S. of over 900 percent since 2003—from $2 billion to over

$19 billion in 2013—and growth in U.S. service exports to India of over 350 percent from $3.7 billion in 2003 to almost $13.5 billion in 2013. In fact, since 2006 the U.S. has had a growing services trade deficit with India, even though the U.S. runs a services trade surplus with the rest of the world.

This services deficit largely reflects the growth in India as a destination for outsourcing by U.S. companies. Outsourcing has given U.S. businesses access to lower cost services inputs that has allowed them to be more competitive in the U.S. and overseas. There have been concerns, however, that outsourcing can negatively affect U.S. jobs.

Total goods trade has also grown substantially—over 400 percent from $18.1 billion in 2003 to $64.2 billion in 2013. The U.S. has a growing trade in goods deficit with India, which was almost $20 billion in 2013, up from $8 billion in 2003.

The U.S. stock of foreign direct investment (FDI) in India has also increased—over 600 percent since 2003—from $4.8 billion in to $28.4 billion in 2012. And while Indian investment in the U.S. has experienced 1400 percent growth, this was off a low base of $350 million in 2002 and was only $5.2 billion in 2012.

- Commit to a deadline to conclude a Bilateral Investment Treaty. This will signal Indian government support for growing U.S. investment and provide a rules-based framework within which this can occur. It will also support growth in services trade which can be provided through FDI.
- Develop a dialogue with Indian regulators to address how India's "Decade of Innovation" can be supported by stronger protection and enforcement of intellectual property rights.
- Affirm the administration's support for extending access to H-1B visas for students having completed postgraduate U.S. degrees.
- India's new government has yet to develop its trade policy. This presents an opportunity to develop a dialogue with

India as to what Indian economic reforms could facilitate it joining either the TPP or the TiSA should it wish to do so.

INDIA US TRADE AND INVESTMENT PARTNERSHIP

India enjoys a long-standing partnership with the US, based on common principles of democracy and shared interests of promoting peace and economic prosperity through trade and investment ties.

The bilateral relationship between the two countries that received an impetus starting with the visit of President Clinton in 2000 has strengthened over the years and continues to gather momentum under President Trump. The forthcoming visit of Prime Minister Modi to US during September 2019 will further catalyze economic ties between the two countries and is a great opportunity for reinforcing this strategic partnership.

Merchandise Trade

The US surpassed China to become India's top trading partner in 2018, while India was its 9th largest trading partner. Total trade between the two countries during 2018-19 stood at around US$ 88 billion, of which India's exports to the US amounted to US$ 52 billion and India's imports from US amounted to around US$ 36 billion.

India-US Trade (in US$ Millions)

Year	2014-15	2015-16	2016-17	2017-18	2018-19
Export	42,448.66	40,336.01	42,212.27	47,878.48	52,406.27
% Growth		-4.98	4.65	13.42	9.46
Imports	21,814.60	21,781.39	22,307.44	26,611.03	35,549.48
% Growth		-0.15	2.42	19.29	33.59
Total Trade	64,263.26	62,117.39	64,519.71	74,489.51	87,955.76
% Growth		-3.34	3.87	15.45	18.08

Source: Export-Import Databank, Ministry of Commerce and Industry, Government of India

Major Indian exports to the United States comprise of pharmaceutical products, textiles, diamonds, organic chemicals, and electrical machinery among others. On the other hand, major imports from the US to India include electrical machinery and equipment, aircraft and parts, petroleum products, plastic and articles, and iron and steel products, among others.

Services Trade

Bilateral trade in services between the two countries has increased rapidly over the last two decades. Total trade in services between India and US stood at around US$ 54.56 billion in 2018 as compared to US$ 51.9 billion in 2017. Of this, services imports into India from US was estimated at US$ 25.8 billion while Indian services exports to US totaled US$ 28.8 billion.

Investment

Both countries are involved in a number of projects and bilateral investments, as part of their multifaceted partnership.

The US is the sixth largest source of foreign direct investment (FDI) to India. Cumulative FDI inflows to India from the US for the period 2000-2019 stood at around US$ 27 billion, constituting more than 6% of total FDI inflows to India. U.S. direct investment in India is led by professional, scientific, and technical services, manufacturing, and wholesale trade.

As per the 2017 CII report, "Indian Roots, American Soil", based on a survey of 100 Indian companies across 50 states in the US, Indian investment to US is estimated at around US$18 billion. India's direct investment in the U.S. is led by professional, scientific, and technical services, manufacturing, and depository institutions.

As per US data sources, cumulative US FDI to India as of 2018 amounted to US$ 45.98 billion while Indian FDI to US for the same year is estimated at around US$ 13.73 billion.

Sectors of Opportunity

Some of the sectors of opportunities which can mutually benefit both countries are in the areas of energy and infrastructure, media and entertainment, defense and aerospace, and healthcare, among others.

Energy: Both countries have a long-standing strategic partnership in the energy sector. India offers one of the largest investment opportunities in the renewable energy space with 175 gigawatts capacity planned till 2022. Potential sectors of collaboration could be in the areas of oil and gas, power, renewable energy and coal, as also India's unconventional hydrocarbons sector and area of fracking of shale gas.

Infrastructure: India could benefit from US participation in developing smart cities while India can help US companies launch and expand businesses in India, focusing on technologies, systems and services in the safety and security, intelligent transportation, water, wastewater, and power sectors.

Defense and aerospace: While US companies stand to gain from India's plan of reviving airport infrastructure through public-private partnerships, collaboration between the two in the areas of drone technology and manufacturing can also mutually benefit both countries. The defense manufacturing companies in the US could leverage India's upcoming defence production corridors and the growing strength of Indian companies for joint production collaborations.

Healthcare: Substantial opportunities exist for technology transfer in the areas of healthcare, with Indian programs such as Ayushman Bharat significantly boosting the demand for innovative and technology-based models. Other sectors of opportunity include medical infrastructure, research, and skill development, among others.

Media and entertainment: The media and entertainment sector also offers many opportunities for collaboration, bolstered by the strong presence of Indian diaspora and greater interest in Indian cinema across the world. VFX/animation, audio-visual co-production, gaming and virtual reality, and digital services are some areas that present huge opportunities for both countries.

The meeting between PM Modi and President Trump is expected to prioritise trade and investment talks that could lead to exciting prospects and further bolster the strong relationship between the two countries.

FOREIGN TRADE POLICY OF INDIA

The integration of the domestic economy through the twin channels of trade and capital flows has accelerated in the past two decades which in turn led to the India's GDP reaching Rs 167.73 trillion (US$ 2.30 trillion) in 2017-18*. Simultaneously, the per capita income also nearly trebled during these years. India's trade and external sector had a significant impact on the GDP growth as well as expansion in per capita income. Provisional estimates of India's GDP during the 2018-19 stood at Rs 190.10 trillion (US$ 2.72 trillion). As per the estimates of Gross Domestic Product (GDP) for the first quarter (Q1) of 2019-20, the growth of real GDP for Q1 of 2019-20 is estimated at 5 percent.

Total exports from India (Merchandise and Services) registered a growth of 1.60 per cent year-on-year during April-November 2019 to US$ 353.96 billion, while total imports estimated to be US$ 408.02 billion, exhibiting a negative growth of 5.30 per cent according to data from the Ministry of Commerce & Industry.Total exports from India (Merchandise and Services) registered a growth of 1.60 per cent year-on-year during April-November 2019 to US$ 353.96 billion, while total imports estimated to be US$ 408.02 billion, exhibiting a negative growth of 5.30 per cent according to data from the Ministry of Commerce & Industry.

The merchandise export stood at Rs 14,89,793.87 crore (US$ 211.93 billion) during April-November 2019 and imports reaching Rs 22,39,900.18 crore (US$ 318.78 billion) for the same period.

The estimated value of services export for April-October 2019 stood at US$ 142.02 billion and import is US$ 89.24 billion.

Thus, the overall trade deficit for April-November 2019 is estimated at US$ 54.06 billion.

According to Mr Piyush Goyal, Minister for Commerce and Industry, the Government of India is keen to grow exports and provide more jobs for the young, talented, well-educated and even semi-skilled and unskilled workforce of India.

Capital Inflows

India's foreign exchange reserves were Rs 32.19 lakh crore (US$ 460.65 billion) in the week up to November 22, 2019 according to data from the RBI.

External Sector

- In December 2019, cabinet approved Memorandum of Understanding between Central Electricity Authority, India and Japan Coal Energy Centre, on Japan-India cooperation for Efficiency and Environmental Improvement for Sustainable, Stable and Low-Carbon supply of Electricity.
- The Memorandum of Cooperation (MoC) between Government of India and Government of Japan in order to constitute the 'India-Japan Steel Dialogue' to strengthen cooperation in steel sector got approval from cabinet in December 2019.
- In November 2019, All India Institute of Ayurveda (AIIA) signed a Memorandum of Understanding (MoU) with Western Sydney University, Australia at New Delhi.
- In November 2019, the Memorandum of Understanding (MoU) signed between India and Finland approved by Cabinet in order to strengthen the cooperation in the field of Tourism.
- In September 2019, four Memorandum of Understanding (MoUs) were signed between India and Mongolia focusing on cultural exchange protocol, disaster management, space exploration and in field of animal health and dairy.
- In September 2019, Liquefied Natural Gas (LNG) importer Petronet entered into agreement with US LNG developer Tellurian Inc. and invest US$ 2.5 billion.
- In August 2019, four Memorandum of Understanding (MoUs) were signed between India and France focusing

on skill development and vocational training, renewable energy, IT services and space research.

- In June 2019, India and Kyrgyzstan signed 15 agreements in main areas, including defence, trade and investment and health.
- In April 2019, India signed a memorandum of understanding (MoU) with the National Bank for Agriculture and Rural Development Consultancy Service (NABCONS) for establishing the India-Africa Institute of Agriculture and Rural Development (IAIARD) in Malawi, South Africa.
- In December 2018, India and the UAE signed currency swap agreement to boost trade and investment ties between the two countries.

Foreign Trade Policy

- In the Mid-Term Review of the Foreign Trade Policy (FTP) 2015-20 the Ministry of Commerce and Industry has enhanced the scope of Merchandise Exports from India Scheme (MEIS) and Service Exports from India Scheme (SEIS), increased MEIS incentive raised for ready-made garments and made- ups by 2 per cent, raised SEIS incentive by 2 per cent and increased the validity of Duty Credit Scrips from 18 months to 24 months.
- In August 2019, Ministry of Commerce plans to introduce new foreign trade policy aimed at providing incentives and guidelines for increasing export in next five financial years 2020-25.
- As of December 2018, Government of India is planning to set up trade promotion bodies in 15 countries to boost exports from Small and Medium Enterprises (SME) in India.
- In September 2018, Government of India increased the duty incentives for 28 milk items under the Merchandise Export from India Scheme (MEIS).
- All export and import-related activities are governed by the Foreign Trade Policy (FTP), which is aimed at enhancing

the country's exports and use trade expansion as an effective instrument of economic growth and employment generation.

- The Department of Commerce has announced increased support for export of various products and included some additional items under the Merchandise Exports from India Scheme (MEIS) in order to help exporters to overcome the challenges faced by them.
- The Central Board of Excise and Customs (CBEC) has developed an 'integrated declaration' process leading to the creation of a single window which will provide the importers and exporters a single point interface for customs clearance of import and export goods.
- As part of the FTP strategy of market expansion, India has signed a Comprehensive Economic Partnership Agreement with South Korea which will provide enhanced market access to Indian exports. These trade agreements are in line with India's Look East Policy. To upgrade export sector infrastructure, 'Towns of Export Excellence' and units located therein will be granted additional focused support and incentives.
- RBI has simplified the rules for credit to exporters, through which they can now get long-term advance from banks for up to 10 years to service their contracts. This measure will help exporters get into long-term contracts while aiding the overall export performance.
- The Government of India is expected to announce an interest subsidy scheme for exporters in order to boost exports and explore new markets.

Road Ahead

India is presently known as one of the most important players in the global economic landscape. Its trade policies, government reforms and inherent economic strengths have attributed to its standing as one of the most sought-after destinations for foreign investments in the world. Also, technological and infrastructural developments being carried out throughout the country augur well for the trade and economic sector in the years to come. Boosted by the forthcoming FTP, India's exports are expected reach US$ 750 billion by 2018-2019 according to Federation of India Export Organisation (FIEO). Also, with the Government of India striking important deals with the governments of Japan, Australia and China, the external sector is increasing its contribution to the economic development of the country and growth in the global markets. Moreover, by implementing the FTP 2014-19, by 2020, India's share in world trade is expected to double from the present level of three per cent.

IN SEARCH OF THE ELUSIVE US-INDIA TRADE DEAL

As leaders and senior officials returned home from nearly a week of meetings and soirees on the margins of the annual United Nations (UN) General Assembly in New York City, observers could finally catch their breath and assess the significance of an unusually high volume of announcements, ranging from climate change and human rights to international finance and trade.

The clear headline grabber on trade was the announcement by the United States and Japan that they had reached an interim deal on tariffs and digital economy—what appears to be a first installment for a possible free trade agreement (FTA). This deal is a stand in for the one concluded during the Obama administration as part of the Trans-Pacific Partnership (TPP), although, by falling short of that example, it is more likely to get serious scrutiny from other countries in the World Trade Organization (WTO) given that it falls short of objective standards of what constitutes an FTA under WTO rules.

Despite high expectations in the run-up to the "Howdy Modi" event before the UN General Assembly meetings and the bilateral meeting between US President Donald J. Trump and Indian Prime Minister Narendra Modi in New York two days later, there was no mini US-India trade deal to compete for the limelight with the US-Japan deal. That is a shame. There was no more auspicious a moment for creating an historic precedent on trade between the two countries—as limited as it was likely to be. We can only hope that the momentum for a deal has not entirely slipped away and that efforts by US Trade Representative Robert Lighthizer and Indian Minister of Commerce and Industry Piyush Goyal bear fruit in coming days.

The US-India relationship, now and for the foreseeable future, is of enormous consequence. Many observers engage in repetitious referencing (and they are correct in doing so) of shared values between the United States and India, as the oldest and largest democracies, and of their growing strategic interests, particularly as China continues to rise. This relationship has the potential to be uniquely strong in ways that will have global implications. And the Indian and broader South Asian diaspora in the United States is an increasingly important contributor to what makes America great as a diverse, open, and innovative society.

That said, the trade relationship has generally been seen as lagging compared to the emergence of the strategic one. As pointed out by Indian External Affairs Minister Dr. S. Jaishankar in his appearance at the Atlantic Council this week, all of the indicators of the economic relationship, including trade, are positive. What has been lacking is a government-to-government shared vision of how to build bilateral trade agreements to underpin the burgeoning commercial relationships.

That can start with a first, even if small, trade agreement to fix a series of immediate priorities. Unlike the Japan deal, a US-India deal may not be a precursor to an eventual bilateral FTA. That's an aspiration for the future and should not be on the immediate horizon. But it could go some distance in building up a new dynamic of mutual interest in resolving trade problems as they crop up and identifying opportunities for promoting regulatory reforms that can nurture the growing commercial ties between the two countries. As the Atlantic Council noted in its recent report on trade with the US-India Strategic Partnership Forum, the two sides can work together to build incrementally a foundation of successes on the trade front—ones which can further nurture the trade and investment interests of their producers and exporters, large and small. With a record of successes, they may find at the appropriate moment that they have reached a point of sufficient mutual trust to seriously explore the ultimate model of bilateral economic integration—a full-fledged, deep, and broad FTA.

While this vision should be sufficient to maintain the impetus to conclude a trade deal in coming weeks, an additional motivation should be the desire to avoid a further inflaming of tensions on trade. That is not a pretty picture. It likely would involve new tit-for-tat actions to restrict trade and investment between the two countries and would deepen the perceptions of their respective stakeholders that the other side will never play fair. At best, this scenario likely would significantly delay the start of a new kind of US-India trade relationship.

Even if the opportunity for an agreement in New York has come and gone, there appears to have been sufficient progress for the two trade teams to conclude a deal very soon. This window may not be open for long and once it has closed, we may find that the trade relationship is again stuck in a longstanding paradigm that does not serve a growing friendship well.

PRESIDENCY UNDER TRUMP BOOST FOR INDIA-US TIES

The US presidency under Donald Trump, a confessed big fan of India and Prime Minister Narendra Modi, is most likely to boost Indo-US strategic relationship with a special emphasis on defence ties and counter-terrorism cooperation.

Trump, 70, had recently described India as "a key, and key strategic ally" and looks forward to deepening the diplomatic and military cooperation that is the shared interest of both countries.

The billionaire businessman who has lauded economic policies of Modi had said he wants to work with him. At an event in New Jersey less than a month from now, Trump had promised to the

Indian-American community in him India would find a true friend at the White House.

"I am a big fan of Hindus and I am a big fan of India. If I am elected president, the Indian and Hindu community would have a true friend at the White House," he had said at an event organised by the Hindu Republican Coalition. Trump said he appreciated "great friend India in the fight against" terrorism.

India has experienced firsthand "brutality of terror" in the past "including the mayhem in Mumbai," he said and described the 2008 Mumbai terror attack and that on Indian Parliament in 2001 as "absolutely outrageous" and terrible. "We will defeat... terrorism. We will stand soldier-to-soldier in this fight. This is so important in the age of Daesh," he said.

"India's is the world's largest democracy and is a natural ally of the US. Under a Trump Administration, we are going to become even better friends.

In fact, I will take the word even out because we are going to be best friends. I look forward to working with Prime Minister Modi, who has been very energetic in reforming the economy and bureaucracy. Great man. I applaud him," he said. "I look forward to doing some serious bureaucratic trimming right here in the US, believe me we need it most," Trump said.

"Your great prime minister has been a pro-growth leader for India. He has simplified the tax code, cut the taxes and the economy is strong growing at 7 per cent year. Excellent," he said. On the eve of the November 8 general elections, a key military advisor to the Trump said that India will have an important role to play in the Trump Administration's Asia Pacific policy of "peace through strength."

"This is a country that shares our values, this is a country that shares a lot of geo-political interest and I think, his (Trump's) work is going to be continuing the tradition of Bush Administration which made a lot of progress in that regard," Alexander Gray, a military adviser and author of several of the ambitious defence policies of Trump, said. "We (at Trump Administration) would be looking to strengthen not just the cultural and economic aspect, but also on the defence side there is so much common ground with India. At a time when India's foreign policy is changing because of China and Pakistan, because of terrorism, we need to be there to greet them with open arms. I think, the Trump Administration is ready to do that," Gray said.

Indian fan club celebrates victory

A far-right Hindu group which has been one of Donald Trump's most avid overseas cheerleaders began celebrating in New Delhi Wednesday as the Republican pulled off a shock US presidential election victory. Vishnu Gupta, chief of the ultra-nationalist 'Hindu Sena' outfit, said supporters had taken to the streets to bang traditional drums even before Trump claimed victory and would also distribute celebratory sweets.

Trump's hardline rhetoric towards Muslims has found favour in some quarters in India, the world's largest democracy which has had its fair share of tensions between the majority Hindu population and its Muslim minority. Indian Prime Minister Narendra Modi was before his 2014 election regarded as an international pariah after deadly communal riots broke out in the state of Gujarat more than a decade ago when he was chief minister. Most of the victims were Muslims.

Trump has called for a ban on all Muslims entering the United States and Gupta said his message had wide resonance. "We predicted that he would win five days ago - there is a huge support for him, his ideas, and we could see that," Gupta said."

Now terrorists will be hunted everywhere in the world, even if they go and hide in a cave. Now only God can help Pakistan. India will now have the support of the US in our efforts against terrorists. We will be together in this.

"Donald Trump will do what no other US president has been able to do before. We are happy. All terrorists should now run and hide. "Gupta's group held a special prayer session for Trump in New Delhi back in May when he was seen as a long shot for the presidency, hailing him as a "fighter and a saviour of humanity". They also celebrated his birth-day in June with a cake, balloons and posters.

Australia wants US to stay focused on Asia

Australia said on Wednesday it was crucial for Washington to stay focused on Asia as Donald Trump won the presidential election, with Canberra keen to see more US involvement in the region, not less. Under President Barack Obama, the United States has pursued a foreign policy "pivot" towards the Asia-Pacific, including stationing marines in Australia, against the background of Beijing's increasing assertiveness.

With tensions high over China's claims in the South China Sea and fears Trump could be a negative for the region's trade prospects, Foreign Minister Julie Bishop said it was critical that the US remain fully engaged. "Countries in our region are looking for more US leadership and not less in the Asia-Pacific," she told Sky News in the first Australian reaction to Trump's win over former secretary of state Hillary Clinton.

As parliament sat on Wednesday, Bishop and Prime Minister Malcolm Turnbull closely watched results flow through on their mobile phones. Bishop said Canberra wanted to continue working closely with any new administration and meet soon "to ensure it focuses on our region and the importance of US leader-ship and a US presence in the Asia-Pacific".

Warm congratulations' sent from Philippines

Philippines President Rodrigo Duterte, who has publicly abused US President Ba-rack Obama and threatened to downgrade ties with the US, on Wednesday sent his "warm congratulations" to US President-elect Donald Trump. "President Duterte wishes President-elect Trump success in the next four years as Chief Executive and commander-in-chief of the US military, and looks forward to working with the incoming administration for enhanced

Philippines-US relations anchored on mutual respect, mutual benefit and shared commitment to democratic ideals and the rule of law," Duterte's Communications Office Secretary Martin Andanar said, GMA news agency said.

Duterte, who has expressed outrage almost daily with the Obama administration and threatened repeatedly to end one of Washington's most important Asian alliances, "hailed the success of US democratic system and the American way of life," the statement said.

7

Trade Agreements and Economic Theory

INTRODUCTION

Almost all Western economists today believe in the desirability of free trade, and this is the philosophy advocated by international institutions such as the World Bank, the International Monetary Fund, and the World Trade Organization (WTO). And this was the view after World War II, when Western leaders launched the General Agreement on Tariffs and Trade (GATT) in 1947.

However, economic theory has evolved substantially since the time of Adam Smith, and it has evolved rapidly since the GATT was founded. To understand U.S. trade agreements and how they should proceed in the future, it is important to review economic theory and see how it has evolved and where it is today.

In the seventeenth and eighteenth centuries, the predominant thinking was that a successful nation should export more than it imports and that the trade surplus should be used to expand the nation's treasure, primarily gold and silver. This would allow the country to have a bigger and more powerful army and navy and more colonies.

One of the better-known advocates of this philosophy, known as mercantilism, was Thomas Mun, a director of the British East India Company. In a letter written in the 1630s to his son, he said:

"The ordinary means therefore to increase our wealth and treasure is by Foreign Trade, wherein wee must ever observe this rule; to sell more to strangers yearly than wee consume of theirs in value. . . . By this order duly kept in our trading, . . . that part of our stock which is not returned to us in wares must necessarily be brought home in treasure."

Mercantilists believed that governments should promote exports and that governments should control economic activity and place restrictions on imports if needed to ensure an export surplus. Obviously, not all nations could have an export surplus, but mercantilists believed this was the goal and that successful nations would gain at the expense of those less successful. Ideally, a nation would export finished goods and import raw materials, under mercantilist theory, thereby maximizing domestic employment.

Then Adam Smith challenged this prevailing thinking in *The Wealth of Nations* published in 1776. Smith argued that when one nation is more efficient than another country in producing a product, while the other nation is more efficient at producing another product, then both nations could benefit through trade. This would enable each nation to specialize in producing the product where it had an absolute advantage, and thereby increase total production over what it would be without trade. This insight implied very different policies than mercantilism. It implied less government involvement in the economy and a reduction of barriers to trade.

The Theory of Comparative Advantage

Thirty-one years after *The Wealth of Nations* was published, David Ricardo introduced an extremely important modification to the theory in his *On the Principles of Political Economy and Taxation*, published in 1817. Ricardo observed that trade will occur between nations even where one country has an absolute advantage in producing all the products traded.

Ricardo showed that what was important was the *comparative advantage* of each nation in production. The theory of comparative advantage holds that even if one nation can produce all goods more cheaply than can another nation, both nations can still trade under conditions where each benefits. Under this theory, what matters is relative efficiency.

Economists sometimes compare this to the situation where even though a lawyer might be more proficient at both law and typing than the secretary, it would still pay the lawyer to have the secretary handle the typing to allow more time for the higher-paying legal work. Similarly, if each country specializes in the products where it is comparatively more efficient, total production will be higher and consumers will have more goods to utilize.

Smith and Ricardo considered only labor as a "factor of production." In the early 1900s, this theory was further developed by two Swedish economists, Bertil Heckscher and Eli Ohlin, who considered several factors of production. The so-called Heckscher-Ohlin theory basically holds that a country will export those commodities that are produced by the factor that it has in relative abundance and that it will import products whose production requires factors of production where it has relatively less abundance. This situation is often portrayed in economics textbooks as a simplified model of two countries (England and Portugal) and two products (textiles and wine). In this simplified portrayal, England has relatively abundant capital and Portugal has relatively abundant labor, and textiles are relatively capital intensive whereas wine is relatively labor intensive. With these conditions, both nations would be better off if they freely traded, and under such a situation of free trade, England would export textiles and import wine. This would maximize efficiency, resulting in more total production of textiles and wine and cheaper prices for consumers than would be the case without trade. Through empirical studies and mathematical models, economists almost universally believe that this model holds equally well for multiple products and multiple countries.

In fact, economists consider this law of comparative advantage to be fundamental. As Dominick Salvatore says in his basic economics textbook *International Economics*, the law of comparative advantage remains "one of the most important and still unchallenged laws of economics. . . . The law of comparative advantage is the cornerstone of the pure theory of international trade."

The law of comparative advantage also holds equally well for many factors of production. In addition to labor and capital, other factors of production include natural resources such as land and technology, and these can be subdivided. For example, land can be land for mining or land for farming, or technology for making cars or computer chips, or skilled and unskilled labor. Additionally, over time factor endowments may change. For example, natural resources, such as coal reserves, may be used up, or a country's educational system may be improved, thereby providing a more highly skilled labor force.

Furthermore, some products do not utilize the same factors of production over their life cycle. For example, when computers were first introduced, they were incredibly capital intensive and required highly skilled labor. Over time, as volume increased, costs came down and computers could be mass produced. Initially, the United States had a comparative advantage in production; but today, when computers are mass produced by relatively unskilled labor, the comparative advantage has shifted to countries with abundant cheap labor. And still other products may use different factors of production in different countries. For example, cotton production is highly mechanized in the United States but is very labor intensive in Africa. The fact that factors of production may change does not nullify the theory of comparative advantage; it just means that the mix of products that a nation can produce relatively more efficiently than its trade partners may change.

Traditional economic theories expounded by Ricardo and Heckscher-Ohlin are based on a number of important assumptions, such as perfect competition with no artificial barriers imposed by governments. A second assumption is that production occurs under diminishing or constant returns to scale, that is, the costs of producing each additional unit are the same or higher as production increases. For example, to increase his wheat crop, a farmer may be forced to use less-fertile land or pay more for laborers to harvest the wheat, thereby increasing the cost of each additional unit produced.

Another key assumption of traditional economic theory is that basic factors of production—such as land, labor, and capital—are not traded across borders. Although Ohlin believed that such basic factors of production were not traded, he argued that the relative returns to factors of production between countries would tend to be equalized as goods are traded between the countries. Subsequently, Samuelson argued that factor prices would in fact be equalized under free trade conditions, and this is known in economics as the factor price equalization theorem. This might mean, for example, that international trade would cause wage rates for unskilled workers to fall in the high-wage country in relation to the rents available from capital and to the same level as wages in the low wage country, and for wages to rise in relation to the rents available from capital in the low-wage country and equal to the level of the country where labor was less abundant.

In static terms, the law of comparative advantage holds that all nations can benefit from free trade because of the increased output available for consumers as a result of more efficient production. James Jackson of the Congressional Research Service describes the benefits as follows: Trade liberalization, "by reducing foreign barriers to U.S. exports and by removing U.S. barriers to foreign goods and services, helps to strengthen those industries that are the most competitive and productive and to reinforce the shifting of labor and capital from less productive endeavors to more productive economic activities."

Many economists, however, believe that the dynamic benefits of free trade may be greater than the static benefits. Dynamic benefits, for example, include the pressure on companies to be more efficient to meet foreign competition, the transfer of skills and knowledge, the introduction of new products, and the potential positive impact of the greater adoption of commercial law. Thus trade can affect both what is produced (static effects) and how it is produced (dynamic effects).

Terms of Trade

Another important concept in international trade theory is the concept of "terms of trade." This refers to the amount of exports needed to obtain a given amount of imports, with the fewer amount of exports needed the better for the country. The terms of trade can shift, either benefiting a country or reducing its welfare.

Assume that the United States exports aircraft to Japan and imports televisions, and that one airplane can purchase 1,000 televisions. If one airplane now can purchase 2,000 televisions, the United States will be better off ; alternatively, its welfare is diminished if it can only purchase 500 televisions with a single airplane.

A number of factors can affect the terms of trade, including changes in demand or supply, or government policy. In the example given just above, if Japanese demand for aircraft increases, the terms of trade will shift in the United States' favor because it can demand more televisions for each airplane. Alternatively, if the Japanese begin producing aircraft, the terms of trade will shift in Japan's favor, because the supply of aircraft will now be larger and the Japanese will have alternative sources of supply.

Under certain conditions, improvements in a country's productivity can worsen its terms of trade. For example, if Japanese manufacturers of televisions become more efficient and reduce sale prices, Japan's terms of trade will worsen as it will take more televisions to exchange for the airplane.

A country can also adopt a beggar-thy-neighbor stance by deliberately turning the terms of trade in its favor through the imposition of an *optimum tariff* or through currency manipulation.

In his economics textbook, Dominick Salvatore defines an optimum tariff as

> that rate of tariff that maximizes the net benefit resulting from the improvement in the nation's terms of trade against the negative effect resulting from reduction in the volume of trade. . . . As the terms of trade of the nation imposing the tariff improve, those of the trade partner deteriorate, since they are the inverse. . . . Facing both a lower volume of trade and deteriorating terms of trade, the trade partner's welfare definitely declines. As a result, the trade partner is likely to retaliate. . . . Note that even when the trade partner does not retaliate when one nation imposes the optimum tariff, the gains of the tariff-imposing nation are less than the losses of the trade partner, so that the world as a whole is worse off than under free trade. It is in this sense that free trade maximizes world welfare.

If both countries play this game, both will be worse off. However, if only one country pursues this strategy, it can gain at its partner's expense.

TRADE IN FACTORS OF PRODUCTION AND SERVICES

Traditional economic theory assumed that goods are traded between countries, but that factors of production (e.g., labor, capital, and technology) and services are not traded from country to country. However, recently capital, technology, and services have been increasingly flowing easily over national borders, and even labor is moving from country to country more frequently. Accordingly, in recent rounds of multilateral negotiations and in U.S. bilateral agreements, negotiators have sought to develop rules governing investment, intellectual property protection, services, and labor.

In economic theory, if factors of production are fully mobile, the costs of all factors of production that could move across borders would result in equal costs in all trading countries. This would mean that the basis of comparative advantage for trade between countries would diminish and there would ultimately be less international trade.

In reality, of course, there are reasons other than trade barriers why factors of production such as capital or labor may not move across borders, even when there are no barriers and higher returns could be gained in other markets. Workers, for example, are reluctant to leave their homelands and family and friends, and investors are reluctant to invest in other markets where they have less familiarity. As a result, even eliminating all governmentally imposed barriers to trade in capital and labor would not lead to the complete equalization of costs between counties.

Like trade in investment and capital, post–World War II economists did not conceive of trade in services. In fact, trade in services was almost considered an oxymoron by early economists, such as Adam Smith and David Ricardo, who assumed that services are not tradable. This was also the view of trade negotiators for three or more decades after the GATT was launched.

Geza Feketukuty, the lead U.S. negotiator on services in the Uruguay Round, gives a wonderful anecdote of early efforts to launch negotiations on trade in services: "The Swiss delegate . . . dismissed trade in services by pointing out how impossible it was for him to have his hair cut by a barber in another country. The chairman of the committee . . . replied that every woman in Germany had benefited enormously from French exports of hairdressing services, and she was confident that the delegate's wife would confirm the same was true in Switzerland."

Not surprisingly, economic theory as it applies to services trade is still being developed. In general, economists today assume that the basic theory of comparative advantage as it applies to goods applies equally well to cross-border trade in services. As Geza Feketekuty says, "The theory of comparative advantage as a theoretical statement about economic relationships should be equally valid whether the products encompassed by the theory are tradable physical goods such as shoes and oranges, or tradable services such as insurance and engineering."

Many types of services, such as telecommunications, are intimately interconnected to other economic activity. Trade liberalization in these areas can have far-reaching economic effects. For example, lowering the costs and increasing the availability of telecommunications services can help manufacturers compete in global markets, it can enable farmers to learn the latest techniques, and it can help other services sectors, such as tourism, that can now reach the world market through the Internet. Liberalization of telecommunications services even facilitated the creation of a new form of enterprise, namely, "off shoring," where companies moved some of their basic operations such as telemarketing call centers to low-cost locations in other countries.

In contrast, liberalizing restrictions in some other sectors, such as tourism, may affect revenues and employment for the providers and the country but will have only a minimal impact on the competitiveness of other sectors within the country. In other words, the liberalization of some services may have multiplier effects throughout the economy, whereas in other sectors the benefits will largely flow only to the affected sector.

Creating Comparative Advantage

The classic Western model of trade was based on eighteenth-century economic realities. Factors of production were relatively fixed: Land was immobile (although its fertility or usage might change), and labor mobility was highly restricted by political constraints. For most of the century, the movement of capital across borders was limited by political barriers and a lack of knowledge of other markets. (However, by the middle of the nineteenth century both capital and labor were flowing more freely between Europe and the Americas.) Technology in the eighteenth century was relatively simple by today's standards and was relatively similar in all countries. Additionally, the production of most products at that time was subject to diminishing returns, which meant that as production increased, the costs of producing each additional unit increased.

In this world, the classic Ricardian model of trade provided a good explanation for trade patterns, such as which countries would produce what products. England would produce textiles based on its wool production and capital availability, and Portugal would produce wine based on its sunshine and fertile soil. If Portugal chose to impose barriers to the importation of British textiles, its own economy would be less well off, and it would still be in Britain's interest to allow the free importation of Portuguese wine.

However, the world economy began to change in the twentieth century, as some products could be produced under conditions of increasing returns to scale. As a company produced more steel, production could be automated and the costs of each additional unit could be significantly reduced. And the same was true for automobiles and a growing number of other more sophisticated products.

By the last twenty-five years of the twentieth century, the global economy was significantly different. Land and labor were still relatively fixed, although capital could again move more freely around the world. However, technology was highly differentiated among countries, with the United States leading in many areas.

An established company in an industry that required extensive capital investment and knowledge had an enormous advantage over potential competitors. Its production runs were large, enabling it to produce product at low marginal cost. And the capital investment for a new competitor would be large.

In this new world, the economic policies pursued by a nation could create a new comparative advantage. A country could promote education and change its labor force from unskilled to semiskilled or even highly skilled. Or it could provide subsidies for research and development to create new technologies. Or it could take policy actions to force transfer of technology or capital from another country, such as allowing its companies to pirate technology from competitors or imposing a requirement that foreign investors transfer technology.

Ralph Gomory and William Baumol describe this well:

The underlying reason for these significant departures from the original model is that the modern free-trade world is so different from the original historical setting of the free trade models. Today there is no one uniquely determined best economic outcome based on natural national advantages. Today's global economy does not single out a single best outcome, arrived at by international competition in which each country serves the world's best interests by producing just those goods that it can naturally turn out most efficiently. Rather, there are many possible outcomes that depend on what countries actually choose to do, what capabilities, natural or human-made, they actually develop.

In the world of the late twentieth century, a country might be dominant in an industry because of its innate comparative advantage, or it might be dominant because of a strong boost from government policy, or it might be dominant because of historical accident. For example, the U.S. dominance in aircraft was probably due to a strong educational system that produced highly competent engineers, a large domestic market with a dedicated customer (the U.S. military), and the historical accident that the aircraft industries of the United States' major competitors—Japan, Germany, and England—had all been destroyed in World War II.

Once such an industry becomes dominant, it is extremely difficult for other countries' industries to compete. The capital costs of entry may be very large, and it is difficult for a new entrant to master the technology. Additionally, the industry normally has a web of suppliers that are critical to competitiveness, such as steel companies and tire manufacturers. However, if such an industry losses its dominance, it is equally difficult for it to reenter the market.

A country with such a dominant industry benefits enormously economically. Because of its dominant position, such an industry may pay high wages and provide a stable base of employment.

Access to other markets plays an important role in this economic model where comparative advantage can be created. Without free trade, it becomes extremely costly for a government to subsidize a new entrant because the subsidy must be large enough both to overcome foreign trade barriers and to jump-start the domestic producer. The WTO and the United States' FTAs also play an important role by setting out rules that govern what actions a country may take in many areas to create comparative advantage; for example, the subsidies code limits the type of subsidies that governments may grant.

Gomory and Baumol note that because countries can create a comparative advantage in goods with decreasing costs of production, there are many possible outcomes to trade patterns: "These outcomes vary in their consequences for the economic well-being of the countries involved. Some of these outcomes are good for one country, some are good for the other, some are good for both. But it often is true that the outcomes that are the very best for one country tend to be poor outcomes for its trading partner."

Although country policies can lead to creation of a dominant industry, such an industry may not be as efficient as if it had occurred in another country. An example given by Gomory and Baumol is Japan's steel industry. Japan has no domestic energy supplies and high wages; by contrast, China "has low labor costs and lots of coal." In theory, China would be the efficient producer of steel, but in reality Japan is the dominant producer. (This example is less valid today, as China has become a major steel producer.)

Although there are many areas where government policies can create comparative advantage, there are still many areas where the classic assumptions of an inherent comparative advantage still hold. The key is whether the industry is subject to constant or increasing costs, such as wheat, or decreasing costs, such as autos, aircraft, or semiconductors.

Neomercantilism

The economic theory based on Ricardo's concept of comparative advantage dominates current thinking in the West and formed the intellectual basis for formation of the GATT/WTO. The doctrine of mercantilism, which dominated thinking up to the end of the eighteenth century, is generally rejected by Western economists today.

However, a number of countries—including Japan, South Korea, China, and some other countries in the Far East—have pursued a neomercantilism model in which they seek to grow through an aggressive expansion of exports, coupled with a very measured reduction of import barriers. These countries seek to develop powerful export industries by initially protecting their domestic industry from foreign competition and providing subsidies and other support to stimulate growth, often including currency manipulation.

The success of some countries pursuing a neomercantilist strategy does not refute the law of comparative advantage. In fact, the reason these countries are successful is that they focus on industries where they have or can create a comparative advantage. Thus Japan first focused on industries such as steel and autos, and later on electronics, where a policy of import protection and domestic subsidies could enable their domestic firms to compete in world markets, and particularly the U.S. market.

To succeed in a neomercantilist strategy, of course, a country needs access to other markets, which the progressive liberalization of trade barriers under the GATT/WTO provided. Neomercantilists generally focus on key industries selected by government, a strategy known as *industrial policy*. A successful industrial policy requires a farsighted government. Japan had an extremely competent group of government officials in the Ministry of Industry and Trade (MITI), which oversaw its industrial policy and was basically immune from political pressures. Although MITI had many successes, it also made some missteps. For example, in their planning to develop a world-class auto industry in the 1950s, MITI officials initially believed they had too many auto companies, and urged Honda to merge with another company. Instead, Honda elected to invest in the United States and went on to become a leading auto producer.

Countries pursuing the neomercantilist model have also generally promoted education and high domestic savings to finance their growing export industries. For example, the savings rate in Japan has often been more than 20 percent of GDP, and it approaches 40 percent of China's GDP today. (By contrast, the U.S. savings rate has been only about 2 percent over the past decade and in some years was actually negative.)

Many economists argue that a neomercantilist strategy may be successful for a while but that over time such a strategy will not be effective. Basically this argument is that the complexities for governments in picking potential winners and identifying how to promote those industries are too great. For example, Japan was very successful with its neomercantilist strategy until the mid-1990s. However, since then the Japanese economy has been stagnating, and many economists believe that Japan will need to change its approach to stimulating domestic demand rather than focusing on export markets. During the past ten years, South Korea and China have also pursued neomercantilist policies, and it remains to be seen if these are effective over the long term.

Additionally, a number of economists argue that government intervention can be effective in promoting a specific sector but that industrial policies are not effective at the macro level of benefiting the economy as a whole. In any case, Western economists and policymakers today almost universally reject the idea that the United States should adopt an industrial policy that picks winners and losers. Opponents of a possible U.S. industrial policy argue that under the U.S. system, such a policy would be subject to political pressures that would ensure failure.

Instead, the real debate among economists and policymakers is whether the United States should respond to foreign neomercantilist practices, and if so, how. Stephen Cohen and his colleagues say:

Free trade advocates argue that imposing import barriers, even if other countries do so, is tantamount to shooting oneself in the foot. The advisability of turning the other cheek to other countries' trade barriers is based on an economic argument traceable to Adam Smith in the eighteenth century: Since consumption is the sole end of production, consumers' interests come before producers' interests, especially those of relatively inefficient producers. Carried to its logical conclusion, this strategy recommends that the U.S. government take no action to offset the de facto subsidies provided to domestic consumers when imports are sold at prices below fair value.

Others argue that the objective of free trade is to promote competition based on comparative advantage, which maximizes global efficiency. Practices such as subsidies or currency manipulation are a movement away from such competition and can produce a result where the less efficient producer dominates trade, thereby reducing total welfare. In these circumstances, taking an offsetting action, such as imposing a countervailing duty, could restore "a level playing field" where trade based on comparative advantage can occur.

Unbalanced Trade

The theory of comparative advantage assumes a world where trade between countries is in balance or at least where countries have a trade surplus or deficit that it is cyclical and temporary. Relaxing the assumption "that international trade among nations is balanced, could lead a nation with a trade deficit to import some commodities in which it would have a comparative advantage and it would in fact export with balanced trade," says Dominic Salvatore. However, he does not see this as a big problem "since most trade imbalances are generally not very large in relation to

GNP. In analyzing the impact of a surplus or deficit, economists often consider "trade" very broadly in definition. Generally, economists do not consider the simple balance in merchandise trade as relevant as the "current account," which includes the balance of trade for goods and services, plus net international income receipts (remitted profits from overseas investments, royalty payments, interest, and dividends) and unilateral transfers (foreign aid and transfers abroad by private citizens). Except for unilateral transfers, all these elements are covered in our trade agreements.

To give a real picture of how the nation is doing, the current account is often measured as a percentage of GDP; as a country grows, a larger surplus or deficit in the current account is not a source of concern because the economy can more readily absorb the impact.

A surplus or deficit in the current account can be affected by the business cycle. Thus, if our economy grows rapidly, the demand for imports will expand as consumers can afford to buy more and businesses need parts and supplies for expansion. Similarly, the United States' exports are affected by economic growth in its trade partners. If it grows more rapidly than its trade partners, in short, that will have a negative impact on the U.S. current account balance. Conversely, if the United States' trade partners are growing more rapidly, that will have a positive impact on its current account balance.

Economists are not concerned with such cyclical trade deficits or surpluses. Additionally, they are not concerned if a deficit occurs because the country is borrowing heavily from abroad to finance investment that will be paid back later. During the nineteenth century, in fact, the United States was in exactly this position when it borrowed heavily to build railroads across the continent, steel mills, and other long-term investments. However, that is not the United States' situation today. Today, it is borrowing heavily from other countries to finance short-term consumption, such as the newest and largest HDTVs from Japan or South Korea, and these purchases do not generate income to repay its debt in the future.

A fundamental accounting concept in international economics is that a country's overall balance of payments, which consists of both the current account and the capital account, has to be in balance. This means that if the current account is in defi cit, the country's capital account has to be in surplus by an equal amount. The capital account consists of purchases or sales of foreign exchange by the central bank or by private citizens. This fundamental accounting principal can be seen as:

Balance of Payments = Current Account + Capital Account = Zero

Two factors that may lead to a deficit or surplus in the current account balance are the level of a nation's savings and investment compared with consumption, and the exchange rate between its currency and that of its trade partners. The level of a country's savings and investment compared with its consumption is inversely related to its trade balance. Joseph Stiglitz puts the matter as follows: "Trade deficits and foreign borrowing are two sides of the same coin. If borrowing from abroad goes up, so too will the trade deficit. This means that if government borrowing goes up, unless private savings goes up commensurately (or private investment decreases commensurately), the country will have to borrow more abroad, and the trade deficit will increase. . . . The reserve country can be thought of as exporting T-bills" in exchange for the import of goods and services.

The second factor that can have an impact on a country's current account balance is the exchange rate. The exchange rate refers to the amount of foreign currencies that can be purchased by a country's own currency. According to economic theory, if a nation is running a persistent trade deficit, its exchange rate would be expected to fall in relation to its trade partners—for example, if the United States runs a persistent deficit, the dollar should purchase less foreign exchange such as euros or yen. This would mean that imported products will cost more, because it would take more dollars for each unit of foreign currency, and this would cause imports to decline. Additionally, the United States' exports should expand, as foreigners can buy more of its products for each unit of their currency.

However, countries can prevent this mechanism from operating by aggressively intervening in the foreign exchange markets. For example, under economic theory, the value of the dollar should decline in relation to the renminbi because the United States has enormous deficits while China experiences comparable trade surpluses. However, China has pegged the renminbi to the dollar and has prevented its exchange rate from rising and thereby restoring a trade balance. China does this by using the dollars it accumulates from its trade surplus to aggressively purchase U.S. currency in the form of Treasury bills. The result has been an overvalued dollar and an undervalued renminbi. (This is similar to what Japan did in the early 1980s when the yen was undervalued and the dollar was overvalued.) In economic theory, an "undervalued exchange rate is *both* an import tax and an export subsidy and is hence the most mercantilist policy imaginable."

THE ECONOMIC EFFECTS OF TRADE LIBERALIZATION

The objective of reducing barriers to trade, of course, is to increase the level of trade, which is expected to improve economic well-being. Economists often measure economic well-being in terms of the share of total output of goods and services (i.e., gross domestic product, GDP) that the country produces per person on average. GDP is the best measurement of economic well-being available, but it has significant conceptual difficulties. As Joseph Stiglitz notes, the measurement of GDP fails "to capture some of the factors that make a difference in people's lives and contribute to their happiness, such as security, leisure, income distribution and a clean environment—including the kinds of factors which growth itself needs to be sustainable." Moreover, GDP does not distinguish between "good growth" and "bad growth"; for example, if a company dumps waste in a river as a by-product of its manufacturing, both the manufacturing and the subsequent cleaning up of the river contribute to the measurement of GDP.

As the result of a multilateral round of trade negotiations under the GATT/WTO, tariffs are reduced during a transition period but are not completely eliminated. In the United States' bilateral or regional free trade agreements (FTAs), however, parties to the agreement completely eliminate almost all tariffs on trade with each other, generally over a transition period, which may be five to ten years.

Although reducing barriers to trade generally represents a move toward free trade, there are situations when reducing a tariff can actually increase the effective rate of protection for a domestic industry. Jacob Viner gives an example: "Let us suppose that there are import duties both on wool and on woolen cloth, but that no wool is produced at home despite the duty. Removing the duty on wool while leaving the duty unchanged on the woolen cloth results in increased protection for the cloth industry while having no significance for wool-raising."

This happens for some products as a result of multilateral trade negotiations. For example, a country often reduces tariffs on products that are not import sensitive—often because they are not produced in that country—to a greater extent than it reduces tariffs on import sensitive products. In an FTA, where the end result is zero tariffs, this would not be an effect when the agreement is fully implemented. However, during the transition period it could well be relevant for some products. Other than this exception, however, reducing tariffs or other barriers to trade increases trade in the product, and this is the intent of the trade agreement.

The benefits to an economy from expanded exports as a trade partner improves market access are clear and indisputable. If the United States' trade partner reduces barriers as a result of a trade agreement, U.S. exports will likely increase, which expands U.S. production and GDP. And suppliers to a firm that gains additional sales through exports will likely also increase their sales to that firm, thereby increasing GDP further.

The firms gaining sales through this may well hire more workers and possibly increase dividends to stockholders. This money is distributed through the economy a number of times as a result of what economists call the *money multiplier effect,* which states that for every $1 an individual receives as income, a portion of it will be spent (i.e., consumption) and a portion will be saved. If individuals save 10 percent of their income, for every $1 earned as income, 90 cents will be spent and 10 cents will be saved. The 90 cents that is spent then becomes income for another individual, and once again 90 percent of this will be spent on consumption. This continues until there is nothing left from the original $1 amount.

In fact, expanded exports increase a nation's GDP by definition. One equation economists use for determining GDP is GDP = Domestic Consumption (*C*) + Domestic gross investment (*In*) + Government spending (*G*) + [Exports (*E*) – Imports (*I*)], or

$$GDP = C + In + G + (E - I)$$

The impact of trade on GDP, therefore, is the net amount that exports exceed or are less than imports. However, this is a static measure. As noted above, expanded exports also have a dynamic effect as companies become more efficient as sales increase.

The economic impact of increased imports is different. By the economists' definition of GDP, of course, increased imports reduce GDP. A way of looking at this is that if a U.S. firm produces a product that suddenly loses out to increased imports, it will reduce its production and employment, and consequently its suppliers will also reduce production and employment, thereby reducing economic output.

This would suggest that the mercantilists were right, that a nation would be well advised to restrict imports. However, almost all economists today would reject that conclusion, and in fact many economists believe that reducing its trade barriers benefits a country whether or not the country's trade partners also reduce their barriers. Adam Smith and many economists after him argue that the objective of production is to produce goods for consumption. Stephen Cohen and his colleagues express this argument as follows: "The theories of comparative advantage (both classical and neoclassical) imply that liberalizing trade is always beneficial to consumers in any country, regardless of whether the country's trading partners reciprocate by reducing their own trade barriers. From this perspective, the emphasis on the reciprocal lowering of trade barriers in most actual trade liberalization efforts . . . is misplaced."

The benefits of unilateral elimination of trade barriers are particularly obvious in those cases where the country does not produce the product; in these cases, eliminating trade barriers expands consumer choice. (As noted above, however, an exception to this occurs in situations where reducing a trade barrier on a raw material or component that is not produced by the country increases the effective rate of protection for the finished product.)

Even where the country does produce the product, increased competition from trade liberalization will likely lead to lower prices by the domestic firms. In this event, some of the consumer's savings will then be spent consuming other products. The amount spent consuming other products will have positive production effects, which will somewhat mitigate the loss in production by the firm competing with the imports.

Increased import competition also has dynamic benefits by forcing domestic producers to become more efficient in order to compete in the lower price environment. Lower prices also may have a positive impact on monetary policy; because import competition reduces the threat of inflation, central banks can pursue a more liberal monetary policy of lower interest rates than otherwise would be the case. These lower rates benefit investment, housing, and other productive sectors.

Economic Models

Economists have developed a number of sophisticated models designed to simulate the changes in economic conditions that could be expected from a trade agreement. These models, which are based on modern economic theories of trade, are helpful where the barriers to trade are quantifiable, although the results are highly sensitive to the assumptions used in establishing the parameters of the model.

One type of model used extensively by economists to estimate the economy-wide effects of trade policy changes, such as the results of a multilateral trade round, is the Applied General Equilibrium Model, also called the Computable General Equilibrium (CGE) Model. James Jackson of the Congressional Research Service notes: "These models incorporate assumptions about consumer behavior, market structure and organization, production technology, investment, and capital flows in the form of foreign direct investment."

CGE models may be used to estimate the impact of a trade agreement on trade flows, labor, production, economic welfare, or even the environment. They may consider the effects of the agreement on all countries involved, and are ex ante; that is, they attempt to forecast changes that would result from a trade agreement. General equilibrium models are based on input-output models, which track how the output of one industry is an input to other industries. General equilibrium models use enormous data inputs that reflect all the elements to be considered.

One of the great strengths of these models is that they can show how the effects on industries flow through the entire economy. One of their disadvantages is that because of their complexity, the assumptions behind their projections are not always transparent. Economic models are useful to give a sense of what might happen as a result of a trade agreement. They give the appearance of being authoritative, but users need to be aware that economic models are not predictive of what will actually happen and that they have significant weaknesses.

First, the results of any model depend on the assumptions underlying it, such as the degree to which imported products and domestically produced products can be substituted for one another, or whether or not there is perfect or imperfect competition. Differing assumptions can produce a wide range of results, not only in magnitude but also sometimes even in the direction of projected changes.

Second, the economic data needed are often weak, not only for developing countries but even for the United States and other developed nations. For example, trade and economic data between countries, and even within countries, are not readily compatible. In the United States, the North American Industry Classification System (NAICS), which is used to collect statistical data describing the U.S. economy, is based on industries with similar processes to produce goods or services. In contrast, data on international trade in goods are collected on a commodity basis. The United States' NAFTA partners, Canada and Mexico, also use NAICS, but the European Union uses a system called Nomenclature of Economic Activities. Although there are concordances between these differing systems, these are far from exact.

Nontariff barriers—such as import quotas, subsidies, standards, and regulations—must be converted to their tariff equivalents, and this is often difficult and unreliable. For new areas covered in trade negotiations —such as services, investment, and intellectual property—efforts to measure the impact of barriers is even more difficult.

Although measuring the impact of tariffs is more accurate than measuring nontariff barriers or services, it is not as straightforward as it would seem. For example, often economists use a weighted tariff by considering the proportion of imports entering under that tariff line. A problem with this approach is that a very high duty will completely block imports, resulting in the false conclusion that that tariff line is given no weight.

In view of the problems with trade models, some economists dismiss their usefulness. For example, Bhagwati says: "I consider many of the estimates of trade expansion and of gains from trade—

produced at great expense by number-crunching at institutions such as the World Bank with the aid of huge computable models . . . as little more than flights of fancy in contrived flying machines." Many economists would consider this criticism extreme, but nonetheless trade models do need to be viewed with a large degree of caution.

TRADE THEORY MEETS NEW REALITIES

From the time of Adam Smith in 1776 to the launching of the GATT in 1947, economic theory of trade evolved fairly slowly. Since the GATT was launched in 1947, however, there have been a number of significant modifications to the traditional Western economic theory of international trade. These modifications largely update the basic theory of trade to reflect the new realities of industry and commerce.

In the times of Smith, Ricardo, and Hecksher-Ohlin, companies were generally small and most international trade was in agricultural or mineral products or produced by small scale manufacturing. By 1947, however, large-scale manufacturing had evolved, and a great deal of trade was in manufactured products.

In 1979, the economist Paul Krugman noted that a great deal of trade was taking place between developed countries that had similar factors of production. For example, the United States and the nations of Europe have broadly similar factors of production, yet conduct an enormous amount of trade generally within the same industries. Thus, the United States will export automobiles and auto parts to Europe and at the same time import autos and auto parts from Europe.

The Heckscher-Ohlin model, which is good at projecting likely trade patterns between countries where factors of production are different, really did not explain this trade pattern. Krugman's theory is based on product differentiation and economies of scale. For example, a Jeep and a Volkswagen are both automobiles, but they are highly differentiated as seen by the consumer. And both benefit from economies of scale; that is, the larger the production, the more costs can be reduced within a broad range of volume. Unlike wheat, where costs increase as volume is expanded, the cost of each additional automobile produced declines as production is increased, although at a very large volume of production costs would likely start to increase. Goods such as automobiles require large, mechanized production runs and substantial capital investment, and it may be extremely difficult for a new entrant to compete with an established firm.

Under trade based on product differentiation and economies of scale, several countries may produce the same product broadly defined and trade parts and differentiated products with one another. Thus, the United States might specialize in producing Jeeps, and Europe might specialize in producing Volkswagens. Clearly, a great deal of production in modern developed country economies is in industries that experience increasing returns to scale, and in these industries returns to factors of production would not tend to equalize as a result of international trade. In fact, returns to labor in a labor scarce economy might well increase, rather than decrease, as would be predicted by the factor price equalization theory.

Western economic theory has also changed in recent years to account for the fact that world trade has increased so much more rapidly than overall economic growth since the early 1970s. In 1973, the ratio of exports to GDP was 4.9 percent for the United States, and by 2005 this had more than doubled to 10.2 percent. For the world as a whole, this ratio was 10.5 percent in 1973, increasing to 20.5 percent in 2005.

What caused exports to increase more rapidly than production is that companies evolved from being domestically oriented to becoming multinational, and now many have evolved to become global. The first six rounds of GATT trade negotiations had reduced developed-country tariffs on industrial goods from the average of 40 percent after World War II to less than half that level by the end of the Kennedy Round in 1967. Additionally, international communications and transportation had improved enormously (the first commercial jet crossed the Atlantic in 1958, and the first satellite for commercial telecommunications was launched in 1965.)

As a result companies in some industries, such as electronics and chemicals, became multinational corporations and increasingly began to purchase and produce parts and materials in a number of countries. Each time these parts and materials cross a border, an international trade transaction has occurred; and then, when the final good is exported, another international trade transaction has occurred.

This trend has increased enormously during the past twenty-five years, and now this cross-border trade occurs in virtually all industries. Many products will have parts and materials from many countries; for example, a new suit may have cotton from West Africa that has been processed into fabric in Bangladesh, and sewn into a suit in China, with buttons imported from India. And then the suit may be exported to the United States. Another example is the first Airbus jumbo jet 380, which had parts and components from more than 1,500 suppliers in twenty seven countries. Many companies today have global supply chains, procuring parts and materials worldwide. Each specific part or material in the value chain is sourced from the country that can produce the part most cheaply, whether because of its endowment of factors of production or because of special incentives, such as tax holidays.

Kei-Mu Yi of the World Bank notes that standard economic models account very well for the increase in world trade through the mid-1970s but cannot explain the growth of trade since then. However, a model that accounts for supply chains does explain the growth in trade, and he believes that such vertical specialization accounts for about 30 percent of world trade today.

Yi notes that tariff reductions have a far greater impact on these global supply chains than they do on traditional trade. To take the suit example, assume that China, Bangladesh, and the United States each reduces its tariffs by 1 percent and that imported fabric and buttons account for half the cost of the suit made in

China; then the cost of producing the suit in China will be reduced by 0.5 percent. Coupled with the 1 percent U.S. tariff reduction, the cost to the U.S. consumer would be reduced by 1.5 percent. If the suit had been wholly produced in China, the cost to the consumer would have been reduced by just the U.S. tariff reduction, or 1 percent.

The emergence of these extensive supply chains has enormous implications. It means that for many products the traditional concept of "country of origin" no longer applies, because many products have many countries of origin. This in turn means that standard trade statistics have limitations in how useful they are for understanding what is really happening in world trade. It has an impact on how countries should approach economic development, because it means that developing countries must become part of these global supply chains as a way to increase the amount of value added in the parts and materials provided to these supply chains. And it has an impact on how companies see themselves—a firm selling globally and procuring its parts and materials globally sees itself as a "global" firm rather than as a "national" firm.

THE ECONOMIC THEORY OF TRADE BLOCS

The drafters of the GATT believed that reducing barriers to trade should be on a multilateral basis to get the greatest benefits of expanded production based on comparative advantage. As noted above, they enshrined this concept in Article I of the GATT (most-favored-nation, MFN, treatment), which requires members to give equal treatment with regard to trade barriers to all GATT members.

However, they also recognized a role for regional integration that would allow the members of a trade bloc to eliminate barriers on trade among themselves, while maintaining a discriminatory tariff on imports from nonmembers. Accordingly, Article XXIV of the GATT provides for a major exception to the MFN principle that allows countries to form customs unions or free trade areas

(FTAs) that may discriminate against nonmembers of the bloc. In a customs union, the members eliminate trade barriers among themselves but erect a common customs tariff on imports from nonmembers. Members of a free trade area also eliminate trade barriers among themselves, but they each retain their own schedule of tariffs on imports from nonmembers.

Customs unions and free trade area agreements may expand trade and global welfare or they may diminish welfare depending on whether they create new trade patterns based on comparative advantage or simply divert trade from a more competitive nonmember to a member of the trade bloc. In 1950, the economist Jacob Viner defined trade creation as the situation where a member of a preferential trading bloc has a comparative advantage in producing a product and is now able to sell it to its free trade area partners because trade barriers have been removed.

Trade creation benefits the exporters in the member of the trade bloc that has a comparative advantage in producing a product and it benefits consumers in the importing member who now can purchase the product at a lower price. Domestic producers competing with the lower-cost imports from its partner country lose, but their loss is less than the gains to the exporters and consumers. Trade creation enhances global welfare through this greater efficiency.

In the case of trade diversion, however, a member gains its sales at the expense of a more competitive producer in a country that is not a member of the bloc, simply because its products enter its partner's market duty free, while the more competitive nonmember producer faces a discriminatory duty. Nonmember country exporters that would have a comparative advantage under equal competitive conditions lose from trade diversion.

Additionally, under trade diversion, the importing country loses the tariff revenue it had collected on those imports which now come in duty free from its bloc partner. The consumer in the importing partner does gain, because the imported good no longer has to bear the cost of the tariff; however, the consumer's gain is necessarily less than or equal to the lost customs revenue, so the nation as a whole is less well off . Thus, trade diversion hurts both the importing country and the rest of the world. These loses are greater than the gains to the bloc member that gains exports due to trade diversion.

If trade diversion is greater than trade creation, formation of the customs union or FTA would diminish world welfare. If trade creation is greater, then global welfare is enhanced.

In addition to trade diversion and trade creation, which are basically static effects, participants in free trade areas and customs unions are also seeking dynamic benefits, such as expanded production as firms take advantage of the increased size of the market to increase output, and improved efficiency as firms adapt to increased competition. Access to a larger market is particularly important for small countries whose economy is too small to justify large-scale production.

To minimize the potential adverse consequences of such trade blocs, GATT Article XXIV requires that the members of a customs union or an FTA must eliminate trade barriers on "substantially all" trade between them, and that all the members of GATT have the opportunity to review the agreement. In the event that a GATT member not a party to the customs union faces higher tariffs on some products as a customs union is formed, Article XXIV requires that that member be compensated for the lost trade. However, as noted in chapter 2, Article XXIV has proven to be totally ineffective in restricting the growth of trade blocs; as a result, trade patterns today are significantly distorted by these preferential schemes.

TRADE AGREEMENTS: THEORY AND REALITY

Ever since the days of David Ricardo in the early 19th century, it has been established, and remains unquestioned to date, that free trade is a win-win for everybody. The key word is "free", meaning without coercion, fully voluntary. Ricardo's clever insight was that trade between nations could be mutually beneficial, even if one nation was more efficient than the other in all commodities.

This was his theory of comparative advantage. Most economists swear by this maxim. The simplest illustration is this: a lawyer may be a faster typist than her assistant, but her time should be spent in legal stuff, not in typing, which should be left to the assistant. The lawyer thus specializes in law, not in typing.

Countries specialize in goods and services in which they have a comparative advantage, and then free trade benefits everyone. It is not possible for one country to be unambiguously worse off due to free trade. But theory has clashed with reality, or its perception. Hence, in response to murmurs of disquiet, the free trade message was slightly modified thus. Sure, free trade might hurt some people, but it's worth it, because in the end everyone is a winner. There are losers and winners, but the net gain to society is positive. The winners can compensate the losers and yet be ahead. The loss of American jobs is more than offset by getting cheap imported stuff at Walmart, which comes from low-wage countries. Unskilled workers in America may lose their jobs to low-cost labour overseas, but they can be redeployed in other sectors, in higher value-adding activity. All good in theory, and immensely seductive logic.

But in reality, the evidence is mixed. For instance, the North American Free Trade Agreement, that came into force in 1994, was supposed to create 200,000 new jobs due to exports to Mexico. But by 2010, the increased trade deficit with Mexico had eliminated close to 700,000 jobs, with job losses in every state. The US-Korea free trade agreement signed in 2010 was supposed to increase American exports, and jobs. But three years later the trade deficit had widened, US exports to Korea had fallen, and of course jobs were lost as well. Globalization, outsourcing, the rise of India and China and competition with low-cost labour have all been variously blamed for the stagnation in wages and productivity in the US. The economy grew steadily by 2% for many years, but median family incomes stagnated. No wonder public support for free trade is dipping. President Barack Obama fought an ultimately losing battle for a mega free trade pact with 12 countries, of which the US would have been the anchor. His successor Donald Trump has scrapped that pact. The rising protectionist sentiment under Trump is not surprising, considering the mixed evidence of gains from earlier free trade agreements. The US, which was traditionally the champion for free trade across the world, has ceded that position to a most unlikely new advocate, China.

India's embrace of free trade became most visible with its aggressive trade liberalization since 1991. Not to forget, however, that India had been a founder member, since 1947, of Gatt (General Agreement on Tariffs and Trade), which eventually morphed into the World Trade Organization in 1995. India's trade-to-GDP (gross domestic product) ratio climbed steeply from around 10% in the early 1990s to 50% now. India has always supported a multilateral approach to liberalizing trade. But the endless delay of the Doha round has led to India flirting with bilateral and regional free trade agreements (FTAs and RTAs). We are in the midst of the 19th round of negotiations seeking to seal the 16-nation Regional Comprehensive Economic Cooperation (RCEP) agreement. This is basically an RTA between Asean (Association of Southeast Asian Nations) plus six, accounting for half the world's population and 30% of world's GDP.

It is here that reality must confront theory, yet again. Here are four stylized facts. Firstly, in the last 10 years, India's exports to non-RTA countries have grown at the same rate as RTA ones. So tariff elimination is not adding any fillip. Secondly, reduction in tariffs in RTAs doesn't increase exports, as much as increase in incomes in destination countries. Thirdly, less than one-fifth of all exporters actually use the RTA route. Maybe they are deterred by the paperwork, procedures or corruption in the "stamping bureaucracy". Fourthly, and most tellingly, India's trade deficit with all the 10 Asean nations, Korea and Japan has more than doubled since the signing of the respective FTAs. So what has India gained in reality? Have jobs grown? Has manufacturing in India benefited? If anything, there is ample evidence of foreign manufactured goods rushing in through the FTA route. In services, where India hoped to gain, there's not much to show. In 2004, Paul Samuelson, the pre-eminent economist of the 20th century, cautioned that free trade can in fact leave workers worse off for long periods. He showed that through a simple analytical model. He especially pointed out the rise of India and China as a threat to American workers. The free trade fundamentalists pooh-poohed this, and said the old man had lost his marbles. But the old man's caution has gained widespread support.

Most governments worry about job creation, not just growth in exports, when they sign up for free trade. Hence strategic policies like non-tariff barriers, local preference in public procurement are some examples of the sand in the wheels of global free trade. Thus, models and reality have to find a middle ground when it comes to free trade. India would do well to keep this in mind in its RCEP negotiations.

TRADE AGREEMENT

A trade agreement (also known as trade pact) is a wide-ranging taxes, tariff and trade treaty that often includes investment guarantees. It exists when two or more countries agree on terms that helps them trade with each other. The most common trade agreements are of the preferential and free trade types are concluded in order to reduce (or eliminate) tariffs, quotas and other trade restrictions on items traded between the signatories.

The logic of formal trade agreements is that they outline what is agreed upon and the punishments for deviation from the rules set in the agreement. Trade agreements therefore make misunderstandings less likely, and create confidence on both sides that cheating will be punished; this increases the likelihood of long-term cooperation. An international organization, such as the IMF, can further incentivize cooperation by monitoring compliance with agreements and reporting third countries of the violations. Monitoring by international agencies may be needed to detect non-tariff barriers, which are disguised attempts at creating trade barriers.

Trade pacts are frequently politically contentious since they may change economic customs and deepen interdependence with trade partners. Increasing efficiency through "free trade" is a common goal. For the most part, governments are supportive of further trade agreements.

There have been however some concerns expressed by the WTO. According to Pascal Lamy, Director-General of the WTO, the proliferation of regional trade agreements (RTAs) "...is breeding concern – concern about incoherence, confusion, exponential increase of costs for business, unpredictability and even unfairness in trade relations." The position of the WTO is that while the typical trade agreements (called *preferential* or *regional* by the WTO) are useful to a degree, it is much more beneficial to focus on global agreements in the WTO framework such as the negotiations of the current Doha round.

The anti-globalization movement opposes such agreements almost by definition, but some groups normally allied within that movement, e.g. green parties, seek fair trade or safe trade provisions that moderate real and perceived ill effects of globalization.

Classification of trade pacts

By number and type of signatories

There are three different types of trade agreements. The first is *unilateral* trade agreement, this is what happens when a country wants certain restrictions to be enforced but no other countries want them to be imposed. This also allows countries to decrease the amount of trade restrictions. That is also something that does not happen often and could impair a country.

The second is classified as *bilateral* (BTA) when signed between two sides, where each side could be a country (or other customs territory), a trade bloc or an informal group of countries (or other customs territories). When both countries loosen their trade restrictions to help out businesses so that they can prosper better between the different countries this definitely helps lower taxes and it helps them converse about their trade status'. Usually this revolves around subsided domestic industries. Mainly the industries fall under automotive, oil, or food industries.

A trade agreement signed between more than two sides (typically neighboring or in the same region) is classified as *multilateral*. These face the most obstacles- when negotiating substance, and for implementation. The more countries that are involved, the harder it is to reach mutual satisfaction. Once this type of trade agreement is settled on, it becomes a very powerful agreement. The larger the GDP of the signatories, the greater the impact on other global trade relationships. The largest multilateral trade agreement is the North American Free Trade Agreement between the United States, Canada, and Mexico.

U.S. regional trade agreements

These are between countries in a certain area. The most powerful ones include a few countries that are near each other in a geographical area. These countries usually have similar histories, demographics and even economic goals.

North American Free Trade Agreement (NAFTA) January 1, 1989 was when it was put into effect, this is between United States, Canada, and Mexico this agreement was designed to get rid of tariff barriers between the separate countries.

Regional trade agreements are very hard to establish and commit to when the countries are more diverse.

Association of Southeast Asian Nations(ASEAN) this was formed in 1967 between the countries of Indonesia, Malaysia, the Philippines, Singapore, and Thailand the reasoning was so that they could engage political and economic encouragement and it helps them all keep regional stability.

By level of integration

There are a variety of trade agreements; with some being quite complex (European Union), while others are less intensive (North

American Free Trade Agreement). The resulting level of economic integration depends on the specific type of trade pacts and policies adopted by the trade bloc:

1. Separate
   - o Trade and Investment Framework Agreement (TIFA)
   - o Bilateral Investment Treaty (BIT)
   - o Preferential Trade Arrangement (PTA)–limited scope and depth of tariffs reduction between the customs territories.
     - – Free Trade Agreement establishing a Free Trade Area (FTA)–extensive reduction or elimination of tariffs on substantially all trade allowing for the free movement of goods and in more advanced agreements also reduction of restrictions on investment and establishment allowing for the free movement of capital and free movement of services
     - – Common market–FTA with significantly reduced or eliminated restrictions on the freedom of movement of all factors of production, including free movement of labour and of enterprise; and coordination in economic policy
   - o Currency union–sharing the same currency
2. Composite
   - o Customs union–FTA with common external tariffs of all signatories in respect to non-signatory countries
     - – Customs and monetary union–Customs union with Currency union
     - – Economic union–Customs union with Common market
     - – Economic and monetary union (EMU)–Economic union with Currency Union
     - – Fiscal Union–common coordination of substantial parts of the fiscal policies *(proposed step between EMU and Complete economic integration)*

Special agreements

- World Trade Organization treaty
  - o agreements in the WTO framework (Textile Agreement and others)
- the now defunct Multilateral Agreement on Investment (in the OECD framework)

By the World Trade Organization

Typically the benefits and obligations of the trade agreements apply only to their signatories.

In the framework of the World Trade Organization, different agreement types are concluded (mostly during new member accessions), whose terms apply to all WTO members on the so-called most-favored basis (MFN), which means that beneficial terms agreed bilaterally with one trading partner will apply also to the rest of the WTO members.

All agreements concluded outside of the WTO framework (and granting additional benefits beyond the WTO MFN level, but applicable only between the signatories and not to the rest of the WTO members) are called *preferential* by the WTO. According to WTO rules these agreements are subject to certain requirements such as notification to the WTO and general reciprocity (the preferences should apply equally to each of the signatories of the agreement) where unilateral preferences (some of the signatories gain preferential access to the market of the other signatories, without lowering their own tariffs) are allowed only under exceptional circumstances and as temporary measure.

The trade agreements called *preferential* by the WTO are also known as *regional* (RTA), despite not necessarily concluded by countries within a certain region. There are currently 205 agreements in force as of July 2007. Over 300 have been reported to the WTO. The number of FTA has increased significantly over the last decade. Between 1948 and 1994, the General Agreement on Tariffs and Trade (GATT), the predecessor to the WTO, received

124 notifications. Since 1995 over 300 trade agreements have been enacted.

FOREIGN TRADE AGREEMENTS: AN ANALYSIS

The current environment of stalled multilateral negotiations has led to a spurt in regional trade agreements and India too has moulded its foreign trade policy to remain in sync with the changing realities. This article evaluates the impact of trade agreements (TAs) on India's trade to gain insights on how it has evolved with its trade agreement partner countries relative to non-partner countries. The study utilises difference in difference approach to estimate the increment of trade flows of India with partner countries. After the conclusion of the trade agreement, growth in trade flows was witnessed between India and the partner countries. One positive impact of TAs has been in the form of increased shipments of capital goods and industrial supplies from trade partner economies. This indirectly would have contributed in enhancing the productive capacity in the country.

After the end of World War II, there was a move towards a multilateral system to facilitate global commerce and countries took initiatives to eliminate trade barriers. With the early efforts in the General Agreement on Tariffs and Trade (GATT) and subsequently under its successor, the World Trade Organisation (WTO), the average value of tariffs in force around the world declined by 85 per cent compared to 1947.

Notwithstanding the benefits arising from multilateral system, the current environment of stalled multilateral negotiations has led to a spurt in regional trade agreements wherein countries have moved towards bilateralism in place of multilateralism. India too has moulded its foreign trade policy to remain in sync with the changing realities. Accordingly, India has signed preferential access, economic cooperation and TAs with about 54 individual countries.

Against this backdrop this article evaluates the impact of trade agreements on India's trade. By dissecting the impact separately for exports, imports and overall trade, the article attempts to gain insights on how India's trade has evolved with its trade agreement partner countries relative to non-partner countries. Historical backdrop along with stylised facts pertaining to trade agreements are set out in Section II. Section III provides a brief review of the relevant literature. Current status regarding India's TAs along with empirical analysis are presented in Section IV. Section V sets out the concluding observations.

Historical Backdrop and Stylised Facts

Trade agreements are arrangements by which countries provide preferential treatment to each other and aid greater ease-of-trade by elimination of tariffs and other trade barriers. TAs can be between two or more countries that primarily agree to reduce or eliminate tariff and non-tariff barriers on substantial trade between them. Formal TAs may cover a spectrum of arrangements, from small margins of tariff preference to full scale economic integration. TAs can take several configurations which can be Partial Scope Agreement (PSA), Free Trade Agreement (FTA), Custom Union (CU), Common Market or Economic Union. Typically, trade agreements aim to reduce trade barriers between the member countries which entails discrimination against trade with non-member countries. By design, TAs have positive as well as negative externalities.

TAs originated primarily among European countries. At the start, TAs had restricted presence and were mainly confined to the geographic influence of the colonial empires and generally took the form of bilateral commercial treaties. The surge in cross-border movement of goods in the nineteenth century led to greater openness and liberalisation and simultaneously altered the nature and scope of bilateral trade treaties. The Cobden-Chevalier Treaty between Britain and France in 1860 may be considered as the pioneer in this regard as for the first time it contained most favoured nation (MFN) clause and led to significant reciprocal tariff reductions between two countries. The Cobden-Chevalier Treaty triggered a spate of bilateral negotiations among other European economic powers. This proved to be a precursor to the competitive trade liberalisation among countries which followed later. Since this new network of treaties was both reciprocal and inclusive (via the MFN clause), it was also essentially interlocking - creating an early form of plurilateral preferential trade agreement (i.e., unconditional MFN treatment among all treaty-signers) and foreshadowing the basic structure of the multilateral system that took shape a century later (Brown, 2003). These bilateral agreements laid the foundations for much of the GATT system after the Second World War.

With the formation of the GATT in 1947, the idea of a wider multilateral agreement moved to the forefront of international trade relations. Nonetheless, the initial signatories to GATT system were just 23 countries. This later evolved to the near universal membership of the WTO. However, the emergence of a multilateral system in the form of GATT did not diminish the significance of bilateral or regional agreements to further international trade relations. Notwithstanding the presence of a multilateral system, the impetus for bilateral/plurilateral agreements outside its purview, especially in Europe, resurfaced within a short span of time. The upshot of this development was concurrent advancement witnessed in both regionalism and multilateralism. In fact, Article XXIV of GATT 1994 encompasses the statutory backing for trade agreements. This Article exempts member states from the Most-Favoured Nation (MFN) principle and permits mutual imports among countries preferentially through the ratification of a trade agreement. The WTO permits three types of trade agreements.

INDIA'S TRADE WITH ITS FTA PARTNERS: EXPERIENCES, CHALLENGES AND WAY FORWARD

In a meeting held on September 10, 2019, at Bangkok in Thailand, India and the group of ten members of Association of Southeast Asian Nations (ASEAN) have decided to initiate the review of the ASEAN-India Trade in Goods Agreement that has been in operation since January 2010. The main objective of the proposed review is to make the agreement more 'user-friendly, simple, and trade facilitative for businesses'. It is an important development for India as there has been a growing concern indifferent quarters including the industry that the benefits for India have been very limited from the Free Trade Agreements (FTAs) that the country has signed and implemented so far, including that with the ASEAN.

It is imperative to note that India has viewed FTAs as an important tool to enhance its trade and investment, and signed a number of trade agreements with various countries or groups. In fact, India is one among top countries in Asia with the maximum number of FTAs either in operation or under negotiation or proposed. According to the Asian Development Bank Institute, as of now, India has 42 trade agreements (including preferential agreements) either in effect or signed or under negotiation or proposed. Out of this, 13 are in effect, one is signed but not yet implemented, 16 under negotiation and 12 are proposed/under consultation or study. Most of India's existing FTAs are with Asian countries which are quite different from each other in terms of the level of their economic development.

At the time when India is negotiating FTAs with a number of countries/groups, including the mega Regional Comprehensive Economic Partnership (RCEP), and has decided to commence the review of India-ASEAN FTA, it is pertinent to examine the progress of trade between India and its key FTA partners. The major FTAs that India has signed and implemented so far include South Asia Free Trade Agreement (SAFTA), India-ASEAN Comprehensive Economic Cooperation Agreement (CECA), India-Korea Comprehensive Economic Partnership Agreement (CEPA) and India-Japan CEPA.

A broad analysis of trade between India and its major FTA partners, mentioned above, shows a significant increase in trade since the agreements have become operational. The SAFTA became effective from January 01, 2006 and as per Ministry of Commerce and Industry data the bilateral trade between India and other SAFTA member countries has increased from US$ 6.8 billion in 2005-06 to US$ 28.5 billion in 2018-19. India's trade with SAFTA has grown faster than its total trade with the world. As a result, the share of SAFTA countries in India's international trade rose from 1.6% in 2005-06 to 2.5% in 2018-19. During the same time, the Indian exports to SAFTA countries haveincreased faster than its imports from them leading to a significant rise in trade surplus with these economies from about US$ 4 billion to US$ 21 billion. The maximum growth in exports to SAFTA region has been recorded with Bangladesh and Nepal.

ASEAN is one of India's most important trading partners. The CECA with ASEAN became effective from January 01, 2010 and the bilateral trade between the two sides has surged from about US$ 43 billion in 2009-10 to US$ 97 billion in 2018-19. As in case of India's trade with SAFTA, the bilateral trade between India and ASEAN has also increased faster than that ofIndia's overall trade with the world, leading to an increase in ASEAN's share in India's global trade from 9.4% to 11.5%.However, contrary to India-SAFTA trade India's imports from ASEAN has increased at a significantly higher rate than Indian exports to ASEAN. Another important point worth to be noted is that the imports from ASEAN grew much faster than India's imports from the world. The faster growth in imports has resulted in a significant increase in India's trade deficit with ASEAN from less than US$ 8 billion in 2009-10 to about US$ 22 billion in 2018-19. The share of ASEAN in India's total trade deficit has increased from about 7% to 12% during the same period.

Along with India-ASEAN CECA, the India-Korea CEPA also became operational from January 01, 2010. During 2009-10 to 2018-19, the bilateral trade between the two countries hasincreased from about US$ 12 billion to US$ 21.5 billion andgrew at a pace more or less similar to that of India's trade with the world. However, Indian imports from Korea have surgedmuch faster than the exports to that country. While India's imports increased at a CAGR of around 8%, the exports to Korea rose at a CAGR of less than 4%. Also, while the imports from Korea have grown faster than imports from the world, the growth rate of exports to Korea has been much slower than India's exports to the world. This again has led to a considerableincrease in India's trade deficit with Korea from US$ 5 billion in 2009-10 to US$ 12 billion 2018-19 and a sizable increase in the share of Korea in India's overall trade deficit from 4.7% to 6.5% during the same period.

The India-Japan CEPA became effective from August 01, 2011. The bilateral trade between the two countries witnessed sharp growth in the year of its implementation e.g. 2011-12 compared to that in the previous year, 2010-11. However, the bilateral trade flow has not only contracted afterwards but witnessed a lot of volatility during 2011-12 to 2018-19. Also, while exports to Japan continued to increase during the year of implementation e.g. 2011-12, they have contracted afterwards. Imports from Japan, on the other hand, have increased but witnessed a lot of fluctuations. As in the case of ASEAN and Korea, however,India's trade deficit with Japan has not only increased during2011-12 to 2018-19 but grown faster than India's trade deficit with the world.

Overall, with the exception of SAFTA, India's experience intrade with its major FTA partners has not been very encouraging. While India has gained substantially in terms of exports from its FTA with SAFTA countries, CEPA with Korea and CECA with ASEAN have been more beneficial to those economies. In the case of CEPA with Japan, however, bilateral trade has either declined or stagnated after the 1st year of implementation but there has been a substantial rise in trade deficit with that country also. Apart from a range of domestic factors that have draggedthe competitiveness of Indian exports and prevented India to leverage the preferential market access in these partner countries, there exist a number of FTA related issues that are seen to be responsible for less than favorable development in India's trade relations with ASEAN, Korea and Japan. Some of these issues include faulty commitments, stricter rules of origin,lack of awareness about the

FTAs and high cost of compliance. It is important, therefore, that India should not remain satisfied with the initiation of a review of India-ASEAN FTA but the existing provisions of CEPAs with Korea and Japan should also be evaluated to make them more trade and business-friendly. It is equally important, however, for India to simultaneously takeall the necessary measures to remove the obstacles that hinder the overall competitiveness of exports in the country.

INDIA-U.S.: ECONOMIC AND TRADE RELATIONS

India is the world's ninth largest economy but only the 18th largest export market for U.S. goods, behind Switzerland and the United Arab Emirates. This stands in contrast to progress across other areas of the U.S.-India relationship over the last decade. Moreover, the absence of Indian participation in the so-called mega-regional trade agreements (the Trans-Pacific Partnership Agreement (TPP), the Transatlantic Trade and Investment Partnership (TTIP) negotiations and the Trade in Services Agreement (TiSA) negotiations) that have been the focus for U.S. trade policy during the Obama administration will leave India worse off, diverting trade from India and making integration into global supply chains even more difficult.

Expanding the bilateral economic relationship and developing mechanisms to minimize the negative impact on India from its absence in these mega-regional FTAs should be a focus for the U.S. and India. Since independence from the British, India has been a relatively minor player in the international economy, reflecting India's orientation that placed a premium on developing domestic means of production. While one of the original parties to the General Agreement on Tariffs and Trade (GATT) 1948, India's record in multilateral trade negotiations has largely been obstructionist, and its FTAs have reflected low levels of ambition.

While India has been discarding non-alignment as an organizing foreign policy principle, its approach to trade has not fundamentally evolved. This is despite the aim of Prime Minister

Narendra Modi's 'Make in India' program to increase India's participation in global value chains - all of which presuppose increased levels of trade and foreign investment.

The U.S.-India economic relationship has also been riddled with challenges. The United States has had a range of market access issues as well as specific concerns over Indian protection of intellectual property rights. For India, greater access for its people to work in the U.S. market has been a key objective.

The U.S. and Indian governments are seeking to deepen economic cooperation in areas such as standards and services trade, however, there is little progress so far. Moreover, India's traditional defensiveness in trade negotiations has resulted in little appetite within the U.S. administration, Congress, and amongst business constituents to include India in the new mega-regional trade negotiations - particularly as India would be unable to meet the high standards being sought in these agreements. It also means that even less ambitious steps to grow the bilateral economic relationship have only tepid levels of support.

The failure to expand the bilateral economic relationship and the possible narrowing of India's global economic horizons due to its absence from the mega-regional FTAs is of concern. This is not only due to potential missed opportunities for growth and prosperity, but it will ultimately also undermine the United States' broader aim for India to play a greater leadership role in its region.

The following recommendations are aimed at expanding the bilateral economic relationship and at supporting India's broader integration into the global economy.

- o India is interested in joining the Asia-Pacific Economic Cooperation (APEC) forum and Obama during his visit to India in 2015 expressed support for this goal. As a non-binding economic forum, APEC would give India an opportunity to experiment with forms of trade liberalization and to familiarize itself with best-practices on economic integration in areas such as standards. APEC could also help India learn about the TPP - connecting APEC members' experiences with India's economic reforms. Obama should reaffirm his support for India's membership in APEC and work with India and other APEC economies to make this a reality.

- o Access for Indian workers to the U.S. economy has been a key Indian trade goal. It has informed India's negotiating position at the WTO and more recently, India has sought WTO consultations with the United States which have so far failed to resolve the issues, likely leading India to seek WTO dispute settlement, alleging the discriminatory treatment of India in terms of visa fees and the allocation of non-immigrant visas. The U.S. should consider establishing a regular bilateral dialogue with India on these issues.
- o The United States is the world leader in services exports and runs a growing surplus in services trade. India also has an increasingly sophisticated services sector which supports a services trade surplus with the United States, worth almost $5.8 billion in 2015. For instance, India is the largest exporter of computer and data processing services to the United States and India-based Tata Consultancy Services is the world's largest computer services firm. Yet India is not a party to the TiSA, which following its completion will result in Indian services exporters facing less favourable market access in key markets such as the United States, European Union, and Japan. The United States and India should establish a working group aimed at preparing India for eventual membership in TiSA, including consideration of the feasibility of a bilateral services agreement.

8

India-Trade Barriers and USA

The US wants India to eliminate trade barriers for American companies and remove restrictions with regard to data localisation to cut the cost of doing business, visiting US Commerce Secretary Wilbur Ross said Tuesday.

"Our goal is to eliminate barriers to the US companies operating here including data localisation restrictions that actually weaken data security and increase the cost of doing business," he said here.

Ross was speaking at the Trade Winds Forum and Trade Mission. He is accompanying a delegation of over 100 American businesses.

He also alleged that India imposes very high import duties on goods like automobiles, motorcycles, agri products and alcoholic beverages.

"... currently US businesses face significant market access barriers in India. These include both tariff and non-tariff barriers as well as multiple practices and regulations to the disadvantage of foreign companies.

"India's average applied tariffs rate is 13.8 per cent and that remains the highest of any major world economy, the very highest. It has for example a 60 per cent tariff on auto, while the US has 2.5 per cent. It has 50 per cent tariff on motorcycles and 150 per cent on alcoholic beverages. Just a few extreme examples," he added.

India imposes bound tariff rates – maximum import duty India can charge under global trade rules of WTO – on agricultural products at the average of an "incredible" 113.5 per cent and some are as high as 300 per cent, he said, adding "they are way too high".

However, India's trade experts counter this by saying that India is not a 'tariff king' and it has all the right to take appropriate measures to protect the interest of specific sectors like agriculture.

"We are working diligently with the Indian government and our private sector partners to address market access issues through the US India commercial dialogue and through the recently re-convened US India-CEO forum," Ross said.

Major obstacles being faced by the US companies include price controls on medical devices and restrictive tariff and inspections on electronics and telecommunications products.

He noted that duties on routers and switches and parts of cellular phones are as high as 20 per cent.

In stark contrast, he said, the duty on these products imported by the US from India is zero.

"Zero versus 20 per cent. That's not a justified imbalance. These high tariffs undermine India's goal of improving digital access and literacy," Ross added.

He expects that the new government would look at these matters.

"In the World Bank's Ease of Doing Business report, India climbed an impressive 23 spots this year but it still ranks 77 out of 190 countries. So, there is lots of room for further improvement," he said.

He mentioned that India is the US's 13th largest export market due to "overly restrictive" market access barriers.

Referring to trade imbalance with India, the commerce secretary said the US accounts for 20 per cent of India's total exports.

Last year, the bilateral trade between the two countries totalled at USD 142 billion, up by about USD 16 billion from 2017.

"In the services sector also, US has a trade deficit with India," he said adding last year it was USD 3 billion.

"This is specially unusual. We generally have services surplus with most countries. But in the case of India, the deficit is largely due to IT services," he said.

Ross also said that as India is pursuing a range of development priorities including revitalisation of urban infrastructure, "we are confident that US technology and expertise can play an important role in serving India's critical development needs".

INDIA - TRADE BARRIERS

Import Licensing

India maintains a nontariff regulation on three categories of products: banned or prohibited items (e.g., tallow, fat, and oils of animal origin); restricted items that require an import license (e.g., livestock products and certain chemicals); and "canalized" items (e.g., some pharmaceuticals) importable only by government trading monopolies and subject to cabinet approval regarding import timing and quantity. India, however, often fails to observe transparency requirements, such as publication of timing and quantity restrictions in its Official Gazette or notification to WTO committees.

For purposes of entry requirements, India has distinguished between goods that are new, and those that are secondhand, remanufactured, refurbished, or reconditioned. India allows imports of secondhand capital goods by the end users without an import license, provided the goods have a residual life of five years. India's official Foreign Trade Policy categorizes remanufactured goods in a similar manner to secondhand products, without recognizing that remanufactured goods have typically been restored to original working condition and meet the technical and safety specifications applied to products made from new materials. The National Trade Estimate Report published recently by USTR indicates that the U.S. stakeholders continue to inform that obtaining an import license for remanufactured goods has been onerous and the U.S. exporters continue to encounter significant tariff and nontariff barriers that impede imports of U.S. products into India.

The Directorate General of Foreign Trade (DGFT) of the Ministry of Commerce is involved in the foreign trade regulation and promotion. DGFT maintains a list of restricted and prohibited items for imports and is updated regularly in their Website: http://dgft.gov.in/

Standards, testing, labeling & certification

The Bureau of Indian Standards (BIS) established by the Indian Government under the BIS Act 2016 and is the National Standards Body of India. The Bureau functions under the Ministry of Consumer Affairs, Food & Public Distribution and is involved in the harmonious development of the activities of standardization, marking and quality certification of goods.

Another agency, the Food Safety and Standards Authority of India (FSSAI), established through the food safety and standards act under the Ministry of Health and Family Welfare; along with the Office of Legal Metrology under the Ministry of Consumer Affairs, Food and Public Distribution; and the Department of Commerce under the Ministry of Commerce and Industries (MOCI), regulate food safety, standards, labelling and packaging requirements of food and agricultural products.

Anti-dumping and countervailing measures

Anti-dumping and countervailing measures are permitted by the WTO Agreements in specified situations to protect the domestic industry from serious injury arising from dumped or subsidized imports. India imposes these from time-to-time to protect domestic manufacturers from dumping. India's implementation of its antidumping policy has, in some cases, raised concerns regarding transparency and due process. In recent years, India seems to have aggressively increased its application of the antidumping law.

Export subsidies and domestic support

Several export subsidies and other domestic support is provided to several industries to make them competitive internationally. Export earnings are exempt from taxes and exporters are not subject to local manufacturing tax. While export subsidies tend to displace exports from other countries into third country markets, the domestic support acts as a direct barrier against access to the domestic market.

The Indian government's Foreign Trade Policy (FTP) 2015-2020 announced on April 1, 2015 is primarily focused on increasing India's exports of goods and services to raise India's share in world exports from 2 to 3.5 percent. The FTP consolidated most of India's existing export subsidies and other incentives into two main export incentive schemes, namely the Manufactured Goods Exports Incentive Scheme (MEIS) and the Service Exports Incentive Scheme (SEIS).

India maintains several export subsidy programs, including exemptions from taxes for certain export-oriented enterprises and for exporters in Special Economic Zones. Numerous sectors (e.g., textiles and apparel, paper, rubber, toys, leather goods, and wood products) receive various forms of subsidies, including exemptions from customs duties and internal taxes, which are tied to export performance. India not only continues to offer subsidies to its textiles and apparel sector to promote exports, but it has also extended or expanded such programs and even implemented new export subsidy programs. As a result, the Indian textiles sector remains a beneficiary of many export promotion measures (e.g., Export-Oriented Units, Special Economic Zones, Export Promotion

Capital Goods, Interest Credit Schemes, Focus Product, and Focused Market Schemes). The GOI in July 2016 further increased the subsidy for the garment sector to boost employment generation in addition to providing for refund of state levies.

In 2017, India graduated from Annex VII of the WTO's Subsidies and Countervailing Measures Agreement. In March 2018, the United States requested consultations on India's export subsidy schemes in the WTO and a formal panel was established on July 24, 2018.

India maintains a large and complex series of programs that form the basis of India's public food stockholding program. India maintains stocks of food grains not only for distribution to poor and needy consumers but also to stabilize prices through open market sales. India uses export subsidies to reduce stocks and has permitted exports of certain agricultural commodities from government public-stockholding reserves at below the government's costs.

As per the USTR updates, India's mid-term review of its FTP (released in Dec. 2017) outlined a renewed focus on promoting Indian exports while highlighting the need to move away from export subsidies consistent with WTO commitments relating to gross national income levels. As a result, India's revised FTP will also focus on reducing the cost of trade internal to the country and has set forth an agenda to address trade facilitation issues impacting Indian exporters.

Procurement

USTR source states that India lacks an overarching government procurement policy and, as a result, its government procurement practices and procedures vary among the states, between the states and the central government, and among different ministries within the central government. Multiple procurement rules, guidelines, and procedures issued by multiple bodies have resulted in problems with transparency, accountability, competition, and efficiency in public procurement. A recent World Bank report stated that there are over 150 different contract formats used by the state-owned Public-Sector Units, each with different qualification criteria, selection processes, and financial requirements. The government also provides preferences to Indian micro, small, and medium enterprises and to state owned enterprises. Moreover, India's defense offsets program requires companies to invest 30 percent or more of the acquisition cost of contracts above the threshold value in Indian produced parts, equipment, or services, a requirement that continues to prove challenging for manufacturers of high-technology equipment.

In 2015, the government mandated that 20 percent of its public procurements be awarded to Indian based micro, small, and medium enterprises, and in 2017, the Indian cabinet approved a public procurement policy encouraging preferences for Indian manufactured goods with a view to promote the "Make in India" initiative. The move is aimed at facilitating local manufacturing and boosting domestic demand for locally manufactured products. As part of this May 2017 policy, the Ministry of Defense approved a model for Strategic Partnerships in certain acquisition programs, although the strong focus on mandatory technology transfer has given many U.S. companies reason to exercise caution regarding participation. A local content requirement has also been extended to the procurement of medical devices, and several government tenders in the last year have included a 30 percent local content mandate. India's National Manufacturing Policy calls for increased use of local content requirements in government procurement in certain sectors (e.g., information communications technology and clean energy). Consistent with this approach, India issued the Preferential Market Access notification, which requires government entities to meet their needs for electronic products in part by purchasing domestically manufactured goods. Subsequently, in June 2017, the Department of Industry Policy and Promotion (DIPP) issued two notifications under the Public Procurement "Preferential Electronics Order" and "Cyber Notification," which require local content for all state and central government procurements mandating preferences for domestically manufactured electronic goods (including medical devices) and cyber-security software products. The notification indicates that this requirement will apply to procurement by government, government companies, and other procuring entities. This notification is the culmination of similar Indian policy proposals over the past year that have outlined discriminatory government procurement policies as a means to stimulate domestic manufacturing of electronics and telecommunications equipment at the expense of foreign companies that have invested heavily in India.

Service barriers

Services in which there are restrictions include: insurance, banking, securities, motion pictures, accounting, construction, architecture and engineering, retailing, legal services, express delivery services and telecommunication. The Indian government has a strong ownership presence in major services industries such as banking and insurance. Foreign investment in businesses in certain major services sectors, including financial services and retail, is subject to limitations on foreign equity. Foreign participation in professional services is significantly restricted, and in the case of legal services, prohibited entirely.

Other barriers

Local Content requirements, Export Duties and Transparency continue to be other barriers for trade.

In 2010, India initiated the Jawaharlal Nehru National Solar Mission (JNNSM), which currently aims to bring 100,000 megawatts of solar-based power generation online by 2022 as well as promote solar module manufacturing in India. Under the JNNSM, India imposes certain local content requirements (LCRs) for solar cells and modules and requires participating solar power developers to use solar cells and modules made in India to enter into long-term power supply contracts and receive other benefits from the Indian government. The United States challenged these requirements through the World Trade Organization (WTO) dispute settlement system. In February 2016, a WTO panel found India's LCRs inconsistent with multiple WTO requirements. These findings were affirmed by the Appellate Body on September 16, 2016, and the DSB adopted the Appellate Body and Panel reports at a special meeting of the DSB on October 14, 2016. On December 19, 2017, the United States requested authorization from the DSB to suspend concessions or other obligations on the grounds that India had failed to comply with the DSB recommendations within the "reasonable period of time" that the parties agreed to. The United States' request was referred to arbitration. On January 23, 2018, India requested the establishment of a compliance panel, asserting that it had complied with the DSB recommendations. The arbitration and compliance panel proceedings are ongoing.

India has steadily increased export duties on iron ore and its derivatives. This includes export duty of 30 percent, ad valorem export duty on iron ore pellets of five percent, an export duty on iron ore containing less than 58 percent iron of 10 percent, and an export duty on chromium ore of 30 percent ad valorem. In recent years certain Indian states and stakeholders have increasingly pressed the central government to ban exports of iron ore. To improve availability of iron ore for the local steel producers, the GOI in March 2016 enhanced and unified the rate of export duty for all types of iron ore (other than pellets) at 20 percent; earlier a 15 percent export tax was applicable on lumps and 5 percent on fines. India's export duties impact international markets for raw materials used in steel production. In addition to the steel-related export duties, India's March 2017 budget also imposed a 15 percent duty on exports of aluminum ores, including laterite. India has also maintained, since February 2012, a 30 percent ad valorem duty on exports of chromium ore.

Lack of transparency with respect to new and proposed laws and regulations affecting traders remains a problem due to a lack of uniform notice and comment procedures and inconsistent notification of these measures to the WTO. This in turn inhibits the ability of traders and foreign governments to provide input on new proposals or to adjust to new requirements. In 2014, India's Ministry of Law and Justice issued a policy on pre-legislative consultation, which was to be applied by all Ministries and Departments of the Central Government before any legislative proposal was to be submitted to the Cabinet for its consideration and approval. The policy also required the central government entities to publish draft legislation or a summary of information concerning the proposed legislation for a minimum period of 30 days. Issuance through electronic media was also encouraged in the policy, as were public consultations. However, despite U.S. requests, the Indian government has provided no information on the implementation of the policy, other than to clarify it is only intended to apply to draft legislation, not regulations or tariff-setting not. U.S. stakeholders continue to report new requirements that are issued with no or inadequate public notice and consultation or without WTO notification. This lack of transparency imparts a lack of predictability in the Indian marketplace, negatively affecting the ability of U.S. companies to enter or operate in the Indian market. The United States continues to raise our concerns regarding uniform notice and comment procedures with the government of India both bi-laterally in the Trade Policy Forum (TPF) and multi-laterally in the WTO and other fora.

TRADE BARRIER

Trade barriers are government-induced restrictions on international trade.

Economists generally agree that trade barriers are detrimental and decrease overall economic efficiency; this can be explained by the theory of comparative advantage.

Most trade barriers work on the same principle: the imposition of some sort of cost (money, time, bureaucracy, quota) on trade that raises the price or availability of the traded products. If two or more nations repeatedly use trade barriers against each other, then a trade war results. Barriers take the form of tariffs (which impose a financial burden on imports) and non-tariff barriers to trade (which uses other overt and covert means to restrict imports and occasionally exports).

In theory, free trade involves the removal of all such barriers, except perhaps those considered necessary for health or national security. In practice, however, even those countries promoting free trade heavily subsidize certain industries, such as agriculture and steel.

Overview

High income countries tend to have less trade barriers than middle income countries which, in turn, tend to have less trade barriers than low income countries. Small states tend to have lower trade barriers than large states. The most common trade barriers are on agricultural goods. Textiles, apparel and footwear are the manufactured goods which are most commonly protected by trade barriers. Tariffs have been declining in the last twenty years as the influence of the World Trade Organization has grown, but states have increased their use of non-tariff barriers.

According to Chad Bown and Meredith Crowley, world trade is "probably" vastly more liberal in current times than was the case historically. According to Ronald Findlay and Kevin H. O'Rourke, "for the nineteenth and twentieth centuries trade barriers and transport costs were the most important barriers to trade". They also write, "during the mercantilist era price gaps were as likely to be due to trade monopolies, pirates, and wars as to transport costs and tariffs, which are more easily quantifiable."

Georgetown University Professor Marc L. Busch and McGill University Professor Krzysztof J. Pelc note that modern trade deals are long and complex because they often tackle non-tariff barriers to trade, such as different standards and regulations, in addition to tariffs. Due to steadily decreasing tariff barriers since World War II, countries have become increasingly likely to enact trade barriers in forms other than tariffs. National firms often lobby their own governments to enact regulations that are designed to keep out foreign firms, and modern trade deals are one way to do away with such regulations.

The barriers can take many forms, including the following:

- Tariffs
- Non-tariff barriers to trade include:
    - o Import licenses
    - o Export licenses
    - o Import quotas
    - o Subsidies
    - o Voluntary Export Restraints
    - o Local content requirements
    - o Embargo
    - o Currency devaluation
    - o Trade restriction

Impacts of trade barriers on business

Trade barriers are often criticized for the effect they have on the developing world. Because rich-country players call most of the shots and set trade policies, goods such as crops that developing countries are best at producing still face high barriers. Trade barriers such as taxes on food imports or subsidies for farmers in developed economies lead to overproduction and dumping on world markets, thus lowering prices and hurting poor-country farmers. Tariffs also tend to be anti-poor, with low rates for raw commodities and high rates for labor-intensive processed goods. The Commitment to Development Index measures the effect that rich country trade policies actually have on the developing world.

Trade barriers are mostly a combination of conformity and per-shipment requirements requested abroad, and weak inspection or certification procedures at home. The impact of trade barriers on companies and countries is highly uneven. One particular study showed that small firms are most affected (over 50%).

Another negative aspect of trade barriers is that they result in a limited choice of products and would therefore force customers to pay higher prices and accept inferior quality. Trade barriers obstruct free trade. Before exporting or importing to other countries, firstly, they must be aware of restrictions that the government imposes on the trade. Subsequently, they need to make sure that they are not violating the restrictions by checking related regulations on tax or duty, and finally they probably need a license in order to ensure a smooth export or import business and reduce the risk of penalty or violation. Sometimes the situation becomes even more complicated with the changing of policy and restrictions of a country.

INDIA TO REMOVE 'UNFAIR' TRADE BARRIERS AS CENTRE SOFTENS STAND

Commerce minister Piyush Goyal has said that India was open to all suggestions on removing 'unfair' trade barriers, reiterating the Narendra Modi government's rush to repair business relations with the US ahead of the prime minister's visit to the US this weekend.

"We have an open mind, if there are any trade barriers in India, we are willing to re-look at that ," Goyal said at Tuesday morning's Asia-Pacific Trade Facilitation Forum event in Delhi, organised by his ministry along with the UN, Asian Development Bank and CII.

Without mentioning the US, Goyal said how the trend of one nation putting trade barriers and the other country retaliating "will only worsen the architecture of free trade in...the world."

In June, the US had removed India from its Generalised System of Preferences (GSP) trade programme that gave about 3,000 export items from India, worth $5.6 billion, duty-free access to the American markets. This is estimated to amount to 12 per cent of India's exports to the US. India had retorted by imposing tariff restrictions on 29 US items a week later.

With Trump slated to appear at Modi's rally in Houston on Sunday, expectations are that an agreement will be thrashed out in time for the two leaders to announce when they meet. Modi is visiting the US to take part in the UN General Assembly's annual event. Hectic negotiations have been going on to work out a solution that will see India getting back on the GSP list, even as it addresses Trump administration's long-standing demand for getting "equitable and reasonable access to its markets".

"We are willing to try and simplify (trade barriers), or eliminate them if they are causing an unfair disadvantage on international trade," Goyal announced. At the same time, the minister pointed out that India's trade policies were transparent and how it was often India that has been at the recieving end, with trade protectionism increasing all over the world in the last year. " We in India very often have not been able to create non-tariff barriers (like other countries). Other countries have often stalled a great number of Indian exports, particularly on the services side."

"It should be a collective effort, on India as well as other countries, to work towards removing these barriers," he exhorted.

US FOREIGN DIRECT INVESTMENT

Although current levels of U.S. foreign direct investment (FDI) are relatively low when compared to China, there is strong private interest in the Indian market for U.S. companies in certain industries. Annual FDI to India from all countries rose from about $100 million in 1990 to nearly $6 billion for 2005, then nearly doubled in one year to more than $11 billion in 2006. About one-third of these investments was made by U.S. firms; in recent years, the major U.S.-based companies Microsoft, Dell, Oracle, and IBM announced plans for multi-billion-dollar investments in India. However, current Indian law restricts foreign ownership in many industries to varying degrees, making FDI less attractive to many U.S. companies.

At present, India strictly prohibits FDI in four industries: retail trade (except single-brand outlets); atomic energy; lottery business; and gambling and betting. For other sectors of interest to U.S.

companies – including broadcasting, pharmaceuticals, banking, financial services, insurance, defence production, mining, oil and natural gas, and telecommunications – FDI limits range from 26% to 100% of total equity, both across and within sectors. In addition, depending on the sector and the size of the FDI, the investment may be subject to administrative approval. In late 2006, India announced it is considering new legislation on FDI. The so-called FDI Promotion Act would cover all aspects of FDI, including entry conditions, dispute settlement, incentive programs, approval procedures. The Indian government is also considering a proposal to create uniform FDI limits within each sector, as well as raise some of the current FDI limits. Prospects for these two proposals are uncertain. However, New Delhi did increase the FDI limit for the telecommunications industry from 49% to 74% in March 2007.

Especially closely watched are opportunities for investment in India's potentially vast retail sector. Foreign involvement in his sector is a sensitive issue for Indians; in March 2005, Commerce Minister Nath said, "We are very clear that if at all FDI is permitted into retail trade it should lead to incremental economic benefits and not substitute ongoing activities. There is no question of replacing or displacing what we have: it must add to economic activity."

New Delhi subsequently commissioned a report on FDI in the retail sector and, in January 2006, Nath announced new regulations that allow foreign investors to own up to 51% of retail outlets selling only single-brand goods. India has a particularly large number of small merchant shops – perhaps the highest per capita number worldwide – meaning that tens of millions of citizens could be adversely impacted by the appearance in India of "big-box" retailers.

Intellectual Property Rights

The U.S. Trade Representative listed India on the U.S. Special 301 Priority Watch List in 2007, despite recognition of improvements in India's IPR laws, regulations and enforcement.

On the administrative side, the United States urged India to "improve its IPR regime by providing stronger protection for copyrights, trademarks, and patents, as well as protection against unfair commercial use for data generated to obtain marketing approval."

The U.S. Trade Representative has also indicated that the United States would like to see India join the World Intellectual Property Organization's (WIPO) Internet Treaties. On the enforcement side, the United States claimed that piracy of copyright materials was "rampant." Opponents of inserting "data exclusivity" clauses into Indian law assert that they constrict India's generic drug industry's ability to compete both domestically and internationally, and place a large financial burden on firms that must repeat expensive clinical trials. By removing the availability of inexpensive and oftentimes life-saving medications, the argument goes, would have a seriously detrimental resulting impact on public health.

India appears to have been active in its IPR enforcement during 2007. On February 6, 2007, India joined 11 other Asia-Pacific entities in a combined sting operation that arrested 870 people and seized nearly 5 million pirate DVDs and VCDs. The operation was called "Operation Trident," and involved operations in Australia, China, Hong Kong, India, Indonesia, Japan, Malaysia, New Zealand, the Philippines, Singapore, South Korea, Taiwan, and Thailand. In India, there were 110 raids, with 118 arrests. Operation Trident occurred while India was hosting the first-ever International Meeting on Intellectual Property and Development. Organized by India's Department of Industrial Policy & Promotion (DIPP), the meeting included representatives from 22 countries, including the United States. The focus of the February 5-7 meeting was on the relationship between intellectual property rights (IPR) and economic development.

In addition, in May 2007, the U.S.-India Business Council (USIBC) in conjunction with the Federation of Indian Chambers of Commerce and Industry (FICCI), implemented a "Bollywood-

Hollywood" anti-piracy initiative aimed at stopping the illegal copying and distribution of U.S. and Indian entertainment videos. The initiative seeks to reduce video piracy both in India and the United States, where the growing popularity of Bollywood movies has given rise to a growing problem of video piracy.

The relationship between IPR and economic development has been of interest to India for several years. In 2003, a group of developing countries, including India, circulated a paper at the WTO making recommendations on actions that could be taken to foster greater technological transfer to developing countries.

The United States and other WTO members objected to the paper's analysis, which suggested that the TRIPS agreement and its IPR protection provisions were hindering technological transfers.

In October 2005, India, Pakistan, and the Philippines submitted another paper on the subject of technological transfer and the TRIPS agreement that focused on ways to encourage technical assistance, promote the performance of technological development work by multinational corporations in developing countries, and facilitate the mobility of scientists and technicians under the GATS agreement. The U.S. response to the second paper was more favorable. The second paper became the focus of discussion in 2006 of the WTO's Working Group on Trade and Transfer of Technology (WGTTT), a body established in 2001 at the Doha Ministerial Conference. According to the USTR's 2007 Trade Policy Agenda, the United States expects that the paper will also dominate WGTTT discussions in 2007.

Beyond the usual concerns expressed by the software, movie, and publishing industries about IPR protection, the U.S. pharmaceutical industry has of late been very actively seeking improved IPR protection in India. In particular, it would like to improve patent protections, secure test data exclusivity, and limit pre-grant opposition to patent applications. India's pharmaceutical industry, for its part, believes that the level of IPR protection sought by the U.S. companies exceeds those provided for in the

TRIPS agreement, and will effectively prevent the introduction of generic drugs in India in the future.

Jewellery

India is a leading exporter of jewellery, especially diamonds and diamond jewellery, to the world and to the United States. In 2006, the United States imported $5.9 billion worth of jewellery (HTS71) from India, or 25.5% of all imports from India. Of this, $3.3 billion (55.5%) were diamonds and diamond jewellery and another $2.4 billion (41.0%) was precious metal jewellery.

The depletion of many of India's diamond mines has pushed its industry to source its diamonds from overseas. In 2005, India imported nearly $10.6 billion worth of diamonds. This has raised concerns about the possible import of so-called "conflict diamonds." In January 2003, India, the United States, and 53 other countries endorsed a UN initiative called the Kimberley Certification Process that certifies that the diamonds do not come from Angola, Liberia, Sierra Leone, and Congo. In 2005, India considered lowering the FDI limit for diamond mines from 100% to 74% in an effort to close a possible back door for the import of "conflict diamonds." However, there are claims that uncut "conflict diamonds" are still finding their way into India, especially into the markets in Surat. If true, then there is high likelihood that "conflict diamonds" could also be making their way into the U.S. consumer market.

Oil

The rapid growth in India's economy has also meant a rapid increase in its demand for oil. Although India has proven oil reserves, production is nearly at capacity, while demand continues to rise. According to the U.S. Department of Energy's Energy Information Agency (EIA), India produced an average of 846,000 barrels per day (bbl/day) of "total oil liquids" in 2006, and used an average of 2.63 million bbl/d of oil, resulting in a shortage of nearly 1.8 million bbl/d. In addition, according to the EIA's estimates, India's oil demand increased by 100,000 bbl/d in 2006, and will increase by similar amounts in 2007 and 2008, leading to the nation's growing "energy deficit."

In order to fill its oil gap, India national oil companies have been actively seeking overseas sources of crude oil, involving the acquisition of equity in some cases. According to EIA, the most active Indian oil company overseas is ONGC Videsh Ltd., which holds interests in 25 oil and natural gas projects in 15 different countries in Africa, Asia, the Americas, and the Middle East. Indian companies have also been actively involved in Sudan's oil industry, as well as the operation of the major oil pipeline and terminus in Port Sudan. India's growing oil demand, along with China's growing demand, are contributing factors in the a tightening global petroleum market and higher crude oil prices. Competition for crude oil and energy in general is becoming an important issue in Asia, pressing nations to develop trade relations outside of the region. For example, India is pursuing closer relations with the repressive regime in neighboring Burma (Myanmar), with an interest in energy cooperation and to counterbalance China's influence there. In response, the United States is exploring ways to foster cooperation with friendly nations with respect to global petroleum market. Legislation specifically on energy cooperation with India has been introduced in both the House of Representatives and the Senate.

Energy Cooperation

There currently is legislation before 110Congress on the subject of U.S.-India energy cooperation. The United States-India Energy Security Cooperation Act of 2007 (H.R. 1186) would "promote global energy security through increased cooperation between the United States and India in diversifying sources of energy, stimulating development of alternative fuels, developing and deploying technologies that promote the clean and efficient use of coal, and improving energy efficiency." Both the Energy Diplomacy and Security Act of 2007 (S. 193) and the Renewable Fuels, Consumer Protection, and Energy Efficiency Act of 2007 (S.

1419) would, *inter alia*, establish a U.S. petroleum crisis response mechanism in conjunction with China and India. The International Climate Cooperation Re-Engagement Act of 2007 (H.R. 2420) would create Foreign Commercial Service attaches and deploy these to India (and China) for the purpose of promoting U.S. exports in clean and energy efficient energy technologies. The New Direction for Energy Independence, National Security, and Consumer Protection Act (H.R. 3221), introduced in July 2007, contains similar provisions. Moreover, and as noted above, an initiative to launch civil nuclear cooperation with India was provisionally endorsed by the 109th Congress in the Hyde Act (P.L. 109-401) and any future "123 Agreement" guiding such cooperation must be approved by Congress.

Immigration

Immigration reform is a major issue for the 110th Congress. The Comprehensive Immigration Reform Act of 2007 (S. 1348), currently being considered by the Senate, would alter the eligibility requirements for H-1B visas under the Securing Knowledge, Innovation, and Leadership Act of 2007 (SKIL Act of 2007), and limit the number of "market-based visas" to 115,000 per fiscal year. While this is an increase from the current limit, it is below the level sought by both Indian and U.S. information technology companies. Nor does the bill address the industry's desire to see the creation of a new visa category for short-term training of foreign nationals in the United States.

Trade in Information Technology

At present, most of the focus of Indo-U.S. service trade is in the information technology (IT) sector. Over the last few years, U.S. companies have been outsourcing many aspects of their IT work to India and other nations. According to one recent study, U.S. banks will increase the share of their IT work overseas from 6% to 30% by 2010, representing a transfer of over $10 billion of IT services. The study also predicted that the nature of the overseas

IT work will shift from "low-level applications" to more sophisticated IT activities. Another study projected that U.S. IT outsourcing would increase at a compound annual growth rate of 5.9% over the next five years, reaching a total value of $17.7 billion in 2011. This later study indicated that an impending shortage of IT skills among government employees will be one of the key stimuli of the outsourcing.

U.S. companies are not limiting their activities in India to IT; they are also utilizing India to provide a growing array of services related to the financial sector. On April 11, 2007, Citigroup announced the elimination of 17,000 jobs – or nearly 5% of its global workforce – and the relocation of 9,500 jobs to "low-cost" locations. However, in the same news story, sources close to Citigroup said that between 5,000 and 8,000 jobs would be moved to India in the near future. Most of these relocated jobs would involve equity research, investment banking, and backoffice transaction-related services.

Meanwhile, India's domestic IT industry is attempting to branch out of the lower value-added activities (such as call centers and payroll processing) into higher value-added services (such as product design, software development, and chip engineering). Many U.S. companies are establishing tech centers in India to take advantage of the greater availability and lower cost of Indian engineers. Plus, leading Indian IT companies – such as Tata, Infosys, Wipro, Satyam, and HCL Technologies – are developing their international IT service capacity.

H-1B Visas. The growth of trade in IT services has placed pressure on the U.S. H-1B visa program. The H-1B visa permits U.S. companies and universities to temporarily employ foreign workers who have the equivalent to a U.S. bachelor's degree. While there is an annual quota of 78,200 visas, exemptions have allowed the U.S. Citizenship & Immigration Services to issue over 100,000 H1-B visas in 2004 and 2005. Recipients of an H1-B visa may remain in the United States for up to six years (ten years for Defence Department related work) so long as they remain employed by the same company. H1-B visas are not transferable. Both U.S. and Indian companies have complained that the current quota is too restrictive, making it difficult for U.S. companies to hire enough engineers and technicians to remain competitive in the global market. Also, some companies would like to see the creation of a new visa category that would allow foreign nationals to work and/or train in the United States for a short period of time. However, there is opposition to the expansion of the current H1-B program.

In May 2007, two senior U.S. Senators wrote letters to nine Indian companies that account for nearly one-third of all H1B visas issued in 2006 and requested further details about their use of the special visa program. The Senators expressed concern that fraud and abuse in such programs may have negative impact on U.S. workers.

The Farm Bill

Many provisions of the current omnibus farm bill, the Farm Security and Rural Investment Act of 2002 (P.L. 107-171), expire in 2007. India, along with Brazil and other nations, have argued that certain aspects of the current U.S. farm program are "trade distorting,' and are pushing the United States to change various agricultural programs, including its farm subsidies.

It was previously hoped that the Doha Round would be completed in time for Congress to consider the enabling legislation under Trade Promotion Authority (TPA), and that any changes in U.S. agricultural policy could be including the enabling legislation. However, since the Doha Round discussions are not completed, Congress is considering the expiring programs without the benefit of knowing the terms of any new WTO obligations. The recently introduced H.R. 2419 provides for the continuation of the expiring farm programs, but may not prove to be in compliance with the results of any agreement coming out of the current Doha Round discussions.

Outsourcing and Displaced Workers

The growth of outsourcing various services to India, as well as other nations, is a serious concern for many U.S. workers. Current U.S. law provides some assistance to "displaced workers" via the Trade Adjustment Assistance (TAA) program authorized by the Trade Act of 1974 (P.L. 93-618), the Worker Adjustment and Retraining Notification (WARN) Act of 1988 (P.L. 100-379) of 1988, and the Workforce Investment Act of 1998 (P.L. 105-220). However, various groups and individuals have called upon Congress to revisit these programs, and strengthen the provisions protecting U.S. workers from job losses caused by outsourcing. There are currently two bills before Congress that offer additional assistance and/or protection to displaced U.S. workers. The Trade Adjustment Assistance Reform Act (H.R. 1729) expands eligibility for displaced textile and apparel workers for trade adjustment assistance, arguably in response to the growth in clothing and textiles imports from India. The second bill, the Worker Empowerment Act (S. 1330), would amend the Social Security Act to provide for wage insurance for dislocated workers.

Foreign Direct Investment

The 110 Congress is considering legislation pertaining to the operation of the Committee on Foreign Investment in the United States, or CFIUS, an interagency committee that overseas the security implications of foreign investments in the United States.

While U.S. laws governing FDI are generally viewed as being very liberal, there has been recent concern about the security implications of some proposed overseas investments, especially their implications for national defence and port security. Proposed legislation would require CFIUS to investigate all foreign investment transactions in which the entity is owned or controlled by a foreign government, regardless of the nature of the business. Given the recent increase in Indian FDI in the United States, this could cause some tension with India, as well as weaken U.S. efforts to persuade India to lower its current barriers to FDI.

9

India's Trade Reform and USA

India could benefit from the fallout in the U.S.-China trade war, experts told CNBC — but much-needed reforms on land and labor could prove to be a challenge for companies trying to do business there.

Trade tensions between Washington and Beijing have caused some manufacturers to shift production out of China, to avoid higher tariffs.

As a result, Southeast Asian nations, such as Vietnam, have often been cited as winners in the trade shifts. India could be a beneficiary too. India could increase its trade footprint in (the) midst of the US-China trade conflict, particularly under categories on which US has imposed tariffs on China," Radhika Rao, an economist at Singapore bank DBS Group, wrote in an August report.

"Apart from trade, diversion in investment flows is an opportunity that India could benefit from, as manufacturers seek alternative origination destinations," Rao added, implying it could attract foreign investments into the country.

India's share of the global export market is relatively small.

Even though Germany's population is nearly 16 times smaller than India's, German exports made up 8.17% of the world's total trade flows in 2017. Comparatively, Indian exports accounted for only 1.68% of world trade that year.

Winning sectors

The top three sectors in India that could benefit from the trade war are: pharmaceutical, chemicals and engineering, Rao told CNBC in an email.

India is already competitive in these industries globally and will likely be well-placed to meet further demand in these areas, she noted.

The South Asian nation's pharmaceutical industry supplies over half the world's vaccine demand, and 25% of medicines in the United Kingdom, according to a July 2019 report from the India Brand Equity Foundation (IBEF).

On the engineering side, India was the world's 12th largest producer of machine tools in 2017, a separate IBEF report said. The country also exports more than 60% of its engineering goods to the U.S. and Europe.

The manufacturing sector may benefit too — particularly the textiles, footwear and electronics sectors, said Rajiv Biswas, Asia Pacific chief economist at IHS Markit, in an email.

That's because exports from the U.S. and China will become more expensive as the tariffs kick in, and some manufacturers may move production to other Asian countries — including India.

"India may be able to benefit from this trend over the medium term, with global manufacturers increasingly focused on the rapidly growing Indian domestic consumer market," Biswas said.

For instance, Taiwan's Foxconn — the largest electronics contract manufacturer in the world, which assembles Apple products — moved production into India from China this year. This was to "diversify their manufacturing supply chain away from excessive reliance on Chinese production," said Biswas.

The Indian economy could benefit by $11 billion from these trade shifts, Rao wrote in the report, citing estimates by the United Nations Conference on Trade and Development.

Challenges for businesses

Businesses in India face two key challenges: land laws and labor regulations.

Land laws are the "biggest hurdle" for manufacturing and infrastructure development, said Societe Generale economist Kunal Kundu in a note to CNBC.

Current land laws make it difficult for the private sector to obtain space for manufacturing units, he said.

That's because land ownership is fragmented across several states, and companies need extended periods of time to obtain land, or bypass legal issues that may crop up.

Another problem is that labor laws in India are "extremely complex," noted Kundu. They comprise about 40 acts and companies are required to adhere strictly to all of them. This makes it difficult for manufacturers.

Land and labor reforms are two of the "most important factors of production" needed, according to Kundu.

Hence, he recommended, a national employment policy should be formulated – particularly one that allows manufacturers to make labor redundant during business down cycles.

Attracting investors

The lack of proper infrastructure could also be a problem, Nomura economist Sonal Varma told CNBC.

That includes connecting manufacturing plants to proper roads and ports, as well as ensuring that power is available.

The government has been seeking to improve some of these policies, but it will be some time before they can be fully realized. It is also trying to boost infrastructure and foreign investment in India through a multi-billion dollar budget.

Recent policy reforms in August were seen as a step forward for investment. For instance, the government approved 100% foreign investment in coal mining, and eased rules in contract manufacturing and retail. "India needs to move fast, through innovative policies and clear focus on infrastructure development ... But (a) lot more remains to be done and done urgently," Kundu said.

More changes to existing laws are needed before India can reap the full benefits of these investments to boost the economy.

As India is a big country, a lot of laws are controlled by the state government – not by the central government, Varma said. "The changes need to be not just ... top down from the central government, but also bottom up from different state governments."

TRADE REFORMS

The policy of economic liberalisation was put into operation with effect from 1991. A highly crucial aspect of economic liberalisation is the liberalisation in the field of foreign trade. Two basic components of the import policy of the government of India before 1991 were import restriction and import- substitution.

The stiff restrictions remained applicable upon imports until 1977-78. The trend towards import liberalisation appeared during 1980's. In that decade, the imports of raw materials and capital goods were liberalised and import facilities were offered to registered exporters and export and business houses. The policy of import substitution, of course, rendered some help in industrial diversification but the cost of import substitution to the economy had been overlooked.

The range of import-substitution remained extremely restricted. This policy promoted the domestic production of luxury goods and not that of the development goods. Industries were protected through high tariff walls. The monopolies gained much strength. The excess capacity emerged in several industries. There appeared serious distortion in prices. The import restrictions and inward-looking trade policies failed to ensure enlargement of exports.

With the object of promoting exports, some policy measures had been adopted even before 1991. They included removal of restrictions on exports, reduction in export duties, subsidisation of exports, institution of organisations in the public sector to enlarge exports, devaluation of rupee in 1966, encouragement to production for exports and upgradation of technology in export industries. These measures, however, failed to induce any appreciable rise in the exports of primary products and non-traditional items.

The bottlenecks in increasing production and making technical innovations in the export industries could not be overcome effectively. The country had to face the unprecedented economic crisis in 1989-90 and 1990- 91. The deficit in trade balance reached the highest level. The balance of payments problem became very acute on account of sharp increase in oil prices due to Gulf war, fall in invisibles, drying up of foreign exchange receipts and external debt problems and servicing thereof. The balance of payment deficit had reached upto the level of Rs. 17,639 crores in 1990-91. It was -3.1 percent of country's GDP in that year. In such dire circumstances, IMF put much pressure upon the government to introduce structural reforms in the economy.

The main features of trade sector reforms introduced by the government after 1991 were as under:

Removal of Quantitative Restrictions on Imports

Prior to trade reforms, there was much complexity in the import policy on account of the existence of different categories of importers, diversities in import licenses and varied ways of making imports. A step was taken in the direction of simplification and liberalisation of imports. In March 1996, import restrictions were removed off 6161 tariff lines. In 2000-01 and 2001-02, quantitative restrictions were removed in the case of 714 and 715 tariff lines respectively. This process continues through regional agreements with SAARC and ASEAN countries.

Reduction in Import Tariffs

In connection with the aim of liberalisation of imports, the government attempted to proceed in accordance with the recommendations of the Chelliah Committee for the rationalisation of tariff structure in the country. In the 1993-94 Budget, the government of India reduced the peak rates of import duty from 110 percent to 85 percent. Subsequently, the government continued to scale down the peak rates of import tariffs in phases. At present, the peak rate of import duty on non-agricultural goods is only 10 percent.

Convertibility of Rupee on Current Account

An important reform in the direction of liberalisation in the fields of trade and payments was related to the convertibility of rupee with other currencies. The partial convertibility of rupee was introduced in 1992-93. The full convertibility of rupee on current account was introduced in 1994-95. Consequently, the exchange rate of rupee no longer remained pegged. It became a market- determined rate.

The government adopted a more cautious approach in respect of convertibility of rupee on capital account. It was decided that the convertibility of rupee on capital account would be introduced in a phased manner. A considerable progress in this regard has already been made.

Decanalisation

The government had set up prior to 1991, the organisations like State Trading Corporation and Metals and Mineral Trading Corporation in the public sector. The imports and exports of several products used to be canalised through them. 20 of the import items and 16 of the export items out of them were decanalised by the government in August 1991. The decanalisation process remained continued in the subsequent years.

Concessions and Exemptions

In order to liberalise imports and to promote exports, the government extended a number of tax concessions and exemptions during the 1990's.

Some important concessions and exemptions were:

(1) Reduction in the peak rate of import duty to 15 percent;

(2) Reduction in the rates of duties in the information technology sector upon certain critical imports;

(3) A 10-year tax holiday to the developers of Special Economic Zones (SEZ) for the building up of infrastructure; and

(4) Extension of facilities and tax benefits to the exporters. In addition, the policy of providing tax benefits to information technology, telecommunication and entertainment sectors was adopted by the government.

Promotion of Exports of Services

In order to promote the export of services, the Exim Policy 2002-07, announced in March 2003, included several measures. The advance licence system was announced for the tourism sector. The firms, under this system, were permitted to make duty-free import of consumable goods and spares upto 5 percent of their average export earnings over the previous three years, provided they were actual uses of the items to be imported.

Special Economic Zones (SEZ) Scheme

In March 2000, the government announced the scheme for the establishment of Special Economic Zones (SEZ) for the boosting up of exports. Such zones could be set up in public sector, joint sector or by the State governments. The essential purposes for setting up the SEZ's were to ensure hassle-free exports and to increase the competitiveness of Indian exports in the international markets. In 2004-05, there were 15 functional SEZ's.

The exports by them in that year amounted to Rs. 18,309 crore. There could be duty-free exports and imports in these zones. The units operating in these zones had been granted 100 percent income tax exemption for 5 years. By 2009-10, as many as 580 SEZ's had been given formal approval and 374 SEZ's had been notified. In that year, their exports amounted to Rs. 2, 20,711 crore and their share in total exports stood at 26.1 percent.

Setting Up of Agricultural Export Zones

The Exim Policy of 2001 put forward the proposal of setting up of Agricultural Export Zones (AEZ). This scheme was meant for promoting agricultural exports and to organise the export effort on the basis of specific products and specific geographical areas. The scheme assured to provide the latest services related to various aspects of agriculture.

Export-Oriented Units (EOU) Scheme

This scheme is complementary to SEZ scheme. It offers more extensive and wide options for the establishment of export-oriented units. These units exported goods worth Rs. 28,896 crore in 2004-05. In 2008-09, exports by them amounted to Rs. 99,688 crore.

Setting up of Trading Houses

The trade policy of 1991 permitted the export houses and trading houses to import a wide range of products. The trade policy of 1992-97 allowed them the duty-free imports. A new category of trading houses called Super Star Trading Houses was introduced under the 1994-95 trade policy. Those trading houses were included in this category in case of which value of exports over the previous three years average of Rs. 925 crore or in case of which the value of exports in the preceding year amounted to Rs. 1387.5 crore.

The government also permitted the setting up of trading houses with 51 percent foreign equity for the expansion of exports. According to Foreign Trade Policy 2004-09, the star trading houses could retain upto 100 percent of their exchange earnings through exports.

Market Access Initiative Scheme

In order to promote the sale of products in foreign markets, this scheme was launched in 2001-02. Under this scheme, in-depth market studies are conducted related to the expansion of export of specific products in some selected countries. For generating the demand for domestic products in foreign markets, trade fairs and exhibitions are organised. The publicity campaigns are undertaken in foreign countries. The efforts are made to upgrade the quality of products in accordance with the requirements of the foreign buyers.

INDIA'S TRADE POLICY DILEMMA AND THE ROLE OF DOMESTIC REFORM

According to Singapore's former prime minister Goh Chok Tong, India currently has the potential to jump-start a stagnating global economy—similar to the way China did ten years ago. But given that India faces massive developmental challenges, is this a realistic assessment? With 1.3 billion people and a $2 trillion economy, the country has more poor people than those in all the sub-Saharan countries put together. Between 1991 and 2013, India's economy produced only 140 million jobs—a fraction of the more than 300 million required; and while 1 million people are currently entering the workforce every month, the presence of 17.7 million unemployed people is a time bomb no government can ignore.

In comparison, China has lifted hundreds of millions of its citizens out of poverty, raising per capita income from $873 in 1999 to $8,027 in 2015. The strength of China's manufacturing sector and a favorable global trade policy setting made this remarkable transformation possible. In 1995, when China entered the WTO, its exports were about $149 billion, with a trade surplus of nearly $20 billion. By 2014, China's exports had risen to $2.3 trillion, with a surplus of $382 billion. China's economic growth accounted for more than three-quarters of global poverty reduction, allowing the world to reach the United Nations Millennium Development Goal of halving global poverty by 2015.

Is India capable of performing similar feats of economic growth and integration into the global economy? Can its manufacturing sector become a major producer of jobs and tradable goods? Can it take advantage of whatever opportunities the fitfully evolving global trading architecture may offer?

The Trans-Pacific Partnership (TPP) and the Transatlantic Trade and Investment Partnership (TTIP) – while both have collapsed – are not the only manifestations of this evolving architecture. Various regional and subregional free trade agreements (FTAs) are already in place or likely to evolve. To maximize opportunities within this environment, India will have to overcome significant trade policy challenges: domestic issues; the evolving global situation; and the need for a positive trade policy agenda, as perhaps the only viable way for India to enhance its economic relationship with major trading partners. The United States – by far the world's largest economy – will continue to set the global trade policy agenda, and the United States itself will have to rework some of its trade policy objectives in light of recent developments. These notwithstanding, the United States will still determine the trade agenda even if a vacuum in leadership is created at the WTO. India could, if it acts wisely and in an enterprising manner, take advantage of that vacuum.

THE INDIAN CONUNDRUM

The greatest challenge to the development of a strong trade policy in India is its poorly developed manufacturing sector. Although it grew after India embarked on focused economic liberalization in 1991, the manufacturing share of the gross domestic product (GDP) has since fallen to 16.2 percent in 2015-2016 – about what it was in 1989-1990 (16.4 percent). The question of how to substantially augment the share of manufacturing is a tough one with no easy answers. Constraints include the limited availability of power and land, lack of access to technology, low productivity, the rising cost of labor, and difficulties doing business. Progress has been made, but it has been insufficient. By far the most serious impediment to the revival of the manufacturing sector is the scarcity of land.

The greatest challenge to the development of a strong trade policy in India is its poorly developed manufacturing sector. In the past decade, India signed FTAs with the Association of

Southeast Asian Nations (*ASEAN)*, the Republic of Korea, Japan, and Malaysia. However, some insiders admit that India's trade partners have gained more from these agreements than India has.

India's experience with regional trade agreements (RTAs) has been less than satisfactory because of the lack of competitiveness of its manufacturing sector and the lack of innovation and investment in sectors such as textiles, garments, and pharmaceuticals. This has resulted in little enthusiasm for adopting a more activist trade policy posture within the government, think tanks, and the trade policy community. Doubts about the attractiveness of international trade agreements grow stronger when global concerns over immigration cause other countries to reject India's demand for the freer movement of professionals (Mode 4 of the General Agreement on Trade in Services [GATS]).

Notwithstanding these challenges and doubts, joining RTAs could bring immeasurable benefits to India. Perhaps most importantly, it would make the country's goods and services more competitive, because it would force Indian industry to adjust to international standards in tech*nical barriers to* trade and sanitary and phytosanitary restrictions—an invaluable asset in the long run.

The real challenge in India . . . is the lack of full understanding of the benefits of trade liberalization, policy paralysis, and consequently the lack of political will. The real challenge in India, as in several other countries, is the lack of full understanding of the benefits of trade liberalization, policy paralysis, and consequently the lack of political will. Crafting a successful trade policy requires an understanding of geopolitics and global economic trends and the ability to negotiate to advantage. Effective negotiating is possible only if decisionmakers have the confidence and capacity to execute the necessary corresponding domestic reforms—some of which require painful adjustments.

Over the years, India has paid insufficient attention to the value of trade policy. In 1996, for example, it was clear that the end of quotas under the Multi-Fiber Arrangement in 2005 would benefit the more competitive exporting developing countries and that the modernization of India's domestic industry was therefore critical. Many policy actions the *Bharatiya Janata Party* government undertook in 2016, such as the enhanced duty drawback scheme, had been suggested in 1996. Policy paralysis, lack of will, and perhaps even lack of full understanding prevented the required steps from being taken in 1996. Had timely action been taken, India's share of global trade in textiles and clothing would have become much larger. Instead, Bangladesh, China, and Vietnam were the big beneficiaries of the end of the quota regime. Between 2000 and 2014, China's share of global exports rose from 10 percent to 36 percent in textiles and from 18 percent to 39 percent in garments.

India cannot serve its economic interests by remaining indifferent to or totally resisting global trade policy developments and the mega-trading blocs that may develop. As Jawaharlal Nehru University Professor Biswajit Dhar notes, "In the long run, no major economy can remain uninfluenced by them because the discriminatory rules regime will have consequences on trade with even nonmember economies."

Thus, the key challenge for Indian trade policy is how to revive the moribund, multilateral trading system anchored in the WTO. It may be in India's interest to encourage shifts back to the WTO, discouraging trade liberalization through just the RTAs and FTAs.

To effect such a change, India's trade policy needs to be bold and imaginative. It should start intensive and wide-ranging consultations among trading countries within the WTO. Depending on the outcome of the consultations, it should put forward concrete proposals for kick-starting negotiations in the WTO, placing the onus on the developed countries to react to India's proposals. Proposals may have to deal with the thorny issues of agriculture, Mode 4 of GATS, and some plurilateral agreements, such as the

Information Technology Agreement (ITA-2), government procurement, and dispute settlement.

India's trade policy needs to be bold and imaginative. It should start intensive and wide-ranging consultations among trading countries within the WTO. India's interest is in most-favored-nation (MFN) trade and the security and predictability associated with the multilateral trading system anchored in the WTO. Ensuring both requires that India not be viewed as a spoiler, as it currently is, in Geneva.

INDIA'S PAST AND PRESENT APPROACHES TO TRADE AGREEMENTS

In 1982, the United States made a determined push to get trade in services included in the General Agreement on Tariffs and Trade (GATT), which was essentially a legal framework covering trade in goods and the imposition of border measures (tariff and nontariff). A discussion between William Brock (the U.S. trade representative) and Shivraj Patil (the Indian minister of state for commerce) at the 1982 GATT Ministerial Meeting is worth recalling. Representing the United States were Michael Smith (the U.S. ambassador to GATT) and Andrew Stoler (who later became a deputy director-general at the WTO). On the Indian side were the late Abid Hussein (then commerce secretary), B. L. Das (India's ambassador to GATT), and the author of this paper. After a brief exchange of pleasantries, Brock enquired, "Mr. Minister, what is India's position on services?" Patil said, "Nonnegotiable." "In that case," responded Brock, "I don't see why I should be wasting your time and mine." That was the India of Indira Gandhi. India's firm stand resulted in a diluted ministerial decision. Given that services account for nearly 57 percent of India's GDP today, it is arguable whether India made the right decision at the time.

In contrast, at the 2015 WTO Ministerial Conference in Nairobi, the Indian representative sat through the deliberations of the select group, acquiesced in the evolution of the package outcome, and then expressed disappointment after the results were gaveled. The

WTO operates on the basis of consensus. Any country can block the outcome if it considers it unacceptable.

Successive rounds of trade liberalization under the GATT and the WTO have resulted in the lowering of MFN tariffs, although there is still a significant differential between the bound and effective rates. In 1990–1991, for instance, the highest Indian tariff stood at 355 percent, and the weighted average tariff stood at 87 percent. By 1996–1997, these tariffs had fallen to 52 percent and 22 percent, respectively. Reductions in tariffs and the removal of quantitative restrictions and other nontariff barriers help expand trade, but they cannot ensure that manufacturing facilities do not move to locations with more attractive tax regimes or seek larger markets offshore. Vietnam, for instance, offers twenty-year tax holidays to new investors. Incentives and what the Chinese have been able to accomplish constitute a major trade policy challenge, not only for India but for several other countries as well, including the United States.

INDIA'S RECENT TRADE POLICY

Announcing a new Foreign Trade Policy in April 2015, Prime Minister Narendra Modi's government said it wished to increase India's share of global trade from 2.1 percent to 3.5 percent and double exports (to $900 billion) by 2020. The policy seeks to integrate the government's Make in India and Digital India initiatives.

Modi elaborated on his thinking and set out a clear road map at a speech in Washington in June 2016:

We will continue to strengthen the "Make in India" initiative. It is not intended for only manufacturing for the domestic market or import substitution. It is as much about making world-class products and services for the whole globe. That is why, for us, improvements towards free trade are important. It is very important for us that developed countries open their markets, not only to goods from countries like India but also to services. I see this as a win-win proposition for the U.S. and for India. India is the future human resource powerhouse of the world with a young hard-working population. In my vision, a partnership between American capital and innovation, and Indian human resources and entrepreneurship can be very powerful I am convinced we can strengthen both our economies through such partnership.

This bold statement, especially in the wake of exports declining for seventeen consecutive months since December 2014, needs to be acted on. But to do so effectively, the government will need to continually assess how these priorities (for example, the partnership between American capital and innovation and Indian resources and entrepreneurship) are playing out within evolving global trends.

Implementation of India's major schemes—the Smart City Project, Make in India, Skill India Program, and Digital India—will require foreign direct investment and a comprehensive rebooting and rejuvenation of India's manufacturing sector. The Modi government has made a good start. In 2015, India attracted more foreign direct investment (FDI) than China and the United States, tripling greenfield FDI, which reached an estimated $63 billion. Indeed, India became the leading country in the world for greenfield FDI, overtaking the United States ($59.6 billion) and China ($56.6 billion).

Implementation of India's major schemes . . . will require foreign direct investment and a comprehensive rebooting and rejuvenation of India's manufacturing sector. The Make in India initiative, however, has possibly run into international headwinds caused by recession, protectionism, and technological developments, such as automation and 3D printing. As a result, Make in India may only affect the Indian market, specifically the defense sector.

RELATIONS WITH THE UNITED STATES

The United States is by far India's largest single country trading partner. Bilateral trade in goods increased from a modest $5.6 billion in 1990 to $66.9 billion in 2014. The value of commercially traded services stood at about $58.8 billion in 2012. During Modi's first ministerial visit to the United States in 2014, the two sides set a target of $500 billion a year in trade in goods and services, without setting a deadline.

Subsequently, on June 8, 2016, Modi addressed a joint session of the U.S. Congress: "Our relationship has overcome the hesitations of history," he said, adding "in every sector of India's march forward, I see the U.S. as an indispensable partner." The trade and economic component of the relationship between the two countries must occupy pride of place, along with issues relating to foreign and security policy, in fashioning a meaningful bilateral strategic partnership.

The importance the two countries attach to enhancing economic and trade ties is reflected in paragraph 29 of the joint statement released after Modi's 2016 visit to the United States:

In order to substantially increase bilateral trade, they pledged to explore new opportunities to break down barriers to the movement of goods and services, and support deeper integration into global supply chains, thereby creating jobs and generating prosperity in both economies.

However, the lofty ideals and pronouncements of heads of state and governments do not by themselves translate into meaningful cooperation and bilateral engagement in the real world of trade negotiations. The strategic convergence the two countries are seeking does not percolate down to the trade segment, which, at its core, continues to be adversarial. The United States has been in the driver's seat, pushing for aggressive trade liberalization, the opening of markets, and mega-trading blocs based on WTO plus commitments.

REGIONAL TRADE AGREEMENTS RELEVANT FOR INDIA

TRANS-PACIFIC PARTNERSHIP

The TPP is a trade agreement among twelve Pacific Rim countries (Australia, Brunei, Canada, Chile, Japan, Malaysia, Mexico, New Zealand, Peru, Singapore, the United States, and Vietnam). The agreement was expected to be completed in 2012; after protracted negotiations, it was signed on February 4, 2016

However, newly elected U.S. President Donald Trump, who had been critical of the TPP throughout the election period, has already abandoned the agreement. It would have come into force when all twelve signatories ratified it or, after two years have passed, when members representing 85 percent of the GDP of signatories ratified it. Given that the United States accounts for 68 percent of the group's total GDP, ratification will not be possible without its signature.

Given that the United States gave its president "fast-track" approval—which means that Congress could reject or approve the agreement without separately considering each provision—the likelihood of a U.S. signature was low in any case. The TPP figured prominently in the U.S. presidential campaign. Democratic candidate Hillary Clinton supported TPP as secretary of state, but under pressure from her primary opponent, Bernie Sanders, a socialist from Vermont, she expressed grave reservations about the agreement and swore to protect American jobs. Republicans have traditionally advocated for free trade, including the TPP; but Trump based his campaign on hostility toward international trade agreements and partners, particularly Mexico and China. His central argument was that such agreements export American jobs, particularly manufacturing jobs. He denounced the TPP.

The same antitrade and antiglobalization rhetoric seen in the U.S. presidential campaign echoed arguments in the Brexit debate. Even if the "Remain" vote had won, half of the British electorate clearly felt alienated. The financial crisis of 2008 and its aftermath of slow growth in developed economies intensified inequities in the sharing of gains and losses, exacerbating inequality and national-level divisions between the better educated and economically well-off and the rest of the population. Both Brexit and the current U.S. stance on trade essentially reflect the inability of advanced industrial countries to cope with slow rates of economic growth.

Given that the United States has rejected the TPP, the agreement will be delayed indefinitely. After some time, however, the United

States and other countries could seek to renegotiate some of its terms. The prospects for finding agreement on whether and how to accommodate new demands by the United States (and other countries) are difficult to predict.

There is more bad news for the TPP. A 2016 report by the International Trade Commission (ITC) finds that the U.S. trade deficit with FTA partners increased by $141 billion (418 percent) from 1989 to 2015. The U.S. trade deficit with all non-FTA partners decreased by $46 billion (6 percent) since 2005. Coming from the ITC, which has traditionally supported FTAs, the report set off alarm bells.

Although the TPP will not be implemented in its current form, it is worth analyzing how India would fare if it would be. In a study prepared for the U.S.-India Business Council (USIBC), C. Fred Bergsten of the Peterson Institute for International Economics argued strongly in favor of India trying to negotiate its entry into the TPP:

India's competitiveness problem is compounded by its absence from the world's new megaregional trade agreements, especially the Trans-Pacific Partnership (TPP) but also the Transatlantic Trade and Investment Partnership (TTIP). If China and the rest of the Asia-Pacific Economic Cooperation (APEC) forum join a second stage of the TPP that continues to exclude India, India's annual export losses will approach $50 billion. India is being left behind by the world trading system.

India could enjoy export gains of more than $500 billion a year (a 60 percent increase, more than any other country) from joining an expanded TPP or participating in the comprehensive Free Trade Area of the Asia Pacific that APEC is now considering. India's national income would expand by a whopping 4 percent (more than $200 billion) as a result. India could further increase its exports by participating in the major plurilateral negotiations on services, environmental goods, and government procurement now taking place at the WTO.

India could further increase its exports by participating in the major plurilateral negotiations on services, environmental goods, and government procurement now taking place at the WTO.

The intersection between trade policy and electoral politics invariably produces fault lines. Globalization and trade liberalization produce both winners and losers. Decisionmakers reach out to unconvinced sections by extolling the virtues of the proposed trade deal often by exaggerating the potential benefits.

In 1993, Gary Hufbauer and Jeffrey Schott of the Peterson Institute projected that the North American Free Trade Agreement (NAFTA) would lead to a rising U.S. trade surplus with Mexico that would create 170,000 net new jobs a year in the United States.

Less than two years after NAFTA's implementation, Hufbauer recognized that his job projections had been totally wrong, noting that "The best figure for the job effect of NAFTA is approximately zero. . . . The lesson for me is to stay away from job forecasting."

The TPP seeks to influence international trade in three ways: by reducing or eliminating tariffs on qualifying products among member countries, regulating the role of state-owned enterprises, and achieving regulatory coherence on an unprecedented scale among its members. Negotiating partners expressed an interest in comprehensively reducing barriers to trade in goods (including agricultural goods) and services, as well as rates and disciplines on a wide range of topics (including new policy issues that neither the WTO nor existing FTAs cover). All these changes would affect India's external trade in ways that are difficult to forecast.

Some Indian commentators have argued off the record that India should aspire to join the TPP. But India was not asked to join the TPP and, even if the agreement was to move forward, would unlikely be invited in the coming years under the current circumstances. The agreement's delay (if not death) gives India breathing space to take corrective domestic actions to manage the consequences of a revised or revived TPP and thereby increase the likelihood of joining a revised TPP at some stage. This provides a best-case scenario for India.

Asia-pacific Economic Cooperation

APEC is a forum for twenty-one Pacific Rim member economies that promotes free trade throughout the Asia Pacific region. India is not a member. A report by the Asia Policy Society Institute suggests why it is an ideal time for India to join APEC and illustrates the benefits of and possible obstacles to its membership.

India's membership in APEC would benefit the government's development programs, which rely heavily on "greater access to foreign markets, investment sources, and value chains to bolster manufacturing and create jobs at home," and prepare Indian entrepreneurs and businesses for the changing global economy. An impressive growth rate, coupled with Modi's persistent efforts at public economic diplomacy in the region and beyond, have given India "hope that it can finally succeed in attaining membership after nearly two decades of disappointment." Joining APEC could be difficult, however, given the reservations of some members who perceive India's policies as insufficiently supportive of more open trade and greater regional integration.

India's membership in APEC would benefit the government's development programs. APEC itself would also benefit from India's participation in the forum, as its members would have better access to the country's labor supply and investment opportunities and to a consumer market that includes a rapidly expanding middle class of 200 million people by 2020 and 475 million by 2030.

Transatlantic Trade And Investment Partnership

In terms of ambition and sheer audacity of scale, the TTIP could be ranked at the level of the proposed TPP.

The Transatlantic Trade and Investment Partnership (T-TIP) is an ambitious, comprehensive, and high-standard trade and investment agreement being negotiated between the United States and the European Union (EU). T-TIP will help unlock opportunity for American families, workers, businesses, farmers and ranchers through increased access to

European markets for Made-in-America goods and services. This will help to promote U.S. international competitiveness, jobs and growth.

Britain's decision to leave the European Union effectively put the TTIP on hold in its present form. The partnership will require renegotiation. Nevertheless, it would be useful for India's Ministry of Commerce to review the chapters on the environment, labor standards, government procurement, state-owned enterprises, and nontariff barriers to at least determine what the country is up against and so that India's industry can be encouraged to upgrade. India has again been granted valuable breathing space, which its industrial sector should not waste.

Regional Comprehensive Economic Partnership

Launched in Cambodia on December 20, 2012, the RCEP is an FTA between ASEAN and its FTA partners (Australia, Brunei, China, Cambodia, India, Indonesia, Japan, the Republic of Korea, Laos, Malaysia, Myanmar, New Zealand, the Philippines, Singapore, Thailand, and Vietnam). The sixteen participating countries account for almost half the world's population, 30 percent of global GDP, and 25 percent of world exports. RCEP seeks to achieve a modern, comprehensive, high-quality, and mutually beneficial economic partnership agreement that will cover trade in goods, services, investment, economic and technical cooperation, intellectual property, competition, and dispute settlement.

India is participating in the RCEP negotiations but appears to be doing so with extreme caution. While there are perhaps valid reasons for this, India should be more forthright because of the following:

- Environmental and labor standards are not big issues in this agreement.
- The agreement gives India an excellent opportunity to negotiate with China, which it has found difficult to do bilaterally.
- India would have to recalibrate its demands on the movement of professionals (Mode 4), so that its partners respond positively.

- India could include some common objectives on environment and nontariff barriers that would not be part of the dispute settlement but would instead be "best-endeavor" clauses.

A ROAD MAP FOR INDIA

India and the United States were among the original signatories to the GATT in 1947. That agreement's preamble encapsulates the rationale for trade policy, which continues to be as valid today as it was then. The first of its two paragraphs cites the goals of "raising standards of living, ensuring full employment, and steadily growing volume of real income." The second cites modalities for achieving them, including "reciprocal and mutually advantageous arrangements directed to the substantial reduction of tariffs and other barriers to trade and to the elimination of discriminatory treatment in international commerce."

For most of the first thirty years of its existence, the multilateral trading system comprised a negotiated framework of rights and obligations governing trade in goods. It set border measures for both tariff and nontariff barriers. The Tokyo Round (1973–1979), the seventh round of multilateral trade negotiations, reduced tariffs and resulted in a number of stand-alone agreements on nontariff barriers. The fragmentation of the trade system dates back to this round of talks. Member countries could accede to the Tokyo Round agreements on an à la carte basis. India chose to do just that, acceding to only some of these agreements.

India found comfort in MFN trade, which became an article of faith—the only exception being the Generalized System of Preferences, a scheme that extended concessions and preferences on a unilateral basis. As long as India benefitted, it liked the scheme. The minute India became subject to conditions and found itself excluded, it protested, albeit without much success.

For valid reasons, India has found it difficult to accept the inclusion of issues relating to Trade-Related Aspects of Intellectual Property Rights (*TRIPs*), the environment, labor standards, and investment and regulatory matters. India has therefore found it difficult to accede to FTAs, which are invariably designed and operated on a WTO plus basis. India's problem today is not with TRIPs per se in the WTO, but with what is known as WTO TRIPs-plus standards. India is now fully compliant with WTO TRIPs standards.

The dilemma now is that the WTO is moribund, and developed countries are unwilling to pursue issues except on their terms. Action is therefore shifting to plurilateral agreements in the WTO and RTAs/FTAs. India is a player in neither; it is not a party to either the plurilateral Trade in Services Agreement (TiSA) or the ITA-2 being negotiated at the WTO, although its interests are at stake in both areas.

At the heart of the trade policy differences between the United States and India is intellectual property. India recognizes the need to reward creativity, innovation, and inventions and to balance that against the requirements of public good. The United States allows multinational drug companies to rake in large profits, as part of a healthcare system that is unaffordable even for the average American citizen. India, on the other hand, is the world's leading manufacturer and supplier of generic drugs. There was therefore understandable concern when the USIBC reported in its submission to the U.S. trade representative that India had given an assurance that it would no longer resort to compulsory licensing. India flatly denied it had provided such an assurance, recalling that it had resorted to compulsory licensing only once. The USIBC's clarification of April 14, 2016, is interesting:

USIBC recognizes and supports the Government of India's sovereign right to issue a compulsory license (CL). However, in order to attract investments that are imperative for innovation to thrive in India, the Council and its members seek transparency, consistency and clarity in the legislation and circumstances under which such compulsory licenses can be issued so as to enable well-informed business decisions.

Innovation is the bedrock of Prime Minister Modi's vision for Make in India, Start Up India and Digital India. USIBC and its members commend the Government of India for its openness to engage in dialogue with the industry in a manner that will grow the economy and bring superior innovation to the lives of Indians.

In May 2016, the government of India released a new intellectual property rights policy. However, if innovation needs to be promoted, perhaps India should have unveiled an innovation incentivization policy, as intellectual property rights are the flip side of the innovation coin. The new policy does not seek to delineate the elements that would promote and incentivize innovation and help release the creative potential and energies of India's youth, especially graduates of the I*ndian* institutes of technology and other leading educational and research institutions. It is not clear how the policy would (1) preserve and promote India's preeminent position as the pharmacy of the world or ensure that India continues to produce drugs and pharmaceuticals of high quality at competitive prices and thus play a role in promoting the basic right to health; (2) protect the right to use the flexibilities under the TRIPs agreement, especially with regard to the issuance of compulsory licensing related to public health; or (3) protect, promote, and enhance India's genetic resources, prevent biopiracy, and protect traditional knowledge and folklore.

If innovation needs to be promoted, perhaps India should have unveiled an innovation incentivization policy, as intellectual property rights are the flip side of the innovation coin.

A POSITIVE TRADE POLICY AGENDA

There is overwhelming evidence that trade has contributed to global prosperity, raised standards of living, and contributed to steadily growing real income. Globalization, however, produces both winners and losers. Trade produces prosperity but also inequality; it can have devastating effects on the manufacturing sector if it is subjected to subsidized or dumped products and exchange rate manipulation. Although the trading system provides remedies against unfair trade practices, little can be done if predatory pricing is institutionally entrenched, when entire systems do not work on the basis of market prices and it is difficult to determine where state subsidization ends and enterprise dumping begins.

Developments in global trade policy confront Indian policymakers with some hard choices. An ostrich-like switch-off mode can only exacerbate the country's problems. A good starting point would be to establish how India went so badly wrong in entering into trade agreements that are so low on ambition and counterproductive to its interests. It is axiomatic that if an FTA results in trade expansion but is in the interest of one partner, it is a badly negotiated agreement. A series of badly negotiated agreements should result in the sacking of trade negotiators, not a turn away from free trade.

India's ill-conceived trade pacts have resulted in inverted duty structures, high import duties on raw materials and intermediates, and lower duties on finished goods that discourage the production and exports of value added items. The Modi government has been bold in conceptual clarity, but it appears to be handicapped by its inward-looking bureaucracy.

There has to be inner consistency and harmony between the objectives of policy and the implementing modalities. It is not possible to want to increase the share of global trade and create millions of jobs by turning one's back on trade policy or relying on a trade policy that isolates India from the major trading arrangements globally taking shape.

Trade and foreign policies must by and large be in sync. Trade and foreign policies must by and large be in sync. The world of trade policy requires give and take. Negotiations for an FTA with the European Union have been languishing since 2007. The European Union is India's largest trading partner, accounting for 13 percent of India's total share of goods and services. A good indicator of a country's external engagements is whether its foreign and trade policies reinforce each other. India has struggled with a foreign policy segment that seeks strategic content with its trading partners and a trade policy segment that is more circumspect and inward-looking, often for good reason. Conceptual clarity is also required regarding actions that could broadly be categorized as trade promotion and actions that would fall under the rubric of trade policy. India's merchandise exports have a narrow account for 78 percent of total exports, and manufacturing exports are rapidly losing competitiveness, primarily because of a poor logistics infrastructure and weak trade facilitation.

India's experiment with special economic zones (SEZs) did not take off. The establishment of free ports or other schemes need to be considered on the merits. One might be forgiven for asking why free ports would succeed if SEZs failed or why the Chinese can organize themselves more effectively than other countries. Meanwhile, a key problem at hand is India's Supreme Court notice to the center and some states on returning unused SEZ land that belonged to farmers. The governments must consider whether to improve or revise the policy.

Under the rubric of trade policy come issues like the real effective exchange rate and the global trading architecture. India has not compensated for its declining exports to the European Union and the United States with increases elsewhere. Clearly, the trade policy bureaucracy has some explaining to do.

India should take advantage of delays in the TPP and TTIP to set its domestic house in order and register as a major trading nation. India should take advantage of delays in the TPP and TTIP to set its domestic house in order and register as a major trading nation. If it does not, the prime minister's grand plan to increase annual trade turnover with the United States to $500 billion and raise India's share of global trade to 3.5 percent will ring hollow.

India should revive the multilateral trade negotiations at the WTO. Doing so requires farsightedness on India's part as well as compromises in some of the positions it has taken on agriculture, Mode 4 of GATS, ITA-2, and government procurement. Its offers can be conditional, putting the onus of taking them forward on India's major developed country partners and the concessions they are willing to grant India. At the end of the day, India's interests are better served by the WTO and MFN trade than by the myriad RTAs and FTAs.

India does not appear to have any option other than to autonomously adjust to world standards on technical barriers to trade, sanitary/phytosanitary standards, and environmental and regulatory standards and to engage in crisis-mode upgrading of the physical infrastructure that is crucial to trade. Unless the industrial sector steps up and assumes responsibility for meeting world standards, there will be limits to what the government can do in terms of improving the country's infrastructure.

Unless the industrial sector steps up and assumes responsibility for meeting world standards, there will be limits to what the government can do in terms of improving the country's infrastructure. The Trade Facilitation Agreement of the WTO—to which India is now a signatory and the cabinet has now approved—would appear to provide the guiding framework within which the required actions can be taken. India needs to work on a road map on a war footing that can bring its goods and services into conformity with the highest standards on technical barriers to trade; sanitary/phytosanitary rules; labeling, packaging, customs, clearance, and freight procedures; and the best or next-best environmental and labor regulations.

Undertaking these actions will require hard decisions, some adjustment costs, and even pain in the short and medium term. These actions are inescapable, however, if India's manufacturing sector is to be given a fighting chance of competing in the global market place. Action is required on the part of both government and industry and related stakeholders.

INDIA'S SUSTAINED TRADE REFORMS UNDER MODI GOVERNMENT

It goes to the credit of Prime Minister Narendra Modi Government for bringing about a turn-around in India's export through sustained trade reforms during the last three years in spite of adverse global economic situation. India is among the few emerging economies, which had escaped the worst of the adverse external environment. This global downturn resulted in severe downturn in global trade and sharp fall in global commodity prices damaging exports all over. It caused the worst damage to oil and mining products exporters among developing economies. But India survived this onslaught because of expanding domestic markets and government's vigorous Make in India campaign. India also benefited because of the falling oil and other global commodity prices like steel and cement, which helped in India's infrastructure push, thereby helping trade as well.

In this difficult global environment, India did well to achieve a booming double digit exports growth in March 2017, surpassing such high growth achieved more than three years ago. India's exports growth, which had been in negative growth mode for nearly two years since October 2014, turned positive in September 2016. It has not looked back since then, thanks to the sustained trade reforms. This double digit growth has happened in India in March this year notwithstanding appreciating rupee, which no exporters welcome. This has only given credence to government's exports reform strategy that more than depreciating rupee, stable currency rate will help to sustain exports growth better. Federation of Indian exporters' organizations President G K Gupta himself acknowledged that the continuous positive growth in exports for more than half a year now is not only very enthusing and encouraging sign but also signifies the dedication, commitment and hard work done by the exporting community and government. It augurs well for India to deliver at challenging times.

The success in trade is mainly because of concerted efforts to promote make in India, push in foreign direct investment, particularly in export oriented industries, ease of doing business, digital India and skill India. All these had ensured not only increased job creation but also swelling foreign exchange reserves. Now that exports have got back to double digit growth, it is quite likely that India's merchandise exports cross $ 500 billion and two way trade to over $ 1 trillion in coming years. If services exports included, the two way trade will go much beyond $1 trillion. One additional factor that is going to promote India's trade is the game changing indirect tax reforms, Goods and Services Tax rollout from July one, this year. One nation, one tax and one common market is going to reduce time lost in logistics as well as lower transaction costs, pushing up trade manifold. DGFT is already working on aligning rates with the rollout of GST.

With Foreign Direct Investment up by 48 per cent from $36 billion in 2014-15 to $53 billion in 2015-16, the trade has been pushed up considerably. In 2016-17 up to December, India received FDI of $47 billion indicating, the flow will surpass last year's $53 billion. The foreign exchange reserves have swelled from $312 billion in 2014 to $365 201. Simplification of rules, scrapping of 1200 redundant and obsolete laws, passage of real estate bill that will lead to establishment of real estate regulators, setting up of e-market for gem industry, a major export item, and so on, have considerably improved the ease of doing business in the last 2-3 years.

The recent cabinet decision approving Supreme Court verdict to retain popular Target Plus Scheme too will help to push exports. Under the Target Plus Scheme duty credit of 5-15 per cent of FOB value is provided to exporters. With growth being positive in 25 of the 30 major exports products in March, the exports are surely back on track and are on the upswing mode. It is bound to bounce back to achieve $325 billion exports in 2016-17, thereby returning to high double digit growth path. The Trade Infrastructure for Export scheme launched by Commerce Minister Mrs Nirmala Sitharaman in March will further boost trade. The challenges faced by exporters on infrastructure is huge and TIES will help create modern infrastructure like last mile connectivity to ports, besides testing labs and certification centres. It will eliminate some of the logistics bottlenecks and address other challenges. The logistics cost in India is one of the highest in the World and this body will help in bringing it down. That apart, Trade Facilitation Agreement at the World Trade Organisation, the first multi-lateral agreement in 21 years, is expected to reduce trade cost on an average of 14.3 per cent. The developing countries like India stand to benefit as it will harmonize global rules for movement, clearance and release of goods. It will make trade related administration easier and less costly, thus helping to provide an important and much needed boost to global economic growth. This will push global growth by at least 0.5 per cent helping the global economy to push growth further. This will provide fillip to exports along with several government measures taken to take India's share in global trade to 5 per cent from the present 1.9 per cent.

With India being the World's fastest growing economy, the Modi government has put in place several measures including reversing inverted import duty structure, to take advantage of the green shoots in the country's exports. The trade reforms that are being implemented will facilitate India's merchandise exports to achieve projected $882 billion by 2020. Coupled with services exports, India's total exports will be around $1.3-1.4 trillion. The total two way trade could exceed $2.5 trillion in such a scenario. This is an ambitious target but achievable in a face of reforms. GST is perhaps one reform that has far-reaching and game changing implications, next only to economic liberalization of 1991.

WILL TRUMP AND MODI BRING A NEW DAWN FOR US-INDIA TRADE RELATIONS?

Firstly China, later India? Over the past few months, US President Donald Trump has hinted that the trade war will not be limited by China. Trump not only threatened to impose trade duties on imported cars from Japan and the European Union, but repeatedly called India the *"king of duties,"* Atman Trivedi writes in an article for Bloomberg.

Trump is simply obsessed with the obsessive Indian high Harley-Davidson motorcycle duties and has repeatedly pointed to India's modest US trade surplus of $24.3 billion. In March 2019, Trump sent Congress a notification that he plans to abolish duty-free treatment for Indian exports of $5.6 billion. He can do this at any time.

It is likely that Trump is not going to stop there. His administration is considering using the same legislative instruments that were used to impose unilateral duties on China in order to establish higher trade duties on Indian imports. Just imagine that one of the largest democracies in the world, which Washington seeks to win over to counter China, may be on a par with the main geopolitical rival of the United States.

India is a ray of light in US foreign policy. With great difficulty, over many years of efforts, Washington's ties with one of the key developing countries have been significantly strengthened. India was once considered an unreliable partner, but now it has become a foothold for the White House's Asian strategy.

Trump's trading tactics seem to be evidence of the US' deep confidence that they can be unceremonious with allies such as the European Union and Japan, without jeopardizing global strategic goals or efforts to contain China. Even assuming that the White House can afford it, given the fact that its long-standing allies need an American security umbrella, it is unlikely that such an approach could be used with respect to India.

India has not yet completely got rid of postcolonial thinking; it highly values its autonomy and its status as a non-aligned country. No matter how powerful and strategic ties have been built over the past few years, India is still not interested in a formal alliance with the United States.

Previous US administrations generally respected India's choice. At the same time, they made efforts to strengthen cooperation with New Delhi. Thanks to a number of initiatives, including a nuclear agreement between India and the United States reached in 2005, previous US administrations have made it clear to India that its development is in the interests of the United States.

If everything was limited only to trade disagreements, then common interests would be enough to maintain a positive relationship. However, Trump is not limited only to trade issues, he demands that India reduce Iranian oil imports to zero, as well as sharply reduce the supply of military equipment from Russia, otherwise India will face sanctions. The US President even belittles India's significant contribution to Afghanistan.

These US actions only increase the doubt among the representatives of India about the reliability of Washington. The Trump administration must remember that the economically more active India will also be a much more confident strategic partner.

It is also worth noting that Trump's comments on India are partly fair. India needs to reform its trade. The new Indian government should abandon the illiberal trade policy that impedes India's regional economic integration and its global competitiveness and labor productivity.

10

India Presents America with a Choice between Geopolitics and Trade

America and India have bickered about trade for years. India's average tariff is high, at around 13%. Its bureaucrats are also keen on other barriers to trade, from obscure rules on packaging to prohibitive red-tape on the import of dairy products. But over the past few years Narendra Modi, India's prime minister, has further inflamed these irritations. His government has increased tariffs on lots of American exports, including telecoms equipment, medical devices and nuts. It has also expanded rules favouring locally made goods in public procurement and has proposed a new law demanding that tech firms store data about Indian customers within India.

THE US-INDIA RELATIONSHIP IS AT A CRITICAL JUNCTURE

The partnership with India is one of the few U.S. relationships that has deepened notwithstanding transitions from the Bush to the Obama to the Trump administrations. But a number of differences are coming to a head over the next few months that could stall or even derail progress.

As Secretary of State Mike Pompeo plans to head to India next week, and President Donald Trump meets recently re-elected Prime

Minister Narendra Modi in Japan during the G20 summit, both these convergences and divergences will be on the agenda. If not handled with care, the latter could overshadow the former, with lasting consequences.

THE POSITIVE SIDE OF THE LEDGER

Over the last two years, there has been steady progress in the U.S.-India relationship. Strategically, both sides have seen the other as playing a crucial role in their Asia strategies—for the U.S., its Free and Open Indo-Pacific strategy; for India, its Act East policy. This has paved the way for deeper diplomatic, defense, and security cooperation. The two countries established a ministerial-level 2+2 defense and diplomatic dialogue last year, their highest-level institutionalized strategic dialogue. Senior bureaucrats and military officials now meet regularly, and their various security dialogues have continued to meet on issues such as defense technology, cyber security, and counterterrorism. Liaisons between the Indian navy and U.S. Naval Forces Central Command in Bahrain, and the countries' defense innovation units, are being established.

A series of agreements—negotiated for years—that would facilitate greater interoperability and technology transfer have finally been signed. The U.S. and India have operationalized the Logistics Exchange Memorandum of Agreement (LEMOA), implemented the Helicopter Operations from Ships other Than Aircraft Carriers (HOSTAC) program, and signed the Communications Compatibility and Security Agreement (COMCASA). They are also negotiating the Industrial Security Annex that will enable greater cooperation between the defense industries, and have restarted talks on the Basic Exchange and Cooperation Agreement that could pave the way for geospatial intelligence sharing.

Their diplomatic engagements also involve other countries. The two countries have upgraded their trilateral with Japan, with the three leaders meeting last fall, and restarted and continued quadrilateral consultations that also include Australia. In 2018, after a decade, they revived their air force exercise (with Japan present as an observer), and this year, they are expected to start a tri-services exercise. In addition, earlier this year, the Indian navy joined USAFRICOM's Cutlass Express exercise for the first time, and American observers (along with some from New Zealand) were included in the Australia-India naval exercise. Moreover, the American and Indian navies undertook a group sail with Japan and the Philippines in the South China Sea recently.

Defense trade has been another plus-point. India has started receiving Apache and Chinook helicopters (both of which beat out Russian offerings), and deploying American equipment like P-8is and C-130s to extend its reach in the Indian Ocean region. The U.S. granting India Strategic Trade Authorization Tier 1 status could further facilitate the export of advanced technology. Washington has reportedly approved the sale of armed drones and multi-role helicopters, and the two countries are also in talks for further deals.

Beyond defense and security cooperation, Washington has proved to be helpful to New Delhi in two crises—during the recent India-Pakistan tension following the February 14 terrorist attack in Kashmir, and, in a quieter way, during the Sino-Indian stand-off at the Bhutan-China-India tri-junction in 2017. In the recent flare-up, it backed India's position, not just rhetorically, but at the United Nations Security Council. It helped draft and push through a statement condemning Pakistan-based terror group Jaish-e-Mohammed and get its leader Masood Azhar designated as a terrorist (a long-standing effort that was being blocked by China). It also took the lead at the Financial Action Task Force to grey-list Pakistan for its lack of action against terror financing. Along with Paris, Washington is now almost playing the role Moscow used to for India in these kinds of forums.

Even U.S.-India economic ties, where strains are pronounced, have deepened over the last few years. In terms of trade in goods, over 2018-19, the U.S. once again become India's largest trading partner (if one includes services, it has held that rank for a while). Not only has U.S.-India trade grown, but, unlike with many other countries, the American trade deficit with India has decreased (from $27 billion in 2017 to $21 billion in 2018). Both American foreign direct investment into India and Indian foreign investment into the U.S. have increased. India is now also importing U.S. oil and gas (and has also benefited from the downward pressure on energy prices that American production has engendered over the last few years). The number of Indian students in the U.S. has increased, and so has two-way tourist flow.

THE NEGATIVE SIDE OF THE LEDGER

However, even as the relationship has progressed steadily on many fronts, a number of problems have arisen. Some stem not from bilateral issues, but from U.S. policies targeting other countries. Indian interests have been adversely affected by the American withdrawal from the Paris climate change agreement, aluminum and steel tariffs, and the change in the U.S. approach in Afghanistan that has led to talks with Taliban (which India remains highly skeptical, if not concerned about). Add to that list Washington's sanctions on oil imports from Iran and Venezuela, both of which have been major Indian suppliers.

Then there's the Countering America's Adversaries Through Sanctions Act (CAATSA) passed by Congress in 2017, which was intended to target Iran and Russia. India's decision to purchase five Russian S-400 long-range surface-to-air missile systems, however, means that it could potentially be the target of sanctions. American officials have also expressed serious concern that the S-400 purchase could limit future interoperability with the Indian military, as well as high-technology cooperation and defense sales.

Legislators have granted the president authority to waive the sanctions, but American officials have made clear that such a waiver is not a given and, among other things, requires India to show it is decreasing its dependence on Russia. And Washington is chagrined that, even beyond the S-400 deal, over the last year,

India has signed additional deals with Moscow for leasing a nuclear submarine, a manufacturing facility for Kalashnikov rifles, and the production or purchase of frigates. These four deals, worth over $12 billion (with additional deals being contemplated), would count as "significant transactions" under CAATSA. They also put in perspective the oft-touted statistic that the U.S. and India have signed defense deals worth $16 billion since 2008. And they have come even as Moscow has deepened relations with Beijing, broadened them with Islamabad, and taken a neutral stance during the India-Pakistan crisis (even offering to mediate between the two countries).

The major bilateral sore spot is on the economic side, where friction over trade, investment, and immigration concerns has only increased. To pre-existing American concerns about market access and price controls on medical devices, the Trump administration has added concerns about India's e-commerce regulations and data localization plans. The Indian government, in turn, has concerns about potential changes to U.S. immigration policies. Recently, the Trump administration ended India's trade benefits under the Generalized System of Preferences, which affects about $5.5 billion of Indian exports. And the Modi government imposed retaliatory tariffs that it had announced last year, but suspended until this past week. Bigger shocks could be coming if the U.S. did indeed launch a broad-spectrum investigation into India's trade and investment practices, as is reportedly being considered (or at least floated as a negotiating tactic).

These trade frictions are of particular concern. For one, it is an issue President Trump cares about deeply, and the grounds on which he measures relationships—far more than what any country does or does not do on the defense and security front. Second, he has shown that he is willing to link national security and trade commitments even with allies—this is a far cry from the last two administrations, which prioritized long-term strategic ties over short-term economic frictions. Third, the basket of issues on which there are differences has expanded. Fourth, given that these economic difficulties involve and affect key domestic priorities and constituencies for both governments, concessions are not easy for either side to make. And finally, both sides seem to believe they are speaking from positions of strength and might feel they do not need to make concessions—Modi after receiving an even stronger electoral mandate, and Trump after garnering concessions from countries like Canada and Mexico.

Add to this another potential issue coming down the pike: the security of India's future telecommunications system. And then there's the possibility of a U.S.-Iran escalation, which could throw a spanner in the works. It would not just complicate India's relations with both countries (not to mention Israel, Saudi Arabia, and the United Arab Emirates), but also be seen as seriously disruptive to Indian interests in the Middle East, which houses millions of Indians and is a key source of the oil and natural gas India consumes. Any escalation would also hinder India's attempt to establish a (non-Pakistan) transit corridor through Iran to Afghanistan. Moreover, it would (once again) distract the U.S. from focusing on Asia, where Delhi sees more converging interests with Washington.

DIVERGENCES VS. CONVERGENCES

This series of differences—coming as they do together—threatens to overshadow the very real progress in U.S.-India relations in the first couple of years of the Trump administration. They have already reinforced traditional concerns that the two countries have about each other. In the U.S., in some quarters, this includes asking whether the relationship with India is worth it; in India, whether the U.S. is reliable.

Advocates of the relationship and of the Free and Open Indo-Pacific concept should not be sanguine that structural and strategic factors—particularly convergence resulting from concern about a rising China's behavior—will naturally keep the divergences from dominating over the convergences. They will have to work hard to ensure that they will not do so.

This will mean the two countries needing to get off their respective high horses and show a willingness to make concessions, find compromises, and strike deals across sectors.

Highly unhelpful, if not, counterproductive is the fact that both sides have forgotten a lesson learned over the last decade and a half—that differences between the two countries are better managed or resolved if they are sorted out behind closed doors. Washington has been particularly guilty of forgetting this over the last few months. Publicly demanding that countries make a certain choice makes it harder for them to make it. In India's case this means that even though the U.S. has now reportedly offered India options if it doesn't go through with the S-400 acquisition, the way this has played out publicly makes it harder for Delhi to walk away from this deal, as it has done with others.

The public statements on S-400 or leaks from sources threatening retaliatory caps on H1-B visas (which is a congressional prerogative) reinforce the image that many still hold in India of an America that makes demands of India in terms of policies or purchases, constrains its choices, and does not take its interests into account. It strengthens the hands—and arguments—of those in the establishment who remain skeptical, if not suspicious, of an Indian partnership with the U.S. This sentiment is not just prevalent on India's left, as a recent speech by the head of the Rashtriya Swayamsevak Sangh made clear. Finally, public pressure muddies independent cost-benefit debates that Indians should be having about the S-400 or telecom policy that have now been framed as making a choice between the U.S. and Russia or the U.S. and China.

India, for its part, cannot complain about American transactionalism, even as Delhi makes plenty of asks too. Moreover, it needs to acknowledge that agreements like LEMOA are not India doing the U.S. a favor—they are in Indian interests, helping it enhance military capability and reach. And, particularly given the slowdown in economic growth, Delhi needs to ask itself whether its current approach to trade and foreign investment is the right one, or whether it can do more to benefit from global engagement (as it has done in the past), and particularly the U.S.-China trade war.

Indian observers need to resist framing everything as a choice imposed by the U.S.

Meanwhile, Indian observers need to resist framing everything as a choice imposed by the U.S. Furthermore, critics cannot first complain about the U.S. not offering India high-end defense equipment and then, when it does offer equipment (often on the Indian government's request), complain the U.S. is demanding that India buy it. This line has become so engrained that critics dismiss or ignore India's *own* concerns about Russian defense companies or Chinese telecommunications companies. They allege, instead, that the U.S. is forcing a choice to benefit its companies, sometimes forgetting that, in many cases, it is European and not American companies that offer the alternatives.

Overall, if the strategic relationship—and the U.S. and India's Asia strategies—is to endure, the two countries will have to remember that the relationship has been strategically and economically mutually beneficial. They will have to step back from the brinkmanship visible in recent weeks. To some extent, both sides are perhaps behaving this way because there's a sense that convergence on China—and mutual need for the other in their respective balancing strategies—will make the other side blink.

But history tells us that is not a given. In the years after the 1962 war, there was a similar shared American and Indian view of a China challenge. But their cooperation to tackle that challenge first slowed and then stalled because of American asks (India-Pakistan talks, limiting defense deals with the Soviet Union, economic reform), and India's inability to deliver on its economic potential. What that led to is limited U.S.-India relations, greater space for China, and increased India dependence—and then overdependence—on the Soviet Union. We should not assume that a similar scenario is impossible today.

AMERICAN PIVOT TO INDIA: THE FUTURE OF INDIA-US RELATIONS

India is an emerging power and going to be a key player in the geopolitical matrix of Asia and the Pacific. It is the second largest country in terms of population and sixth largest in GDP. India also has a huge fertile territory. Since the post-World War II ear, India-US relations have been determined by the dynamics of the Cold War. Geopolitical considerations, not mutual relations - determined American policy towards India in the hot and tumultuous days of the Cold War. There was an invisible curtain between the two nations due to India's non-aligned position during the Cold War. The future of India-US relations will not resemble the past.

After the independence from the British Crown, Jawaharlal Nehru, the first prime minister of India visited the United States in October 1949. It was the beginning of a new era in India-US relations. President Eisenhower was the first serving President to visit India. Washington supported New Delhi in 1962 China-India war. America even provided military hardware to India during the war. However, relations were not always that smooth afterwards. Historically, we have witnessed ups and downs in Indo-US bilateral relations. The United States' support of Indian position in the Kargil War in 1999 was the first gesture of its policy reorientation in recent history. Relations between the two countries got renewed momentum during the presidency of George W. Bush. India–United States Civil Nuclear Agreement and Logistics Exchange Memorandum of Agreement have taken their relations to a new height. Treaties, agreements and mutual interests will guide the future of India-US relations. Washington considers New Delhi as a strategic partner. Joint military exercise, technology transfer and defense cooperation point towards a convergence in their mutual interests. India and the United States has a shared vision regarding the geostrategic architecture of the Asia-Pacific. They also share common values and principles as both of them are democracies. Trade and commerce are growing steadily every year. Today, they enjoy nearly 115 billion dollars of two-way trade. India is one of the major destinations for the United States' foreign direct investment.

The rise of China and its rapid military modernization has caused apprehension and discomfort in Washington and New Delhi. China's assertive behavior in the South China Sea has amply demonstrated its regional and global ambitions. America has committed its naval and military resources and political capital to counter the influence of China. The United States' rebalancing or pivot to Asia is explicitly designed to box in the influence and power of Beijing within the confines of East Asia. Washington alone cannot implement the policy of rebalancing. It needs key states from Asia-Pacific region to form a balancing coalition against the dragon. India, Japan, Australia, South Korea, Vietnam and the Philippines are the most suitable candidates for this job. However, India and Japan are anchor states in the United States' policy of New Containment or Containment Version 2.0.

The United States' government has published the National Security Strategy paper (NSS) on 18th December 2017. It has identified China and Russia as possible threats to American global interests. According to the National Security Strategy paper, "China and Russia challenge American power, influence, and interests, attempting to erode American security and prosperity." The NSS has also stated, "China and Russia are developing advanced weapons and capabilities that could threaten our critical infrastructure and our command and control architecture." The Trump administration sees especially China as a strategic rival because it can compete with the United States in multiple domains, namely military, politics, technology and economics. Notably, the paper has used the term Indo-Pacific instead of Asia-Pacific. It has also placed particular importance on the Indo-Pacific region to indicate India. Page 68 of the document mentioned, "We welcome India's emergence as a leading global power and stronger strategic and defence partner. We will seek to increase quadrilateral cooperation with Japan, Australia, and India." Now, it appears to many scholars that India is too important a player in the Asia-pacific region. So, the statement "American pivot to India" is not an exaggeration. The future of India-US relations is on an upward trajectory.

Current geopolitical dynamics or structure of the international system is encouraging both Washington and New Delhi to coordinate their actions. India is very concerned about the intentions and capabilities of the Peoples' Republic of China. Beijing's aggressive behavior and refusal to accept the verdict of international tribunal regarding the South China Sea have fuelled further geostrategic competition and rivalry in the region. The recent Doklam standoff has sown the seeds of distrust in the heart of India.

China has nearly four times the GDP of India. Beijing has shown marked improvement in designing and producing major military weapons where India is still facing enormous challenges. The communist country has emerged as a fourth largest exporter in the global arms trade, in contrast, India is the number one importer of military hardware. All these developments have pushed India into the arms of the United States. Only America can reliably help it recovering its weakness. The groundwork for the future of India-US relations has already been done. The coming days will attach flesh to the skeleton of their present relations.

America and India will get even closer in the coming days. Distribution of power in the international system, shifts in the geopolitical settings and rise and fall of great powers determine the status of major power relations. A tectonic shift in the fabric of geopolitical landscapes makes a previous friend a foe and an enemy a friend. Einstein's law of relativity is also applicable to the domain of international relations to some extent. Friendship and enmity are relative, not absolute and they also revolve around a strong gravitational force called the balance of power. America and India are on the same page in the geostrategic space-time continuum.

US-INDIA RELATIONS AT THE CROSSROADS

U.S. Secretary of State Mike Pompeo is scheduled to visit New Delhi this week to prepare the ground for a meeting between Prime Minister Narendra Modi and President Donald Trump on the sidelines of the G-20 meeting on June 29 in Osaka. S. Jaishankar, India's new foreign minister, must convince Pompeo that the unnecessarily hard-line trade policies of the Trump administration will only cloud the geopolitical promise of a closer strategic alignment between India and the United States.

It is time to redefine the parameters of Indo-American ties. Pompeo needs to be told unambiguously that if trade tensions are allowed to persist, the very foundation of Indo-U.S. strategic partnership will be called into question. It is not in Washington's interests for trade frictions to powerfully drive India's domestic political debates in policymaking toward the United States.

Modi has begun his second term as prime minister at a moment when the Trump administration's unilateralist impulses are uncontrollable. As Trump's campaign for the U.S. presidential election next year is likely to be more muscular and nationalistic than Modi's campaign this year, India's relationship with the United States is at a crossroads. Despite plenty of positive momentum, many sticky issues threaten future progress in Indo-U.S. relations.

On the positive side, ties between India and the United States have seen considerable improvement in the last two decades with a convergence of views on many issues. Successive presidents from Bill Clinton through Donald Trump have ensured that the project of deepening ties between the India and the U.S. remains on track. Immediately after assuming the presidency, Trump began to woo Modi, who lost no time in carving out a personal relationship with him. The Trump administration made India eligible for defense-related technologies under a "strategic trade authorization," going a step further than the Obama administration, which had designated India as a "major defense partner."

The term "Indo-Pacific region" has now replaced the term "Asia-Pacific region" in the American diplomatic lexicon. The Trump administration has consistently described India as one of its major allies in the Indo-Pacific region; it renamed the former U.S. Pacific Command as Indo-Pacific Command, emphasizing the strategic linkage between the Indian and Pacific Oceans. There is greater clarity now that the arc of authoritarian resilience threatening both India and the U.S. is no longer localized to the Asian landmass but can potentially stretch from the Pacific Ocean to the Indian Ocean. The democratic voices in territories falling between these vast oceans are calling for the creation of new security architecture premised on international law.

There has been a growing realization in Washington that closer ties with India can help the United States become stronger once again in Asia, where China has begun to flex its military muscles. On the other hand, India feels constrained in its options due to China's growing global footprints. As New Delhi is trying hard to make its presence felt at the international level with enhanced engagements, China's reluctance to acknowledge India's global rise is having a negative impact on India's engagement in its immediate neighborhood. India seeks to ameliorate many of its strategic challenges by deepening ties with the United States.

Modi's previous tenure witnessed a series of defense-related agreements that would enable the two countries' militaries to work closer together. Continuing the momentum, the Modi government would like the U.S. to help India add more teeth to its military capabilities. This is particularly important for India to become a net provider of security in the Indo-Pacific region.

The Basic Exchange and Cooperation Agreement (BESA), the last of the three "foundational agreements," is likely to be signed soon. The Logistics Exchange Memorandum of Agreement (LEMOA), which allows the Indian and American forces to use each other's facilities, was signed in 2016. The Communications Compatibility and Security Agreement (COMCASA), which allows the United States to transfer communication equipment to India for the secure transmission of data and real-time information, was signed during the inaugural "two-plus-two" talks in 2018.

American concerns about Chinese President Xi Jinping's most ambitious geopolitical project, the Belt and Road initiative (BRI), have found echoes in New Delhi, which views the initiative as undermining India's security interests. India and the U.S. seem determined to counter China's maritime expansion, which is seen as a threat to their trade routes in the Indian and Pacific Oceans. Beijing is increasingly using the carrot and stick policy for increasing its geopolitical influence in countries in South Asia and the Indian Ocean region.

It is expected that at the end of this year India and the United States will conduct a new bilateral triservices exercise, which was announced at two-plus-two dialogue. Last month, two Indian naval ships - INS *Kolkata* and INS *Shakti* - participated in a joint naval exercise with the United States, the Philippines, and Japan. This significant naval event has been viewed as India offering support to the Philippines in its claims over disputed parts of South China Sea.

The Quadrilateral grouping, uniting India, the U.S., Australia, and Japan, has been revived with meetings being held at regular intervals. The Trump administration has been more vocal than previous administrations when it comes to U.S. support for New Delhi's fight against terrorism. The listing of Jaish-e-Mohammed leader Masood Azhar as an international terrorist by the UN is an example of uncritical American support to India. The Trump administration has also thrown its weight behind the International Monetary Fund (IMF) to reinforce the Financial Action Task Force (FATF) demands on Pakistan. Recently, the White House has made it clear to Islamabad that the onus for regional peace is on Pakistan, which should take irreversible steps to shut down terrorist groups. In other words, American views on Pakistan seem a lot closer to India's thinking, and this is an achievement.

Therefore Modi finds it far easier to deepen ties with the United States as support for closer ties with America has grown among India's strategic elite. He has been remarkably successful in projecting a strong image of India, putting New Delhi in a leading position to play a larger role on the international stage. Following his tremendous electoral victory, Modi will find more maneuvering space to resist Chinese assertiveness while deepening ties with Washington. But it does not mean that the relationship is free of frictions, as rhetorical ambition and practical constraint are two different things. Despite an unmistakably positive turn in Indo-U.S. relations, Modi will find that the United States is mounting pressure on India on multiple flanks.

India cannot ensure its global rise without a stable global economic order, but Trump's America is challenging the basic foundations of economic globalization. The U.S.-China trade and technology conflict is rising, with huge consequences for a global economy already under stress from several directions. Washington seems to relish bullying traditional American allies, as has become a norm in its foreign policy conduct during the last few years.

The Trump administration's extremely thoughtless approach toward its allies by degrading the strategic value of NATO, threatening to impose tariffs on the European Union goods in connection with trade disputes, unilateral withdrawal from the Iran nuclear deal against European consensus, and raising doubts about America's commitment to Japan and South Korea are just a few visible examples of the senseless application of "America first" policy. With Washington flexing its economic muscles, India has begun to face heat.

New Delhi has been forced to stop concessional oil imports from both Iran and Venezuela, and these heavy-handed American tactics have led to sharp rise in India's oil import bill. India's energy security requires a stable Middle East and New Delhi cannot be expected to downgrade its profile in the region. But more that, the U.S. attempts to undercut India's strategic ties with Iran are going to pose serious challenges for Indian foreign policy. The common concerns of India and Iran about threat of jihadist terrorism emanating from Pakistani territory make Iran an important geopolitical partner of India. India's attempts to reach Central Asia are also likely to suffer if New Delhi's ties with Tehran show downward trend. So far, the United States has exempted the Iranian port of Chabahar - which lets India bypass Pakistan to create a transportation corridor to Afghanistan - from punitive sanctions, but many in India remain deeply suspicious of America's future intentions. If Chabahar port stops receiving preferential treatment, it would be a classic case of short-term American unilateralism trumping long-term strategic thinking.

The United States has also been critical of India's bid to purchase the Russian made S-400 air defense system. Washington argues that if India buys the S-400, it will violate the Countering America's Adversaries Through Sanctions Act (CAATSA); America's ties with Turkey are also under strain as the latter is planning to buy the same S-400 system. Former US Defense Secretary James Mattis was the biggest advocate for a presidential waiver for India, but his absence from the Trump administration has made the threat of CAATSA sanctions a real possibility. The biggest challenge New Delhi faces is that if it defies American diktat, there would be economic sanctions as well as restrictions on high-tech defense cooperation with Washington. But if India cancels the S-400 deal, its traditional ties with Russia are bound to suffer.

Trade ties are also a source of tensions. India has been a huge beneficiary of the Generalized System of Preferences (GSP) program, but the Trump administration is moving ahead to end it. The GSP is a preferential trade program that gives developing countries like India easier access to the American market by reducing duties on their exports. Meeting many American trade demands on medical devices is not possible without having a deleterious impact. Washington also wants India to relax e-commerce rules. Many rounds of talks on a comprehensive trade package have failed to yield any breakthrough.

So far, the strength of Indo-U.S. strategic relationship has allowed overall ties to endure the jolts on the commercial side. But

America's provocative and unilateral actions in the economic sphere will only exacerbate the Modi government's challenges in balancing India's multifaceted relationships with Iran and Russia. If the thinking in Washington is that these actions would force India to become more closely aligned with American position, then it is an essentially faulty way to breathe a fresh life into the Pax Americana. Every time Trump takes a strictly transactional approach to India, bilateral ties will come under strain, and the differences between Washington and New Delhi will then appear too large and the need for a common approach too weak. It therefore needs no further elaboration that the role of Iran and Russia in the Indo-U.S. bilateral dynamics needs to be addressed urgently.

Perhaps most importantly, the real danger is that if the Trump administration does not soften its quarrelsome trade attitude toward India, it may end up projecting an image of America as unreliable and insensitive. Hyper-nationalism and a combative approach has fundamentally defined the motivational structure of Modi's foreign policy. Therefore America's narrowly-conceived actions may revive the dormant tendency in India's diplomatic establishment for the vigorous pursuit of "strategic autonomy."

If a more coherent response to the BRI in the form of multiple infrastructure initiatives is to emerge in near future, the United States cannot continue to behave like an arrogant, nonchalant, and unilateral actor. It is tempting to suggest that the U.S. should offer incentives and rewards to India rather than continue to make demands, if it is really serious about reversing China's economic and strategic onslaught.

The Indo-U.S. ties have gathered momentum fuelled by strategic realities and political convergence. Strategic dialogues and military exercises between the two have become more sophisticated and elaborate. Therefore, leaders on both sides need to chart out a pragmatic vision of what is achievable over the next half decade, with concrete steps along the way. The interlocutors of the Modi government must convincingly argue before Pompeo that a long-term American commitment to India in the Indo-Pacific region is the only way to operationalize the vast potential in Indo-U.S. strategic relationship into concrete policy outcomes while preparing India as a credible counterweight to the Chinese power in Asia.

GEOPOLITICAL BLUNDER OR PRO-AMERICAN PIVOT?

The globally renowned Japanese financial newspaper Nikkei published a thought-provoking analysis on India's refusal to join RCEP earlier this week. "India makes historic blunder in abandoning RCEP trade deal", written by James Crabtree, an associate professor in practice at the Lee Kuan Yew School of Public Policy at the National University of Singapore and author of "The Billionaire Raj", made the case that the country surrendered its regional influence in ASEAN to China by capitulating to intense public opposition against the deal which he says wouldn't have made much of a difference anyhow had it entered into practice since "it is shallow in its ambition, acting mostly to tidy up existing bilateral agreements." In his opinion, "Modi's decision makes China the overwhelmingly dominant voice in a new deal" and "sends alarming signals about India's commitment to both trade and domestic economic reform more broadly." All of this is true, but it misses the point that this probably wasn't a mistake at all, but a preplanned move to justify the country's ongoing pro-American pivot.

Debunking The Economic "Balancing" Narrative

The argument can be made that it would have "been better" from an American perspective for India to "balance" China within the bloc, during which time it could seek to expand its influence in ASEAN together with Japan through their joint "Asia-Africa Growth Corridor" (AAGC) in order to provide a credible alternative to Beijing's Belt & Road Initiative (BRI). That viewpoint, however "theoretically sound" it may be, fails to take into account the reality that neither India, Japan, nor their combined economic potentials are capable of competing with China, and that the ASEAN states' decision to go ahead with RCEP without India's participation as a so-called "counterbalance" proves that they're keenly aware of this and would rather "bandwagon" with China than "balance" against it. The very fact that anyone would seriously consider India at this point in time as being capable of "competing" with China in the economic sense speaks to the effectiveness of New Delhi's Bollywood-like infowar narrative that the still-developing South Asian state is supposedly already a "global power".

It's not, nor will it ever be anytime in the coming future except in some long-term scenarios because its socio-economic and political foundations at home are much too weak for it to project any meaningful influence outside of its immediate neighborhood in South Asia, though that nevertheless doesn't mean that it lacks latent potential and could eventually fulfill this role with time and massive external support. Prime Minister Modi himself is obviously very well aware that his country is "all bark and no bite" in this respect, as well as its so-called "success story" being mostly an illusion that's conveniently decontextualized and then overamplified upon narrative manipulation by wishful thinking stakeholders within his homeland and beyond who have a geopolitical interest in propagating it abroad so as to portray India as the "predestined counterbalance" to China. This isn't just done for reasons of so-called "prestige" or simply to "bluff" the People's Republic (which never fell for it in the first place), but to encourage more foreign direct investment from the West.

The Pro-American Pivot In Practice

India's decision makers have decided to stake their country's future on a military-strategic alliance with the US that they hope will eventually reap economic dividends for them if they can convince America that they're the perfect re-offshoring destination for the Western companies that leave China as a result of the so-called "trade war". The two sides have already signed military logistics and communications agreements over the past few years, and the US has suddenly emerged as India's third-largest defense partner in the span of only a decade, so it's clear that each country's military, intelligence, and diplomatic bureaucracies ("deep states") are already working very closely together with the unstated intent of "containing" China through the Pentagon's "Indo-Pacific" strategy. India's (declining) military partnership with Russia is mostly the result of the historic inertia of their ties and is nowadays relied upon as a convenient excuse to deflect any criticism that it's actually pivoting towards the US by claiming that it's still practicing the policy of what it unconvincingly calls "multi-alignment".

As part of this ongoing pivot, India knows that it needs to eventually transform its nascent military-strategic ties with the US into lasting economic ones, but it'll be unable to retain America as its new top trading partner without entering into a free trade agreement with it, though that would have been practically impossible in the current context had it gone ahead signing one with China instead. The domestic opposition to RCEP is real, but it was indirectly stoked by the same pro-government oligarchs (especially from Gujurat, Haryana, and Rajasthan) that stand to lose the most from the emergence of China as a credible competitor in what has hitherto been a largely protectionist domestic marketplace that's kept their spheres of economic interest safe from foreign rivals. Prime Minister Modi depends on these groups for support and can't risk their ire, especially not after they proved just how capable they are of mobilizing intense opposition against RCEP in recent weeks, so any speculative doubts in his mind about the wisdom of rejecting this deal were surely dispelled.

Westward, Ho!

It's therefore not a coincidence that his government's Commerce and Industry Minister Piyush Goyal declared just a day after India rejected RCEP that "At present, India is exploring trade agreements with the USA and the European Union, where

Indian industry and services will be competitive and benefit from access to large developed markets", which was the dog whistle needed for Indian media such as the The Times Of India to editorially describe this as a "strategic shift". Some casual observers might be surprised by this since they were probably under the mistaken impression that the two sides were engaged in a fledgling "trade war", though like the author noted back in June, "Delhi And Washington Are Just Trying To Get A Better Trade Deal" from one another through their hardball tactics against the other, all of which are aimed at improving their negotiating positions and extracting concessions from their counterpart. India may have tried to play those developments off as an "emerging rift" with the US over the past few months with the hope of extracting concessions from China and thus signing RCEP instead of an eventual free trade agreement with the US, but that's no longer the case now that New Delhi has officially shown that it's openly returning to Washington's economic embrace, with Indian media even reporting that Goyal will travel there next week to continue trade negotiations.

India is much more confident talking about its desire to reach a free trade deal with the US after blaming China for its failure to sign RCEP by claiming that the terms of the agreement wouldn't have been beneficial for the average Indian. The innuendo is that China was trying to "take advantage" of India through economic means but the country's "wise leader" saw through this "scam" and saved his country from certain doom. That's of course not what really happened, but it's the impression that was made upon average Indians. The narrative groundwork has now been set for taking the developing Sino-Indo split even further by adding an economic dimension to India's military-strategic alliance with the US, though India will still have to carry out domestic economic reforms prior to the signing of any forthcoming free trade agreement just like it would have had to eventually do with RCEP, but the pro-government oligarchs are unlikely to rally the masses to resist them as long as their core interests remain protected. The genie is out of the bottle, however, and it can't be guaranteed that there won't be just as loud of an outcry against a deal with the US like there was against the one with RCEP.

Concluding Thoughts

Far from being the "blunder" that it's being portrayed as, India's refusal to join RCEP was most likely the next phase of its preplanned pro-American pivot, which was proven in hindsight by its Commerce and Industry Minister immediately talking about his country's interest in reaching a free trade deal with the US right after. It was unrealistic to ever expect India to "balance" China in RCEP, so its decision not to join actually didn't change much other than making it increasingly obvious how much economic influence the People's Republic wields in Southeast Asia nowadays, but the geopolitical implications of this move were to widen the Sino-Indo split and create the "justification" for "balancing" Beijing with Washington after the weaponized infowar narrative was implied that New Delhi's neighbor was trying to "take advantage" of it through the deal. The military-strategic basis of the Indo-American alliance will therefore likely grow to include an economic dimension with time, and while the terms of any forthcoming free trade agreement with it might even be comparatively worse than the ones that RCEP proposed, they'll likely protect the interests of the pro-government oligarchy and thus ensure the establishment's support for this "strategic shift".

INDIA AND GREAT POWER POLITICS IN THE INDO-PACIFIC

As China managed to convince the ASEAN this week to move forward with the Regional Comprehensive Economic Partnership (RCEP), great power politics was clearly the elephant in the room at the summit in Bangkok, Thailand. The US-China contestation was out in the open once again at the annual East Asia Summit (EAS) and ASEAN was forced to respond to it in a manner where it has to balance the contending claims of two major powers.

The Trump administration has overturned decades of political consensus in Washington about integrating China in the global order. It is now openly confronting China at multiple levels. Most significant of the problems is in trade where the tariff war between the two most powerful economic powers has escalated. China's economy has been hurt and its growth rate has fallen. Despite a trade pact between China and the US on the horizon, the two powers are trying to shape regional geopolitics in the Indo-Pacific to their own ends.

Yet where China managed to present itself as a positive actor trying to shape regional economic future via RCEP, questions abound about America's commitment to the region and if ASEAN at all figures in Trump administration's strategic priorities. This was most visibly manifest in Washington's decision to downgrade its presence at the EAS to the lowest level since the Obama administration joined it in 2011. While US President Donald Trump managed to attend in 2017, he sent Vice President Mike Pence last year, and followed it up by sending the lowest-ranking delegation to the EAS, led by White House national security adviser Robert O'Brien.

This was seen as a snub by most ASEAN member states who reciprocated by downgrading their level of representation at the US-ASEAN Summit. While the leaders of Thailand, Vietnam, and Laos attended the summit, other seven member states sent their foreign ministers. The ASEAN states got Trump's invitation for a special summit in early 2020 in the US which would provide 'an excellent opportunity' for leaders to 'broaden and deepen our cooperation on matters of great importance'. It remains to be seen if Washington follows this up and if the summit that it has proposed delivers some concrete results.

Whatever be the case there, it is clear that Southeast Asia is preparing for a different regional order when the US centrality to the region would be not that significant. This despite the fact that the US State Department suggesting that 'President Donald J Trump has made US engagement in the Indo-Pacific region a top priority of his administration.' The region's concerns have been growing since Trump's decision to withdraw from Trans-Pacific Partnership and Trump's stress on 'America First' policy at a time when China has been all out in wooing the region, emerging as ASEAN's largest-trading partner for the last decade with bilateral trade reaching $580 billion and mutual investment more than $200 billion.

Strategically, China is now facing a stronger pushback in the wider Indo-Pacific where regional powers are arranging themselves in new coalitions to challenge China's aggressive projection of its power. Like-minded countries see a need for a new security architecture in the region which can manage China's rise. While a formal system will take time to emerge, informal coalitions are now growing in numbers and issue-based coalitions are the norm. With the credibility of the US declining, regional states are now willing to shoulder greater burden themselves.

It is against this backdrop that India-ASEAN strategic co-operation assumes greater significance. While India's decision not to join RCEP will lead to many questioning India's Indo-Pacific vision, structural changes shaping the region are having a significant impact on the way regional actors are re-evaluating their external outreach. This will continue to underscore India's regional relevance.

India has welcomed the ASEAN's outlook on the Indo-Pacific as it sees 'important elements of convergence' with its own approach towards the region. India has been categorical that it is 'for something' in the Indo-Pacific and 'not against somebody', seeking to carefully calibrate its relations with the US and China in this geopolitically critical region. As External Affairs Minister S Jaishankar suggested "[and] that something is peace, security, stability, prosperity and rules".

With the ASEAN finally coming to terms with its own role in the Indo-Pacific, the ball is now in the court of other regional stakeholders to work with the regional grouping to shape a balance of power in the region which favours inclusivity, stability and economic prosperity.

India needs to do a more convincing job as a beneficial strategic partner of the ASEAN by boosting its domestic economic reforms agenda, enhancing connectivity within the region, and increasing its presence in regional institutions. The ASEAN nations too should be clearer and more specific in their expectations from New Delhi and nudge India for a deeper, more broad-based engagement. Despite the RCEP setback, there is much at stake for both sides.

INDIA-US TIES IN A TRUMP PRESIDENCY

On 9 November, Prime Minister Narendra Modi spoke with US president-elect Donald Trump to congratulate him on his victory. In no previous change of administration—either in the US or in India—did India rise to the next-day call list. For that matter, in no previous US election did a major party candidate release a campaign ad in Hindi. Or attend a Bollywood-and-anti-terrorism-themed jubilee in Edison, New Jersey.

The Trump administration thus heads into office positively disposed towards India, and will likely continue to pursue stronger ties with the world's largest democracy, in keeping with a general bipartisan consensus on India. But Trump has signalled throughout his campaign that he will focus on "America First". The direction the US takes will affect US-India ties as a result. India will likely benefit from impending geopolitical shifts, but will likely find itself at odds with a balance-sheet approach to trade and economic policies.

From the George W. Bush administration forward, the US has actively supported India's rise towards great power status and a larger role in the world. While it remains unclear how actively a Trump administration would champion a permanent seat for India in the UN security council—in fact, he has said little about his approach to the UN—it seems clear that in their approach to global security concerns, Trump and Modi will find commonality on the urgent threat Islamist terrorism poses.

The Trump administration will need to develop its approach to the US effort in Afghanistan—its longest war, where the Islamic

State has now spread. Based on his promise to crush the IS and to calibrate a limited but strong role for the US military abroad, we can anticipate a more counter-terrorism focused approach to Afghanistan than a larger, full-scope governance and democratization assistance effort.

This has direct implications for Pakistan, provider of safe havens for the Afghan Taliban and other terrorist groups like the Haqqani network, and groups focused on India. The Obama administration and the US Congress have grown weary of Pakistan's insufficient actions to counter terrorist groups, and we are likely to see a Trump administration flatly tell Pakistan that the American well of patience has run dry. New Delhi will find this firmer approach helpful.

The US and India have dramatically strengthened defence ties over the past decade, and naval cooperation in particular has leaped ahead. Trump has promised to renew and expand the US navy just at the time India is expanding its navy to ensure its role as the pre-eminent Indian Ocean power. Look for this aspect of India-US ties to develop further.

Trump will enter office with a fully de-hyphenated view of India and Pakistan. He has spoken about India as a land of economic opportunity, has pursued property developments in India, and admiringly cited India's high economic growth rate during the third presidential debate. He has spoken of Pakistan as the most dangerous country in the world, and said that only India can "check" Pakistan.

He is suspicious of the net benefits the US derives from traditional alliances in Europe and Asia, believing that US allies do not carry their own weight in American security cooperation. A US foreign policy approach that places less emphasis on traditional alliance relationships, becoming more focused on ties premised on reciprocity, could open more mental space for India (on the other hand, the pursuit of measurable reciprocity could result in low marks for New Delhi). Trump is suspicious of China, particularly its mercantilist interests and island-building in the

South China Sea. India has an opportunity by contrast. And Trump's notable admiration for Vladimir Putin points to a less-adversarial approach to Russia, which may eliminate an occasional source of stress for India.

Trump's campaign contained a seven-point agenda on trade. He has spoken frequently of the damage trade agreements have done to the American economy, and promised to bring jobs back. He has called for immigration reform to limit and better control who crosses into the US. He has said he would end the H-1B high-skilled worker visa programme—a programme with which India has been dissatisfied (although it is the top recipient of all US H-1B visas issued each year); New Delhi filed a trade dispute on these visas in the World Trade Organization against the US this past year. A Trump administration is likely to push back hard on the dispute and in bilateral conversations about visas.

Trump is likely to seek further economic opening on India's part, as all previous US administrations have. A Trump administration will likely continue to perceive India's patent law as insufficiently protective of innovation, so long-running differences, especially over pharmaceutical patents, will likely continue. India can breathe a sigh of relief, however, about the Trans-Pacific Partnership, which many in India saw as an "anti-India," exclusionary trade pact. Trump said he will tear it up.

Trump views climate change dimly and has spoken of cancelling the Paris agreement. He has said little about clean energy, likely not a priority. This means that one of the most successful US-India areas of partnership—clean energy research and development—has just lost its American champion.

Over the past eight years, clean energy collaboration has quietly become a singularly successful technical partnership between Washington and New Delhi, with billions of dollars mobilized with government seed funding and private sector matching funds.

Look to see this shift into low gear for Washington, even as clean energy remains a high priority for India due to its lack of domestic oil and gas resources, its tremendous energy needs, and its ample supply of sunlight.

As the Trump team begins to take shape, more clues about the next US administration's approach to India will emerge. For now, it seems clear that broad policy continuity with previous administrations will result (a rarity these days), but the Trump approach to larger geopolitical and geo-economic questions will likely pull ties between Washington and New Delhi in new directions.

STRATEGIC PARTNERSHIP WITH US UNDER DONALD TRUMP'S PRESIDENTSHIP

With Donald Trump set to take charge as the next US president, New Delhi needs to pitch for a more energetic strategic partnership with Washington. We need to especially focus on policy cooperation in the domain of power and energy. It would have very favourable implications for the global environment, and hugely boost infrastructure and investments. The capital markets have been very buoyant since his election, and surveys suggest that consumer confidence in the US is also up. The dollar has also strengthened since the November election.

Trump has confidently stated that he would double the rather lacklustre US economic growth rate. 'Make America Great Again' was his campaign slogan. It remains to be seen how he can, now in office, rise to the occasion and walk the talk.

The world's largest economy, after all, has had a weak and hesitant recovery since the global financial crisis of 2008, which was, of course, home-grown in the US. Yet, it would make eminent sense to boost fiscal policy and step up investment. Which, in turn, should boost the growth momentum there.

The figures show that net of depreciation, US public capital investment has been falling as a share of national income for years. While it was 3% in the 1960s, the figure dropped to as low as 1.3% of GDP in 2007. It rose for a few years after the financial crisis, but has fallen since, pegged at a lowly 0.4% in 2014. It should be possible for Washington to chalk out a medium-term plan to build and construct infrastructure, so as to coagulate funds on the groundand raise the growth momentum.

The US and India need to join hands and rev up thermal efficiency at power plants in both economies. Power producers in the US have indeed been able to demonstrate cutting-edge technology to quite dramatically increase productivity in conventional thermal stations. But the know-how needs to be commercialised and adapted to suit Indian conditions and resource endowments. To diffuse leading-edge technologies for power plants across India would require huge long-term resources at fine rates. For this purpose, we would need to gainfully seek multilateral funding.

Meanwhile, the policy of ultra-low interest rates in the US since the crisis seems, ironically, to have raised the value of all capital assets across the board. And the consequent power of corporates to be in a position to shift production across national boundaries — often simply to seek tax benefits — may have been one of the main reasons why Trump won more than enough electoral college votes in the so-called 'rust belt' states, although he did comprehensively lose the popular vote.

Trump unambiguously opposed such production shifting during his campaign, threatening to slap steep duties on the finished items shipped back to the US. And the threat seems to have worked, at least for now. Major automobile and white goods producers have reportedly decided to stay put in the US. The phenomenon of ultra-low interest rates raising the value of capital assets across the mature markets but especially in the US is real. It may well explain Trump's rather unexpected victory in last year's close race to the White House.

The point is that the bond market is massive and thriving in the US. The lower the rate of interest, the greater the capital value of bonds. This is because in a regime of low interest rates, the prices of bonds are high at maturity, taking into account the low (coupon) rates. But there is no reason why the rise in capital value remains confined only to bonds. It would favourably affect all capital assets and raise value, particularly in those markets where there is much recourse to arm's-length bond finance. It can raise corporate power as well.

The capital value of any asset is the (discounted) value of its future earnings. A lower rate of interest does increase the value of all capital assets. It essentially raises total wealth. The wealth appreciation can have untoward implications, like corporates seeking to move production (and attendant jobs) purely for reasons of tax arbitrage. Hence the rationale for a proactive policy such as penal duties to stem the capital flight at least temporarily, which anyway is due to distorted interest rates in the first place. It seems notable that Trump had his ear to the ground in the rust-belt states.

The US-India energy engagement needs to boost efficiency in conventional thermal stations, shore up capacity-building in the proposed International Solar Alliance here, and speedily actualise India's long proposed membership of the Nuclear Suppliers' Group (NSG).

INDIA'S FOREIGN POLICY AND FOREIGN RELATIONS

The end of Cold War political constraints and the rapid growth of India's economy has allowed New Delhi to more energetically engage global diplomacy. Expanded engagement is evident through the huge increase in the number of bilateral defence arrangements the Indian government has made in the past decade, more than tripling from 7 in 2000 to at least 26 today. During the latter half of 2010, every major world leader paid a visit to India, including those from all five permanent U.N. Security Council members. Much of the international attention on India is due to the country's vast market potential—the retail sector alone is worth an estimated $450 billion.

Some observers argue that the New Delhi government acts too timidly on the global stage, and that the country's regional and domestic difficulties continue to hinder its ability to exert influence in geopolitics. As a rising power, India has appeared unwilling to take the kinds of policy stances expected of major global players, in particular those who sit on the U.N. Security Council, as India has been in 2011. From vague positions on Middle East uprisings to the appearance of fence-sitting on issues such as U.S.-led efforts to isolate Iran and Burma, New Delhi's leaders may be finding it increasingly difficult to avoid taking on the responsibilities many in Washington and elsewhere are looking for.

One example is New Delhi's largely hands-off response to uprisings in the Arab world, with External Affairs Minister Krishna saying India would not "jump into the fray" unless invited and would maintain a "very cautious" approach to the Libyan conflict. In March 2011, India officially opposed NATO's military action in Libya and notably abstained—along with Brazil, China, Russia, and Germany—from voting on U.N. Resolution 1973, which approved of such action. More recently, Secretary of State Clinton has sought greater Indian assistance in pressuring the faltering Syrian regime. Human rights activists have joined foreign governments in prodding India to be more proactive on key foreign policy issues, even those in India's own neighborhood such as in Burma and Sri Lanka. One such observer has criticized New Delhi for issuing "bland propositions" that "can convey indifference to the plight of subjugated people." She challenges India's leaders to "stand with people or with dictators."

Many analysts view India's foreign policy establishment—its foreign service, think-tanks, public universities, and relevant media—as being too small and/or too poorly developed for India to achieve true great power status in the foreseeable future. By one substantive account, without a major modernizing and revamping of this establishment, "India's worldview will be parochial, reactive, and increasingly dominated by business rather than by strategic or political concerns." Thus, even as India's rising stature commands greater attention in many world capitals, the country's diplomatic influence remains limited—especially in comparison to that of China—and the central government continues to concentrate mainly on domestic development and poverty alleviation. Indeed, India's domestic and social indices continue to rank it as a developing country, or what one former senior Indian diplomat called a "premature power." Moreover, Indian bureaucrats' prickly and sometimes distrustful attitude toward their American counterparts survives long after the Cold War's end, and is sometimes evident in New Delhi's vehement reactions to what many Americans would consider minor and essentially meaningless slights.

TRUMP: A GEOPOLITICAL OPPORTUNITY FOR INDIA

In India, public support during the American election campaign have been overwhelmingly in favour of Democratic candidate Hillary Clinton. This also holds true for the majority of the 3.3 million Indian Americans. Altogether five Indian Americans - the highest number ever - have been elected into both houses of Parliament, all Democrats. The Indian government, and Prime Minister Narendra Modi in particular, will be pragmatic in their approach to this new situation.

The USA is India's leading foreign trade partner. Former Foreign Secretary Kanwal Sibal predicts that the current dynamic of bilateral relations will slow down in the immediate future. India will have to learn about the new personnel, who will be largely unknown. Nirupuma Rao, a former Foreign Secretary and ambassador to Washington, noted that "the American President-elect is generally not acquainted with the salient details of the India-U.S. strategic partnership."

Geopolitical implications of the Trump Presidency

Substantial geopolitical changes are expected under Donald Trump, who, in his political style and some of his opinions, is quite similar to Narendra Modi. From an Indian perspective much will depend upon his relationship with China, particularly in view of the sharpening differences between India and China.

Since Trump is against the 'US pivot to Asia', this would permit China to assert itself more in the western Pacific and allow it to expand faster into the Indian Ocean. This would be contrary to the strategic vision built with Obama for the Asia-Pacific and Indian Ocean regions, which was supposed to counter Chinese muscle-flexing. If this does happen, India must either try to influence the expected American strategy or to fill the expected vacuum. C. Raja Mohan, director at Carnegie India, has pointed out that Trump's election presents a rare opportunity for Delhi to expand its own influence and agency in the Eurasian region, rather than being the 'lynchpin' of the US pivot to Asia, and indeed become a leader in its own right.

Improved relations with Russia under Trump are seen in India as another good opportunity, in that Russia will lean less towards China and cooperate less with Pakistan, creating changes in the Middle East that could benefit India. Here a coordinated partnership between India, the EU and Britain could be envisaged.

A statement from former Ambassador Rao was telling: "Trump came across during the campaign as having a much more rational and less prejudiced approach to the situation in Syria and Russian involvement in the region, and it is hoped that his advent to office will see more collaborative, well-reasoned policy approaches and dialogue with Moscow to defeat the Islamic State instead of just pursuing the prospects of regime change in Damascus."

Others have suggested that Trump's election could have indirect implications for Pakistan, in that Trump could pull Putin away from Chinese premier Xi Jinping, and thereby ruin Pakistani ideas of a Beijing-Moscow-Islamabad axis.

Economic implications

The prospect of protectionist policies being put in place by Trump are only partly seen as directed against India. It has been noted that India is not necessarily ready for major free-trade agreements, and that the country could benefit geopolitically from the negative economic effects that American protectionism could have on China. That said, if Trump does start to fine outsourcing companies, as he has said he would, this could have a negative effect on the Indian IT industry.

According to Shyam Saran, a former Foreign Secretary and architect of the Indo-US Nuclear Deal, the strategic community in India is confident that in view of the consensus about good bilateral relations and a "strengthening of the strategic relations with India", no negative tendencies are to be expected with the new administration.

There is are similarities between the Hindu-nationalist NDA-government's economic and social policies and what can be expected from Trump. Therefore it is to be expected that in India there will be less criticism of Trump's domestic politics and a greater focus on his future foreign policy.

11

The Need for Catalysing Indo-US Trade

The Indo-Pacific Region is strategically and economically significant. It accounts for two-thirds of all global trade. These countries are seeking high-quality goods and services to sustain and develop their economies.

US companies are extremely well positioned to meet these demands, including in the important area of infrastructure. The Asian Development Bank estimates that $1.7 trillion needs to be invested in the region's infrastructure every year.

But, with its strong and growing economy, India is key to the Administration's approach to the Indo-Pacific region. Last year, India's real GDP reached an estimated 7.1 per cent growth; and is projected to increase by a very healthy 7.4 percent this year.

India's population has grown by an astonishing 341 million people over the past 20 years to 1.35 billion. Just the growth since 2000 is greater than the total population of the United States.

Combined with the 281 million people in India between the ages of 20 and 35, there are almost 600 million people either in – or soon to be entering – their primary years for consuming goods and services.

India is already the world's third largest economy, and by 2030, it will become the world's largest consumer market because of the rapid growth of the middle class.

Yet, today, India is only the US's 13th largest export market, due to overly restrictive market access barriers. Meanwhile, the US is India's largest export market, accounting for something like 20 per cent of the total.

CRAFTING NEW FRAMEWORKS FOR INDIA'S DIGITAL ECONOMY

India has charted an ambitious target to create a US$ 1-trillion digital economy by 2025. The legal and regulatory environment that the GOI establishes around data flows and digital commerce will help drive sustained innovation, investment, and job creation from the private sector. However, recent attempts to regulate the digital economy have also introduced some degree of uncertainty into the business landscape and created several challenges for multinational tech companies and startups looking to deepen investment in the Indian market.

These include:

Regulatory uncertainty: Indian ministries and regulators are attempting to keep pace with rapid technological change and disruption by quickly advancing various new regulatory measures or overhauling existing frameworks. These frameworks should be aligned with the further evolution of new technologies, the investment cycles of businesses, the ease of technology adoption by first- or secondgeneration Internet users, and the right to privacy of all Indians. While it may not be possible to strike a golden balance between these considerations in all cases, Indian policymakers must reorient their regulatory tendencies with a clearly articulated framework that represents the nation's considered, best interests.

Overlapping policy frameworks: Lack of alignment among ministries and sectoral regulators — including the Ministry of Electronics and Information Technology (MeitY), the Reserve Bank of India (RBI), the Department for Promotion of Industry and Internal Trade (DPIIT), and the Telecom Regulatory Authority of

India (TRAI) – has given rise to either disconsonant, or else overlapping e-commerce, data protection, data localisation, and content liability frameworks.

Limited stakeholder consultations: Ministries and sectoral regulators have often provided limited opportunities for stakeholder consultations, with little time, if at all, offered to stakeholders to comment on proposed rules and regulations.

Balancing privacy, innovation, and national security: Governments across the world are attempting to navigate interlocking challenges in technological innovation, data privacy, and national security. India is no exception to this trend, with lawmakers, industry, and civil society groups seeking to create new frameworks to safeguard user privacy, shape data practices of platforms and industry, and mediate lawful government access to private user data.

Protecting user privacy: A string of high-profile data breaches of multinational companies has heightened global sensitivities to create new personal data protection frame-works. Public debates around data privacy have accelerated in India over the past two years – especially after the Supreme Court enshrined privacy as a fundamental, constitutional right in August 2017; thereafter, the Srikrishna Committee submitted its recommendations on data protection. These recommendations are a useful starting point to address any trust deficiencies that may exist between global technology giants and their users in emerging markets. The bilateral relationship must nudge the US private sector to absorb the concerns of Indian users, and respond adequately with strong privacy frameworks.

Facilitating legitimate access to cross-border data

Alongside these efforts, law enforcement and national security officials have triggered a new round of debates focused on government access to user data – especially data generated by users of popular social media, encrypted messaging, and payment platforms. The delays in securing cross-border access to data –

sometimes by as much as a year in response to their requests – have prompted Indian authorities to press for swift access to user data that can aid investigations into criminal or terrorist activities. A lack of a timely response from jurisdictions that currently host and hold data has added an urgency for governments around the world, including India, to seek data localisation and message tracing.

Navigating bilateral India-US trade tensions

India's approach to data and e-commerce regulation has drawn criticism from the White House and senior members of the Trump administration. US trade officials have focused primarily on the RBI's data localisation circular, MeitY's data protection bill, and DPIIT's Press Note 2 and e-commerce policy to date, alleging that these measures are creating unfair market access barriers that harm foreign companies. India, meanwhile, has criticised the US approach to Indian requests for access to cross-border data, pointing to shortcomings in the mutual legal assistance treaty (MLAT) as an important rationale for its data localisation measures. Moreover, the US market is difficult to navigate and is often inaccessible to all but a few Indian entrepreneurs and businesses, despite the long legacy of cross-border cooperation in IT services. Indian policymakers are also keenly aware that India's transformation from a low- to a middleincome country would be affected by its ability to retain the largest share of the value that accrues from the data economy, and they believe data policies must privilege greater investments in India and Indian enterprises. While both sides initially tried to separate these challenges from broader trade discussions, the data suite of issues are likely to persist in Washington and New Delhi.

Keeping pace with international digital economy frameworks

The global cyber norms-making process has stalled, and the political stalemate at the recently concluded G20 summit at Osaka is evidence of it. Earlier this year, the United States expressed reservations against a proposal floated at the G20 meeting of finance ministers to levy a "digital tax" on large technology companies. India is one of the prime movers of this proposal, which has gained traction in the international community amid concerns in New Delhi that the explosive growth of Silicon Valley companies over the past decade has generated insufficient economic value in the local jurisdictions in which they operate. As a result, New Delhi and other emerging markets have expressed wariness over participating in multilateral conversations on digital commerce. The stalemate does little to advance diplomacy around digital issues, which India and the United States are uniquely positioned to lead.

Recommendations to unlock the India-US digital potential

India 's digital economy is likely to see continued growth as new netizens, startups, and companies deepen engagement and investments in the market. Unlocking the potential of India-US digital cooperation, however, will require policymakers and private sector leaders on both sides to navigate critical challenges and proactively seize opportunities to promote growth and development. To advance this goal, TAG and ORF outline the following ten recommendations for government, private sector, and civil society leaders:

1. Champion narratives that secure data and generate economic value for the digital economy: Most policy debates in India have focused on creating local value from data. The equitable distribution of economic advantages on account of data generation and curation is undoubtedly a matter of concern to any regulator. National policies must also enhance data's ability to "teach" and inform economic growth, understand changing consumer behaviour, pilot e-governance initiatives, and generate sustainable skills to weather the disruptions caused by 21st century technologies. To this end, US and Indian companies should collaborate to put forward practical solutions on data portability and sharing, with a view

to generate local value for the digital economy, while respecting the privacy and security of users. This effort must be driven by establishing engagement forums between security communities, civil society and enterprises in India and the United States so as to ensure that domestic players and multinationals are able to navigate the two ecosystems productively. Fintech regulations in the United States must also reflect the desire for Indian entrepreneurs to build global products, which often require the expertise and resources available in advanced economies. India needs to enter into agreements that will allow Indian products and platforms to become global in the coming decade.

2. Lead on articulating and legislating cross-border data flow regimes with key economies: Rapid growth across India's digital economy has the potential to make India the receptacle of world's data and a digital superpower in its own right. This fundamental insight should be the foundation for India's technology policy frameworks. As such, India should aim to put in place data protection legislation that promotes open and freer exchange of data across borders consistent with emerging international norms. Moreover, India should engage at the WTO, G20, and RCEP forums to lead on issues pertinent to cross-border data flows, helping craft a suitable framework that preserves open data flows as the heart of the global digital economy. Such frameworks must be based on reciprocity, equitable market access and consistency across IPR regimes.

3. Develop processes that institutionalise 'Multistakeholderism' in practice: The Government of India (GOI) and the US Government should facilitate robust and inclusive consultation processes that give all players – foreign and domestic industry, as well as civil society groups, big and small – adequate time and opportunity to carefully consider draft measures and to submit inputs prior to promulgation of a final law or order. Creating standard processes and timelines for stakeholder comments is important to exchange ideas and interests, and align future proposals on regulating the digital economy. As the two largest digital democracies, it is

incumbent upon both countries to make each of their policymaking processes more inclusive and representative.

4. Convene an annual standing conference to promote Indian leadership in "Digital Public Goods" as articulated by Prime Minister Narendra Modi: India is pioneering innovation in e-governance and the mass application of technology through its IndiaStack suite of "digital public goods" – especially Aadhaar, UPI, DigiLocker, and eKYC. The success of IndiaStack programmes and their wide-ranging impact on India's development trajectory offers New Delhi a powerful diplomatic asset in its engagement with other developing countries and established digital economies. As India, the United States, Japan, and other partners seek to promote digital development across the Indo-Pacific, New Delhi should create a new diplomatic initiative to train and equip countries to implement local versions of IndiaStack programmes. To further these efforts, the Ministry of External Affairs and MeitY could host an annual international e-governance conference in New Delhi that would draw representatives from developed and developing economies as well as leaders from the private sector. This annual conference could aim to foster discussion on best practices and use cases in e-governance, new innovative technologies created in the developing world, as well as opportunities for countries to partner with tech companies on their key development priorities. The United States and other likeminded countries must serve as founding partners of such an effort.

5. Harness private sector technology innovation for the Sustainable Development Goals: Companies should proactively seize opportunities to demonstrate the applications of their technologies for the public good, working with state and central government authorities as well as civil society groups to tackle some of India's most pressing development challenges – from education and skilling, to women's empowerment and digital infrastructure. To catalyse this engagement, the GOI could entrust NITI Aayog with developing a series of public-private working

groups on specific development challenges and how they could be advanced through unified cooperation with tech companies. These efforts must be closely aligned with the impact investment community in the United States that is engaged with meeting the sustainable development goals (SDGs). A technology-for-development bridge must be created between the two countries.

6. Create a working group focused on international data regimes during India's G20 presidency in 2022: India's presidency of the G20 in 2022 presents a critical opportunity for New Delhi to articulate an ambitious, forward looking vision on cross-border data flows and digital commerce. Over the course of 2020 and 2021, the GOI should help create and actively participate in a working group comprised of government leaders, industry experts, and policy stakeholders to help develop specific workstreams and recommendations for India to put forward at the G20. The recommendations could cover cross-border data flows, e-commerce, digital taxation, and data privacy. TAG and ORF are well-positioned to help support and advance this group, drawing on both institutions' unique ability to engage relevant stakeholders.

7. Establish new advisory boards in India and the United States to build trust among industry and security officials: The GOI and the USG should create Advisory Boards in both countries that would convene leading tech companies — both foreign and domestic — as well as national security and law enforcement officials for ongoing conversations on the pressing privacy and security issues of the day.

8. Set up India-US working groups to coordinate approaches to emerging technologies: India and the United States should set up bilateral working groups to coordinate their responses to the new risks to national security and international stability posed by emerging technologies and actors. The security concerns around 5G are perhaps only the first of many such disruptions that both countries will grapple with. A permanent India-US working group alert to such development should discuss digital connectivity in the Indo-Pacific, the need for updated legal regimes, and interest

based cooperation on global norms-making processes. India and the United States should also lead the incubation of new global arrangements to prevent the proliferation of weaponised digital technologies.

9. Strengthen India-US cooperation on data sharing through a new bilateral agreement: India and the United States should aim to sign a bilateral data-sharing agreement – potentially modeled on the Clarifying Lawful Overseas Use of Data (CLOUD) Act – which could help both sides reduce digital trade frictions, resolve conflicts of law, and harmonise enforcement regimes across jurisdictions. As part of this, both sides sh ould look to create new mechanisms and appropriate safeguards to help law enforcement swiftly obtain evidence stored in India and the United States. Addressing issues of legitimate data access through a bilateral data-sharing treaty would also eliminate one of the central justifications for data localisation policies, which has emerged as an irritant in India-US trade ties.

10. Bolster Indian leadership on combating cybercrime: India should better coordinate with other digital economies on preventing cybercrime, a transnational challenge that poses massive threats to Indian citizens and businesses. New Delhi should help craft new institutions and arrangements that reflect and carry forward the spirit of the Budapest Convention, while "updating" it for a wholly new set of challenges posed by the advent of IoT and AI. Participating actively in these discussions will help bolster India's status as a leading digital power and deliver cross-cutting benefits if New Delhi looks to advance digital norms as part of its G20 presidency in 2022.

A GLOBAL PARTNERSHIP FOR PRINCIPLES, PEACE, AND PROSPERITY

The Ministers reiterated their commitment to a free, open, inclusive, peaceful, and prosperous Indo-Pacific region. Appreciating the convergence in their respective Indo-Pacific visions, they reiterated their support for ASEAN centrality, rule of law, freedom of navigation and overflight, peaceful resolution of disputes, and sustainable and transparent infrastructure investment. They reaffirmed that closer India-U.S. cooperation is instrumental to promoting security and prosperity in the broader Indo-Pacific region and beyond.

The Ministers reaffirmed their shared vision for greater connectivity in South Asia and the Indo-Pacific and noted the progress of ongoing initiatives being undertaken by India and by the United States for the development of infrastructure and connectivity in the region.

The Ministers welcomed the enhanced diplomatic consultation and coordination between India and the United States, bilaterally, with other partners and in regional and international fora to sustain and enrich the international rules-based order. In this context, the United States reaffirmed its strong support for India's permanent role in a reformed U.N. Security Council and for India's early entry to the Nuclear Suppliers Group.

The Ministers valued the recent India-U.S.-Japan trilateral summit meetings and welcomed the India-U.S.-Australia-Japan Quadrilateral Ministerial meeting in September 2019, as means to promote practical cooperation in infrastructure development, cyber security, counterterrorism, and regional connectivity.

Reiterating their shared interest in strengthening UN peacekeeping, the Ministers intend to collectively work for capacity-building of peacekeepers from Indo-Pacific countries that would follow the successful India-U.S. training program for African peacekeepers.

In view of the importance of greater regional and global collaboration to reduce risks from natural disasters, the Ministers welcomed the United States joining the recently created Coalition for Disaster Resilient Infrastructure. In this regard, they also welcomed ongoing technical cooperation, including with the National Disaster Response Force (NDRF). The Ministers appreciated Prime Minister Modi's Indo-Pacific Oceans Initiative and noted their nation's shared interest in collaborative efforts to secure an open, inclusive and free maritime domain, as well as the health of the oceans. They recommended building on the India-U.S. Oceans Dialogue to advance shared oceanic priorities, including combating pollution, fisheries enforcement, scientific exploration, and species documentation in the Indian Ocean.

The Ministers conveyed their shared interest in a peaceful, secure, stable, united, democratic, inclusive and sovereign Afghanistan. They expressed support for Afghan-led and-owned negotiations that culminate in a sustainable peace, cessation of terrorist violence and preservation of the gains of the last 18 years. They applauded India's efforts to build trade linkages and multi-modal connectivity infrastructure for Afghanistan to enhance its regional connectivity to sustain growth and development over the long term.

The Ministers supported freedom of navigation and uninterrupted maritime trade in the Strait of Hormuz, and reaffirmed the importance of ensuring peace and stability on the Korean peninsula, including through North Korea's dismantlement of all weapons of mass destruction and ballistic missiles in accordance with relevant United Nations Security Council resolutions.

Building an Enduring Defense and Counterterrorism Partnership

The Ministers committed to a common vision for the India-U.S. Major Defense Partnership (MDP) that recognizes their countries' shared desire to build a comprehensive, enduring, and mutually-beneficial defense partnership and to expand all aspects of their security and defense cooperation. Consistent with this vision for MDP, the Ministers seek to expand military-to-military cooperation and improve the defense and security partnership in the coming year.

In this context, the Ministers welcomed the growing and increasingly sophisticated cooperation between their two Navies.

In particular, the Ministers noted the continued high level of operational interaction achieved in the MALABAR naval exercise. The two sides also applauded the establishment of the new tri-service, amphibious exercise - TIGER TRIUMPH - as a tangible demonstration of the growing scope and complexity of military cooperation. The Ministers decided to hold TIGER TRIUMPH annually, in formats to be decided mutually. The Ministers committed to enhanced cooperation between the Indian Navy and the U.S. Navy Fleets under U.S. Indo-Pacific Command, Central Command, and Africa Command and intend to expand similar cooperation between their respective Armies and Air Forces.

In support of shared interests in enhancing maritime security and naval cooperation, and building on the success of the fourth India-U.S. Maritime Security Dialogue, the Ministers welcomed the assignment of an Indian officer to liaison with U.S. Naval Forces Central Command in the near future and noted their intent to explore further military liaison relationships. The United States applauded India's leadership in establishing an Information Fusion Centre for the Indian Ocean Region (IFC-IOR), and decided to explore placement of a U.S. liaison officer at the Centre to advance cooperation on maritime security across the region.

The Ministers recognized the importance of maritime cooperation, including with other partner countries in the Indo-Pacific. In this regard, the United States welcomed India's invitation to join the 2020 MILAN multilateral naval exercise and plans to participate.

Building on the success of India-U.S. naval cooperation, the Ministers emphasized the importance of enhancing other areas of military-to-military cooperation. The Ministers reaffirmed their commitment to strengthen joint and service-to-service interaction and cooperation. They discussed ways to enable closer Army-to-Army and Air Force-to-Air Force ties and to explore cooperation between Special Operations Forces. They also noted that the senior-most military dialogue, the Military Cooperation Group, should review military cooperation on an annual basis and plan forward-looking cooperative activities. The Ministers affirmed their commitment to enable defense information-sharing at the joint and service-to-service levels. The Ministers noted their respective commitment to supporting capacity building efforts in the Indo-Pacific.

The Ministers also emphasized the importance of defense enabling agreements, which allow Indian and the U.S. militaries and defense industries to expand cooperation in key areas. The Ministers noted rapid progress to implement the Communications Compatibility and Security Agreement (COMCASA), which has already enabled valuable cooperation. They called for the quick installation of secure communication capabilities between the Armed Forces, including the Armies and Air Forces. Both sides noted that continued COMCASA implementation would further enable growing military cooperation. They also decided to continue the discussion on the Basic Exchange and Cooperation Agreement (BECA) in 2020 to enable greater geospatial information-sharing.

The Ministers welcomed the signing of the Industrial Security Annex (ISA) which will facilitate the exchange of classified military information between Indian and the U.S. defense industries. Both sides also expressed intent to meet in 2020 to discuss ISA implementation. The Ministers welcomed growing India-U.S. defense trade, the shared commitment to defense innovation cooperation between their respective agencies, and India's increased contributions to the global defense supply chain. The Ministers were pleased to announce important progress under the Defense Technology and Trade Initiative (DTTI), including the finalization of a Statement of Intent to co-develop several projects. The Ministers welcomed the finalization of the Standard Operating Procedure for setting forth implementation guidelines for projects under DTTI and the Industry-to-Industry Framework, which will establish a standing mechanism for dialogue between Indian and U.S. defense companies and their governments on defense technology and industrial cooperation.

The Ministers noted their intent to explore collaboration on testing and certification in defence and aerospace sectors and establishment of Maintenance Repair and Overhaul (MRO) facilities in India. Both sides note that the development of Defence Industry corridors in India offers opportunities for defence industrial cooperation.

Condemning terrorism in all its forms, the Ministers called for concerted action against all terrorist networks, including al-Qa'ida, ISIS/Daesh, Lashkar e-Tayyiba, Jaish-e-Mohammad (JeM), Haqqani Network, Hizb-ul Mujahideen, TTP and D-Company. The Ministers called on Pakistan to take immediate, sustained and irreversible action to ensure that no territory under its control is used for terrorism against other countries in any manner, and to arrest and prosecute the perpetrators of cross-border terrorist attacks, including 26/11 Mumbai and Pathankot. India appreciated U.S. support at the United Nations for terrorist designations, including of JeM leader Masood Azhar, and the United States welcomed changes in Indian law that will facilitate further cooperation on terrorism designations.

Taking note of the judicial cooperation on terrorism cases between the National Judicial Academy in Bhopal, India and the U.S. Federal Judicial Center, the Ministers intend to facilitate further cooperation between them in new areas and through joint judicial workshops for third-country partners. To strengthen security cooperation on international supply chain and cargo security, the Ministers looked forward to an early finalization of a Mutual Recognition Arrangement (MRA) between their Authorized Economic Operator (AEO) programs.

Recognizing the serious threats posed by malicious cyber actors, and recalling the successful recent meetings of the India-U.S. Cyber Dialogue and Information and Communication Technology (ICT) Working Group, the Ministers reaffirmed the importance of cyber security cooperation, promoting responsible state behavior in cyberspace, and supporting open and transparent platforms and technologies that will safeguard privacy and sovereignty as per domestic legal framework, particularly in emerging ICT technologies including 5G networks. Both sides also expressed intent to initiate discussions on cyber defense issues in the coming year.

Economy, Energy, Environment and Mutual Prosperity

The Ministers applauded the record levels of trade between India and the United States and welcomed discussions by India's Ministry of Commerce and Industry and the United States Trade Representative to reach an understanding on various bilateral trade issues raised by the two sides to facilitate trade, improve market access and address issues of interest to both sides. The Ministers looked forward to the swift conclusion of discussions that will advance their shared objective to support prosperity and job creation in both countries and foster greater investment and innovation in their economies.

Welcoming enhanced energy and resource cooperation between two of the world's largest energy users, the Ministers emphasized the importance of building on the India-U.S. Strategic Energy Partnership to modernize power grids in support of India's goal to provide reliable and affordable energy to its population; develop greater integration of modern energy sources into India's power systems; and increase the focus on energy efficiency and combatting air pollution. They emphasized knowledge exchange for reform in electricity distribution as well as the recently launched Flexible Resources Initiative under the U.S.-India Clean Energy Finance Task Force.

The Ministers applauded growing exports of U.S. LNG, crude oil, and other energy products to India, totaling $6.7 billion to date. They look forward to greater investments in each country's energy sector, including in oil and gas exploration and production (E&P) sectors and in development of gas infrastructure.

The Ministers welcomed the Memorandum of Understanding signed between India's Ministry of Jal Shakti and the U.S. Geological Survey to promote technical cooperation in areas such as water quality and management. Recalling the historic India-U.S. civil nuclear deal, the Ministers welcomed continued progress by the Nuclear Power Corporation of India Limited and Westinghouse Electric Company toward a techno-commercial offer for the construction of six nuclear reactors.

Noting the excellent cooperation between India and the United States in civil aviation, the Ministers appreciated efforts towards establishment of standard operating procedures to allow U.S. carriers to conduct ground handling operations under the India-U.S. Air Transport Agreement. The Ministers also expressed hope for an early completion of a new Civil Aviation Memorandum of Agreement between the Indian Ministry of Civil Aviation and the U.S. Federal Aviation Administration.

Shared Leadership in Science and Space

The Ministers welcomed the conclusion of a new Science and Technology (S&T) Agreement, which will further strengthen collaboration on science and technology, particle research, and innovation.

Celebrating the 50th anniversary of the Apollo 11 mission and the founding of the Indian Space Research Organisation (ISRO), the Ministers recognized space cooperation, including on Earth science and lunar exploration, as a unique facet of the India-U.S. partnership. They applauded the close collaboration between their space agencies to launch the jointly developed NASA-ISRO Synthetic Aperture Radar (NISAR) satellite in 2022.

The Ministers welcomed growing cooperation through the biennial India-U.S. Civil Space Joint Working Group that spans cutting-edge Earth observation capabilities to interplanetary exploration and supported new opportunities for collaboration, including in the areas of human space flight and exploration. The Ministers also welcomed the sharing of bilateral Space Situational Awareness information, which will catalyze efforts to create the conditions for a safe, stable, and sustainable space environment.

Both sides expressed intent to discuss areas of potential space defense cooperation in the next year.

Building Bonds Between Our Citizens

The Ministers recognized the unique and enduring foundation that people-to-people ties, including the presence of a four million strong Indian-American diaspora in the United States, have created for the India-U.S. partnership.

The Ministers welcomed the recent growth in the number of Indian students in the United States to over 200,000, and acknowledged the role of expanding university research partnerships in fostering mutual understanding, entrepreneurship and scientific innovation. In this context, they commended the enduring success of the Fulbright-Nehru Program, which will celebrate its 70th anniversary in India in 2020. The Ministers expressed intent for establishment of a bilateral India-U.S. Young Innovators Initiative, which will support internship opportunities for emerging young leaders in key areas of scientific and economic endeavor.

Applauding the entrepreneurial spirit of Indians and Indian-Americans that has benefited both nations, the Ministers noted the important role of people-to-people linkages in strengthening economic ties. Both sides look forward to the upcoming India-U.S. Consular Dialogue to further increase cooperation and discuss issues of mutual concern, including visas and familial issues related to marriage, adoption and child custody.

Reflecting the widespread popular and political support in both countries for a robust India-U.S. partnership, the Ministers looked forward to the establishment of India-U.S. Parliamentary Exchange to facilitate reciprocal visits by Parliamentarians of the two countries.

Secretaries Pompeo and Esper expressed appreciation to the Government of India for its continuing support to the Defense POW/MIA Accounting Agency (DPAA) as it works to repatriate the remains of U.S. service members missing from World War II.

For the 150th birth anniversary of Mahatma Gandhi, the United States joins India in celebrating his life and message, which has inspired generations of Indians and Americans.

TRUMP ADMINISTRATION WOULD BE GOOD FOR INDIA

"I think US needs India for its presence in the region itself," Mukesh Aghi, president of US India Business Council (USIBC), a representative body of top American businesses having a footprint in India, told PTI. Noting that geopolitically as India sits in a very turmoil arena, New Delhi needs Washington more.

"We feel that from the Indo-US relationship perspective, Trump administration will be good for India," Aghi said, adding that two principles could drive Indo-US relationship. "First, this administration sees that the economic prosperity of India is good for America. Second, it also sees the military growth of India as a stabilising factor in the region itself," he said.

"We believe that India wants to see the US as a strong nation, sending a strong message out there because at this stage while India is trying to grow economically you do not want too much disruption in global order. We feel that the ties between the Trump administration and Modi government will be positive and much more deeper also," Aghi said. Trump and Modi will also look at Indian IT companies to create and hire more Americans, Aghi said.

"The Indian companies will restart hiring Americans in the US. Geopolitically, India will stand by the US and US will support India. "I feel that the partnership is going to reach a higher level as it settles down and the team takes shape in the US itself," Aghi added.

Trump and Prime Minister Narendra Modi are expected to meet sometime later this year. Foreign Secretary S Jaishankar is currently in the US, probably for preparing ground work for Modi's visit and draw a road map of Indo-US ties under the Trump administration.

In addition to the political and strategic partnership, the two leaders in their forthcoming meeting are expected to talk about enhancing the economic and trade ties, Aghi said. "I also believe that Make in India and Buy America, Hire America is not in conflict. They basically support each other.

"Make in India is more for domestic market. India is not a very large export benefaction country. India can support the US very much on pharma side. Indian pharma companies provide cost benefits to American companies and the country. Trump wants to bring the cost down. So he looks at Indian companies to help from that perspective," Aghi added.

TRUMP CAN IMPROVE TIES WITH INDIA

Beyond the din of post-election protests lies a place where many Americans - as well as like-minded observers in India and elsewhere - who lament the selection of Donald Trump as president of the United States can seek relief from their dismay and anxiety. There, concerned Americans will find a role that is critically important to the capable functioning of a democratic system.

It has various names, including the "loyal opposition." The point is that - without questioning the legitimacy of a government that emerges from a free and fair election - those who find themselves philosophically in disagreement with it have every right to speak out in a clear voice and hold the new leadership accountable.

That way, the political system has a chance to evolve, rather than devolve (as some observers pessimistically predict for the United States). It is also not too early to be thinking about the next election; better results happen when strategizing and follow-up efforts are proactive instead of reactive.

In the meantime, the United States cannot afford disruptions in its work as a nation, either domestically or abroad. More specifically, relations between the United States and India, as well as other countries, must proceed.

So, how might Indo-U.S. ties develop under the incoming Trump administration? For insights, I turned to various specialists, including Ronak Desai, an affiliate of the India and South Asia Program at Harvard University's Belfer Center for Science and International Affairs, and a Fellow at New America, a think tank and civic enterprise in Washington, D.C. Desai says "if a Clinton presidency would have represented continuity in U.S.-India relations, a Trump triumph has injected some uncertainty." On the one hand, Desai continues, Trump expressly declared last month that the United States and India would be "best friends," should he win the White House. Such sentiments are consistent with the bipartisan consensus that has formed around the growing strategic partnership between the United States and India over the past decade and a half.

However, Trump's views on multiple issues could potentially generate friction between the two countries. This is particularly likely in areas such as trade, immigration and climate change. Trump's "isolationist and nativist tendencies also remain cause for concern," according to Desai, especially if the president-elect follows through on his promises to dramatically reduce immigration and diminish U.S. engagement in the Asia-Pacific region. Still, Desai notes, there is reason to remain cautiously optimistic that Trump will align his effusive rhetoric for stronger U.S-India ties with reality.

In that event, the bipartisan consensus supporting the strategic partnership is likely to endure.

What are the key issues that demand attention from the United States and India at present? They remain largely the same, Desai observes: strengthening strategic and economic ties, increasing trade, combatting extremism, and promoting regional and international stability. In his opinion, combatting extremism and enhancing security cooperation will likely garner greater prominence and importance under Trump. The central question, which Desai correctly identifies, is "whether the full range of issues affecting U.S.-India ties, and on which the two countries cooperate, will be afforded the same level of priority moving forward."

I also sought input from Brigadier General (ret.) Stephen Cheney, CEO of the American Security Project (ASP), a non-partisan public policy and research organization in Washington, D.C., and his staff. Cheney and Andrew Holland, ASP's director of studies and a senior fellow for energy and climate, indicate that - like everything in America's international relations - the U.S. relationship with India is suddenly open to reinterpretation under the incoming Trump administration. They do not anticipate significant changes, though. According to Cheney and Holland, "there are no major trade deals that Trump would want to 'renegotiate' (like he wishes to do with NAFTA or the Trans-Pacific Partnership), nor is there a treaty alliance between the nations that he has questioned (like the U.S.-Japan alliance or NATO)."

If anything, Cheney and Holland say, Trump may lean more towards India. Why? Because that posture would provide a counterweight to China in Asia, and strengthen India's role as a partner in anti-terrorism operations across South Asia and the Middle East.

On the issue of climate change, Cheney and Holland suggest the major discontinuity between the Obama and Trump administrations in the context of Indo-U.S. relations will be over international climate policy. While the United States has worked with India and pressed it hard on climate policy in both the Montreal Protocol and the Paris Agreement, Cheney and Holland say, the Trump approach will likely not follow suit and may even seek to abrogate American commitments to those treaties. In response, they advise, India should push the new U.S. administration to ensure that it meets America's climate commitments.

Further, Cheney and Holland are right to remind us that the United States remains concerned about tensions between India and Pakistan, especially in light of their nuclear arms. The two countries need to show restraint, embrace cooperation and resist military confrontation, Cheney and Holland recommend, and they feel confident Trump's administration will share their view.

Lastly, I talked with Akhil Gupta, director of the Center for India and South Asia at the University of California, Los Angeles. He expects the new administration will be very friendly towards India, will likely take tougher stances on China and Pakistan, and could move closer to Russia. That might create a new geopolitics in South Asia, Gupta says, prompting Pakistan to get cozier with China and distance itself from the United States. If that happens, he anticipates seeing greater military and diplomatic cooperation between the United States and India.

The major issue for India, Gupta says, will be free trade in services and other goods. If the incoming Trump administration "clamps down on B-1 visas and IT enabled-services exports, it will impact the Indian economy in a big way," he cautions. As for other issues, the sale of military hardware and nuclear power will be important items for the bilateral agenda. Gupta also warns that if racist attacks against people of Indian origin in the United States go up, it will put a strain on relations between the two countries.

Gupta notes that the top priority for India should be to improve the lives of large numbers of people living in abject poverty, but immediately adds that such an outcome is unlikely to gain the attention of policymakers in either New Delhi or Washington. Aside from that issue, Gupta believes the chief priorities should be the danger of nuclear conflict between India and Pakistan, and the achievement of a peaceful political solution in Kashmir.

To the opinions expressed above, I would add the following, specific suggestions for President-elect Trump to set Indo-U.S. relations on the proper course upon taking office:

1. Immediately extend a firm hand of friendship, respect, consultation and cooperation to India.
2. Designate Indian-Americans for key appointive positions in the Trump administration, especially in areas that affect U.S.-India ties.

3. Invite Prime Minister Narendra Modi to visit the White House as soon as possible.
4. Begin planning for a reciprocal trip by Trump to India early in his term.
5. Publicly recognize India as the linchpin U.S. relationship in South Asia.
6. Re-commit to closer coordination with India in areas such as global and South Asian security, defense and counter-terrorism.
7. Strongly support India's bid to become a permanent member of the U.N. Security Council.

An opportunity exists during the next few months for the Trump transition team to take a careful look at U.S.-India ties, and prepare the new administration to define for Americans and Indians what the nature of that relationship will be. It is time to move past fulsome campaign rhetoric, and embrace substantive policy positions that will shape and reinforce America's much-needed strategic embrace of India.

12

The US-China Trade War Dynamic: How it may Impact India

As British people agonise over Brexit, Farage, and the oh-so disappointing finale of Game of Thrones, a real life, world-changing global conflict is happening. It has the potential to define our reality here in the UK for many years to come, to a far greater extent than any other issue currently in play.

That no one in our political debate seems to have the slightest idea what to do about it or the slightest influence in shaping these grand events is yet another indictment of Britain's political class, though to dwell on that is to offer little new to the debate.

Instead, here are five things that emerged for me as I experienced the anxiety and sense of helplessness on the ground from those whose lives are already being directly affected by the real-life Game of Thrones happening between Washington and Beijing.

War of economic models and culture as much as it is war of currency and trade

China's centrally planned economic operation is a source of much angst among the Trump administration. For some of its members, China is both it is both a strategic adversary and a philosophical enemy.

Trump is a self-proclaimed champion of a certain type of free market economics. In a campaign speech in 2011 he called the

Chinese "motherfuckers" - and got a round of applause. In that speech and many times after, he claimed the way to deal with China was to put a man who understands how to negotiate - The Donald himself - in charge. In many ways the China conflict is the whole point of Trumpism. It is likely that Trump will do and risk anything to fight this battle, no matter the cost.

And that cost is likely to be significant given the considerable rise in cumulative trade between US and China prior to the start of the trade wars.

Cultural difference is not just about presentation, however. It is about strategy. The Chinese are able to take a multi-decade and even multi-generational approach to economic planning, so long as domestic living standards are improving at a rate that keeps the current regime in power.

In contrast, the US faces a four-year election cycle that leaves only narrow windows where short-term pain can be suffered, without risking a change of leadership.

The Chinese maintain an advantage - unless tariffs are raised to such a level that other suppliers substitute their wares for those offered by the Chinese, a process that inevitably takes time. Trump knows this: for him an escalation in tub-thumping and in tactics is the only route to success in 2020.

THE US-CHINA TRADE DISPUTE: WHAT IMPACT ON THE CIRCULAR ECONOMY?

In the latest development in the trade dispute between the US and China, the Trump administration has announced a delay to the newly planned 10 per cent tariffs on another $300 billion of Chinese goods until the end of 2019. Since a recent round of negotiations did not bring about any resolution to the dispute between both countries, there is now increasing evidence that the trade war between the two countries is hurting both economies. Furthermore, the trade dispute is yielding negative spill-over effects for different areas of global concern, including the climate, environmental protections and waste management, while also dampening trade in circular goods and services between the two countries.

The circular economy - an economic model in which waste is eliminated by design, goods are reused, repaired and recycled, and asset-sharing is prioritized over individual ownership - is a crucial strategy for reducing the resource footprint of industrial development and for tackling the global waste crisis. China and the US, both key players in this space, are vital for the success of the global circular economy, and the two countries have enjoyed a healthy symbiotic relationship through the trading of goods until now, particularly the trade in secondary raw materials and waste products for re-processing and recycling.

However this relationship is now under threat. China's retaliatory tariffs cover multiple categories of scrap metals, copper waste and other secondary materials including recovered fibre and paper pulp from recycled paper and cardboard in the US - all relevant resources for the circular economy. Consequently, the impact of these tariffs has been significant. China has been the top importer of US recycled paper for decades: before the tariffs in the first half of 2018, it imported 2.73 million tons of US cardboard and 1.4 million tons of other US-sourced recovered fibres. By July 2019, China's imports of paper and cardboard reduced by more than one third.

Initially, the loss of China as the principal export market for American recycled paper has left many municipal recycling programmes in crisis, facing increasing costs and reduced revenues. More recently, the US recycling industry has been experiencing a revival partly through Chinese investments. For example, the Hong Kong-based company Nine Dragons, one of the world's largest producers of cardboard boxes, invested $500 million to buy and expand production at US paper mills to avoid trade tariffs. While another Chinese company, Global Win Wickliffe, is reopening a shuttered paper mill in Kentucky, thereby creating US jobs and revitalizing the community.

In China, recycling operators and urban mining pilot projects, which were already facing a shortfall of secondary raw materials after China placed restrictions on foreign plastic waste imports at the start of 2018, are now suffering from the new import tariffs. Urban mining operations and industrial parks are short of feedstock, with some having had to stop their operations, as there are not enough secondary resources from domestic Chinese sources. As such, the fall-out with the US risks undermining China's efforts to support the growth of a domestic circular economy: urban mining and recycling operations, developed through the support of policy over the last decade under the Circular Economy Promotion Law, now face an uncertain future. To maintain and expand these operations, it is necessary to provide more domestic supplies of high-quality recyclables, a goal the government aims to achieve with ambitious pilot projects introduced only in July 2019 in Shanghai for the mandatory sorting and recycling of household waste.

These recent developments point out certain challenges that governments and businesses will need to address as the global circular economy evolves. Most countries and businesses are not able to make use of all the waste and secondary materials that they generate as by-products. International cross-border trade is therefore essential to generate markets for circular goods and services. But, in a highly interconnected network of global circular value chains, businesses and governments are exposed to sudden market disruptions. Governments will need to take a twin-track approach to managing the risk of such disruption.

To do this, they firstly will need to support the development of their reuse, repair and recycling capacity at home and support the development of domestic markets for circular goods and services. Current uncertainty about future trade relations risks dampening innovation in the circular economy and discouraging the development and trial of new business models and products. Domestic markets matter for the circular economy to generate value and create new employment locally. This can be achieved through supportive policies that encourage local repair businesses and start-ups with digital solutions for optimizing resource use and facilitating asset-sharing.

Secondly, they will need to engage to enable closer cooperation within the framework of a rules-based international system to govern trade in a way that works for the circular economy - not against it. This requires taking into account the perspective of global value chains and the full life cycle of goods and services. Despite this, the role of global and regional trade in the circular economy remains little understood. As more countries are developing national circular economy strategies, it is important to understand how these will relate to the trade rules of the global economy.

What is needed is a clearer analysis and understanding of the physical trade flows of waste products and secondary resources in a wide range of sectors and across borders. A new Chatham House circular economy project will look more closely into these complex trade issues to inform the design of effective national and international trade policies in support of the circular economy.

US-CHINA TRADE WAR: HOW IT MAY IMPACT INDIA

The ongoing trade tussle between world's two major economies — the United States and China — is fueling fears about damage to global economic growth. The US and China have locked horns over tariffs, leaving the world on the brink of a trade war. China has said it would impose higher tariffs on $60 billion of US goods from June 1 in retaliation against Washington's tariff hike on Chinese goods.

How US-China trade dispute began

It all started in March last year when US President Donald Trump had slapped heavy tariffs on imported steel and aluminium items from China and it responded by imposing tit-for-tat tariffs on billions of dollars worth of American imports.

The dispute intensified after the US demanded that China must reduce its $375 billion trade deficit with the US and give more access to American goods in Chinese markets.

The International Monetary Fund (IMF), in a report earlier this year, had stated that the US-China trade tension was one factor that contributed to a "significantly weakened global expansion" late last year, as it cut its global growth forecast for 2019. IMF chief Christine Lagarde had also said that fresh trade tensions between the United States and China were threat to the world economy.

Impact on India

For India, a significant shift in the manufacturing sector is awaited and this could be a golden opportunity for India, especially if it is properly positioned. Although, if the tension persists for long, then there could be a slowdown in the economy too.

The United Nations had said in a report that India is among few economies that stand to benefit from the trade tensions between the world's top two economies.

What Xiaomi founder has to say

In an interview with TOI, Lei Jun, the 49-year-old founder of Xiaomi, the Chinese mobile phone and electronics giant that has raced to $26 billion in turnover in less than a decade of existence, said that he believes that growing trade tensions between China and the US could see Chinese investment flow being increasingly directed towards India.

Jun, who is called by some as the 'Steve Jobs of China', describes India — where the company leads in smartphone sales — as Xiaomi's most important market outside China, and says the company is getting set to launch a range of new products in India to complement the existing line-up of phones and televisions that it already sells. These could include refrigerators, washing machines, ACs, water purifiers, and possibly even electric vehicles.

Opportunity for exporters?

As Chinese goods are being taxed at a higher rate in the US, this implies that the Indian exporters can explore this opportunity to fill the gap. But, currency factor will be an important factor to watch.

Apple shifting base

Foxconn Technology Group chairman Terry Gou had said the iPhone will go into mass production in India this year, a shift for the largest assembler of Apple Inc's handsets that has long concentrated production in China. Gou had stated that Prime Minister Narendra Modi has invited him to India as his Taiwanese company plans its expansion in the country. Apple has had older phones produced at a plant in Bangalore for several years but now will expand manufacturing to more recent models.

"In the future, we will play a very important role in India's smartphone industry," Gou had aid at an event in Taiwan. "We have moved our production lines there."

Stock markets bleeding

World stocks hovered near two-month lows, although slightly more optimistic comments from the US and Chinese officials on trade brought some comfort a day after equities suffered their worst selloff so far this year.

Domestic stock markets are facing the heat too. The benchmark BSE sensex shed 1,941 points in just nine trading sessions. However, some experts have said that the uncertainty in markets can also be due to the pending results of the 2019 general elections. Equity indices are expected to bounce back after the results are announced on May 23.

THE US-CHINA TRADE WAR DYNAMIC: WHAT'S IN IT FOR INDIA?

26 December marked the 125th anniversary of Mao Zedong's birthday. Speaking in the mid-December celebration of the 40th

year of reform and opening up, President Xi Jinping hailed Mao for laying the foundation for the successful transformation of China. 1 January 2019 will mark the 40th anniversary of the establishment of the diplomatic relations between the United States and the People's Republic of China, though it is unlikely that this event will be celebrated at this fraught juncture in Sino-US relations.

The two countries are locked in what began as a conflict over trade and tariffs, but has now become all-consuming and is affecting their relationship across the board. Relations between them are probably the worst they have been since 1979.

Reports say that a US team will travel to Beijing on 7 January to hold trade talks with Chinese officials. It will be led by the Deputy US Trade Representative (USTR) Jeffrey Gerrish and will also include Treasury Undersecretary for International Affairs David Malpass. These will be the first face-to-face discussions since Presidents Trump agreed in his meeting with President Xi in Argentina, to postpone the imposition of additional sanctions on $200 billion worth of Chinese goods (imposed until 1 March).

Beijing is now battling an economic slowdown, as well the headwinds in its relations with the US. The economy continues to be weighed down by debt and the impact of US tariffs are only now beginning to tell.

The latest signals coming from Beijing, through the outcome of the Central Economic Work Conference (CEWC) that concluded last week signals that the Chinese will make efforts to stimulate their economy and at the same time work towards a trade deal with the US. This is a key meeting of top officials chaired by Xi Jinping that was aimed at setting the tone of the Chinese economy for 2019.

The third quarter saw the slowest quarter of growth since 2009. It stood at 6.5 per cent. Some are forecasting Chinese growth to slip below 6.5 per cent in the coming year. The World Bank, however, says China's economy "remains resilient" and has projected China's growth rate in 2018 to 6.5 per cent and 6.2 per cent in 2019. The CEWC signalled that that China planned to continue to promote the development of high-end manufacturing and make China a "high end manufacturing powerhouse." More important, the CEWC statement struck an upbeat note declaring that "China is still and will be in an important period of strategic opportunity for development for a long time to come."

Meanwhile China is signalling that it is willing to adjust its policies to meet what has now become near-universal criticism. As a result of the G20 meeting, China announced a third round of tariff cuts on 700 goods from 1 January to open up the economy. China also removed retaliatory duty on US automobiles and began buying US crude oil, LNG and soybeans again.

Meanwhile the US continues to pile on pressure on China. In November the US Commerce Department asked for public comment on putting tough export controls on a list of 14 new technologies which could have dual national security implications such as genomics, computer vision and audio manipulation technology, AI chips, quantum computing, mind-machine interfaces and flight control algorithms.

The Huawei drama continues to unfold in slow-motion. Its CFO Meng Wanzhou was released on bail earlier in December and even though China has taken three Canadian nationals hostage, it is unlikely that Ottawa will unbend on the issue. As of now the US has not formally sought her extradition.

Last week, the US Justice Department announced charges against two absconding Chinese nationals for participating in a global hacking campaign to steal tech company secrets and IPR, including the data of more than 1000,000 US Navy personnel. According to the legal documents, the two, operating in conjunction with the PRC's Ministry of State Security stole information from at least 45 US companies in a campaign that began in 2006.

Later that day, in coordinated announcements by UK, Australia, Canada and New Zealand, attacked China for its 12-year campaign of cyber-espionage targeting their technology companies. According to reports, initial plans were for a simultaneous announcement of financial sanctions on those implicated in the hacking.

The CEWC did make favourable noises about quickening reform, enhancing foreign investor access, protecting IPR of foreign companies, and removing ownership caps in more areas and "implement the consensus from the China-US summit (in Argentina)." But so far the Chinese have not provided any detailed concessions that could meet the heightened expectations of the Trump-Xi meeting. Indeed, what they are worried about it US piling on demands in the face of Beijing's concessions.

Who is winning and who is losing the trade war

According to a study by European Network for Economic and Fiscal Policy Research (Europe Econpol), 20.5 per cent of the cost of the 25 per cent tariffs that the US has imposed on $250 billion worth of Chinese goods will fall on Chinese producers, while the US consumers will only pay 4.5 per cent.

A September 2018 survey by the American Chamber of Commerce (AmCham) China and the American Chamber of Commerce (AmCham) Shanghai says US companies doing business in China have been hurting. They based their findings on a survey of 430 companies doing business in China. Nearly two-thirds of respondents said that cross-tariffs of $50 billion each imposed by China and the US were already affecting their business operations. Additional tariffs would affect a higher proportion of businesses, the survey noted. However, all but a handful of them said they would remain in China for the near future.

A study by Nomura Global Research suggests that there could be companies, industries and even some small economies that could benefit. According to the study some would benefit from import substitution, others from production relocation. A country like Malaysia, for example, could gain in the area of electronic integrated circuits, while Pakistan could benefit in cotton yarn. India, along with Malaysia and Singapore could benefit from a diversion of FDI and production from China. More detailed analysis in the study shows that India does not benefit from the import substitution by countries on account of the US tariffs on Chinese imports. Whereas it does gain marginally from the import substitution on account of Chinese tariffs on US imports.

India's gains could come from the diversion of production and FDI from China which could occur were the trade war become prolonged. 43 per cent of China's total merchandise exports depend on foreign investment, pointing to their potential for relocation. This may not hurt China's giant economy, but would certainly benefit the economies to which the diversion occurs.

India's market size and potential make it a likely destination of countries wanting to relocate. But the Nomura Production Relocation Index puts India at the fourth position after Vietnam, Malaysia, and Singapore.

Looking forward

At this stage the outcome of the US-China negotiations remain in the realm of speculation. The Chinese could decide that it was prudent to keep on the right side of the US and make the changes in their economy that the Americans wanted, which would actually amount to carrying out the reforms they have themselves sought but have been unable to make.

On the other hand, they could double down and refuse to make the changes and hope to buy off the US by increased purchases of energy and agricultural products like soybeans and put on a show that they are working hard to meet US goals. As speeches go, Xi's have a mixed record. In his major speech on the anniversary of reforms, Xi took a hard line and insisted that only the Communist Party of China (CPC) dominance would allow China to continue its remarkable economic transformation. On the other hand, the statement at the CEWC, chaired by XI signalled that China was willing to make a deal.

To show that they are serious in addressing US concerns, a standing committee of China's legislature, the National People's

Congress, recently began discussion a draft proposal that would prohibit the forced transfer of technology to domestic companies using administrative measures. Just how this would work is not clear since the draft agreement speaks of promoting "voluntary technological cooperation based on business rules." Critics, however say that the draft law is a formal document, whereas technology transfers take place in actual practice. It's not clear when the NPC will actually pass the new proposal as a law. It could actually take another year and more for the process to be completed.

A great deal of the US-China trade outcome depends on just at what point does the US wants to compromise. The American position, of course, is known only to President Trump. He could have his officials negotiate hard with the Chinese and then cut a deal which would meet his trade demands, but cut the Chinese some slack on the issue of its industrial policy. For Beijing, that could well be a best case scenario which would drastically reduce the current antagonism and prevent what is clearly looking like a train-wreck in Sino-US relations. He has so far, for example, not only let of ZTE off the hook, but also signaled that he may be willing to have a look at the extradition of Meng Wanzhou, if the Chinese so requested. One disturbing development for Beijing, however, is that despite the US going it alone, its allies are now lining up behind it to raise the issue of China's industrial policy and cyber espionage in a united front.

There are hazards not just for India, but the global economy in the event of the trade war deepening. Among the more dire ones is the decoupling of the two economies into two mutually exclusive Chinese and American camps. China took the lead in the process by walling off its internet from the global product. Now, counter-moves are afoot to exclude Chinese companies from the United States.

Countries like India, which are not major players, be forced to choose, but they will also be compelled to be part of this or that global value chains. A wrong choice will obviously have you on the losing side.

CAN INDIA CAPITALISE ON US-CHINA TRADE WAR?

The US-China trade war has reached unprecedented levels. After having levied tariffs on imports worth $250 billion, US President Donald Trump has not toned down his rhetoric. He has threatened to impose tariffs on another $267 billion worth of imports, which should pretty much cover all of China's exports to US. Either side is determined not to blink first. Trump wants China to capitulate while Beijing has made it clear that it does not intend to do so. The global economy is consequently feeling the chill. Amidst this development, is there a real opportunity for India to warm up to?

To answer this question, one needs to understand the evolving US-China relationship. Over the last few decades, the nature of their relationship was one of 'nether friends nor foes' and all they wanted was a 'win-win economic engagement'. In other words, they were 'co-operating rivals'. But that changed post the 2008 global financial crisis, which narrowed the gap between their economies.

In 2007, the US economy was four times that of China but by 2012, thanks to the great recession, it reduced to two-times. There is growing anxiety in the US about China's growth. The Chinese, on their part, believe that the US is actively working to prevent their country from taking the rightful place in the world order. It is not just economic growth that has sowed seeds of discontent.

China has been flexing its muscle militarily by spending heavily. China's military, vexed at the US control over trade routes, has been trying to test its strength in the South China Sea. The two nations have had their share of skirmishes there. Also, President Xi Jinping's Belt and Road initiative has unnerved the US which sees it as an attempt by China to play a larger role in the world. It is clear that China does not like the idea of a uni-polar world but the US wants to keep it that way.

That apart, the two nations do not see eye to eye when it comes to political values nor do they have common security interests. So this trade war is not just about trade. Going forward, their relationship would at best remain frosty.

De-risking operations

This puts US companies in a piquant position. Over the years, taking advantage of low costs, they have increased their dependence on China for their supply chain needs and manufacturing. Such is the depth of the arrangement that over 50 per cent of the products HP, IBM, Dell, Cisco, Microsoft and Intel or their suppliers use come from China. It is the second largest exporter of auto parts to the US auto giants (after Mexico). The list of sectors heavily dependent on China is long and US companies are realising the need to de-risk their operations — supply chain as well as manufacturing.

The US is already pushing ICT players to reduce their dependence on China. Investors are also beginning to question US companies on their fall-back plan if US-China relationship goes into a spiral.

This situation presents a clear opportunity for Indian companies. After all, the US and India see each other as natural allies. Former US President Barack Obama even described the relationship as 'one of the most defining partnership of the 21st century'. Trump too wants a close relationship with India, a democracy with shared values. Not surprising that US companies have already started making enquiries about sourcing from Indian players, especially in the auto-component space.

But taking a share of China's supply chain or manufacturing is easier said than done. Over decades China has invested a lot in upgrading its infrastructure. Also, the scale of manufacturing is such that it will be difficult for India to match in terms of cost. But the silver-lining is that the recent imposition of tariff by the US has levelled the playing field, at least in select sectors.

Competitive enough

These sectors have certain common traits that help them to be as competitive as those in China. They have good scale thanks to a strong domestic market in India. They have also built a solid supply-chain network (this is critical as India cannot grab a share of the ICT exports from China as it lacks proper supply chain, especially in semi-conductors). They also export a fair share of their production and, consequently, their quality is tested and is as good as anywhere in the world. Auto components, leather and textiles are some sectors that top the list.

The government must direct its 'Make in India' initiative on these sectors with suitable incentives. However, low manufacturing cost alone is not enough. Logistics cost, to move the manufactured goods from the factory to the destination, is critical. China excels here. India has been building roads, improving port infrastructure/ connectivity to the hinterland through Sagarmala and Bharatmala programmes.

It is also trying to enhance coastal shipping and boost transportation through inland waterways. To rival China on logistics costs, it has to redouble its efforts. In developed markets, companies outsource 70 per cent of their logistics operations that can be outsourced to lower costs. In India it is just 35 per cent. Even though India's steep climb in the recent 'ease of doing business' ranking is noteworthy, it still has a long way to go in reforming labour laws and the land-acquisition process which are essential for lowering costs further.

Indian entrepreneurs, for their part, must take advantage of the situation and invest aggressively. De-risking from China will remain a long-term strategy for the US and European companies. Higher exports will also help in neutralising domestic cycles that plague some sectors such as auto components.

It will be a difficult call for Indian entrepreneurs to make as many of them have been investing abroad to de-risk their investments in India. It is a leap of faith.

If they take it, India will not miss the manufacturing bus, as it did in the 1980s and 1990s that saw emergence of East Asian Tigers and China as manufacturing hubs for the world, yet again.

INDIA DRAWS UP PLAN TO GAIN FROM US-CHINA TRADE WAR

With the US-China trade war intensifying, India is keen to increase its market share in both countries and has carried out a detailed analysis identifying items where there is potential to increase exports.

In a recent study, the Commerce Ministry has identified 203 products where exports could be increased to the US, replacing Chinese goods, and 151 items where exports to China could rise.

"The list of items where exports from India can be increased to the US and Chinese markets will be shared with the respective line Ministries and Departments and industry organisations so that sectoral plans can be made. India will also bilaterally seek more access for these products from the US and the Chinese governments by asking them to remove non-tariff barriers wherever they exist," a government official told *BusinessLine*.

Per the analysis, there are at least 203 lines where India has the potential to replace Chinese exports to the US as it already has market access for these items and is a competitor of China. Since the US has increased tariffs for China on these items, it would be easy for India to increase exports. These items include electrical machinery and equipment and base metals and articles.

US imports from China of these items are worth $30.6 billion, while India's exports to the US are only worth $2.4 billion. The fact that India has the capability of increasing exports to the US is evident from the fact that India's total exports of these items to the world are worth $22.2 billion.

A number of agricultural items and chemicals, too, have the potential for greater export to the US.

In the case of China, where different levels of retaliatory tariffs have been imposed on US goods, the Commerce Ministry has carried out a commodity-wise analysis. "The specific lines in which India can potentially expand exports to China immediately ... and also those in which concerted efforts need to be made to acquire market access have been identified," the official said.

The outright advantage

Of the items on which 25 per cent duty has been levied by China on the US, India has the outright advantage to displace US exports to China in 47 lines as it is a strong exporter of these items, according to the analysis. These include some chemicals, granite, inverters, copper ore and concentrates.

Of the items on which China has imposed 10 per cent duty on the US, there are 29 lines in which India is a strong exporter and can displace the US. The top lines include chemicals, equipment for transmission of voice/data in a wired network and tubes and pipes and hoses of vulcanised rubber.

Of the items imported from the US on which China has imposed retaliatory tariffs of 5 per cent, India can displace US exports for 25 lines, including engines, diesel, x-ray tubes and some antibiotics.

UNPACKING THE US"CHINA TECH TRADE WAR

For global technology executives, following developments on the trade front can be gut wrenching. Until very recently, the technology industry was, for the most part, left out of the tit-for-tat tariff increases announced by Washington and Beijing. But suddenly, the tech industry finds itself at the center of an escalating trade war.

This should come as no surprise. The tech industry is a major contributor to the US trade deficit with China. Consumer electronics such as smartphones, personal computers, and TVs alone accounted for around $130 billion of the 2018 trade gap in goods of $419 billion, which the current US administration has stated it wants to slash nearly in half. Achieving that target only through increased

Chinese purchases of such US products as soybeans, liquefied natural gas, and commercial aircraft, as China has reportedly offered to do, is mathematically impossible. If trade deficit reduction is the primary US objective in negotiations, technology products will inevitably have to be on the table.

While the headlines may be dominated by tariffs, there are other major issues regarding the technology industry that further complicate the US view of its trade relations with China and are shaping its policies. They include treatment of intellectual property, access to markets for digital services, and government intervention in support of national champions in strategic sectors such as semiconductors. These issues are all arising within a context of heightened cybersecurity concerns and a race for global leadership in critical new technologies, such as 5G cellular networks and artificial intelligence.

It's impossible at this point to predict how the current trade dispute between the US and China will play out. But it is becoming increasingly likely that—for better or worse—there will be no returning to the previous status quo for the tech industry. Any "deal" that may emerge from talks between Washington and Beijing will be just one step in a long process of working through geopolitical tensions in the growing strategic competition between two superpowers, both of which regard technology leadership as a critical advantage. These dynamics are likely to redefine the global context for the technology industry for the next one or two decades. As explained below, we see several potential scenarios for how the new US"China technology trade relationship will unfold, ranging from what we call "true reciprocal access" to "technology cold war." And since any deal will cross many industries, it can present substantial challenges or opportunities to any given tech sector and product line.

Given the uncertainty, a wait and-see approach may at first seem logical, based on the assumption that either a deal will eventually be reached or nothing can be done anyway. But we think it's not only possible but critical for technology CEOs to think proactively and start taking steps to adapt quickly to the new context. Companies should evaluate potential scenarios for each of their different businesses, products, or services and take actions to mitigate risk, make their organizations and supply chains more resilient to shifting trade rules, and prepare strategies to seize any competitive advantage that the changes may afford them.

And this is important not just for US and Chinese companies. Every major technology company that has substantial operations in China or the US, and for which either nation is a primary end market, will be affected by these changing trade dynamics and needs to be prepared.

WHY THE TECHNOLOGY TRADE "DEFICIT" IS HARD TO RESOLVE

The large US"China deficit in technology products reflects the structure of the technology industry, with its large, truly global supply chains. For many finished electronics goods, China is the primary assembler of imported components and materials. With its massive manufacturing capacity, China accounts for nearly half of worldwide exports of electronic devices. The US is particularly dependent: approximately 70% of its combined imports of major consumer electronics such as smartphones, laptops, and TVs originate in China. The next three largest suppliers—Mexico, South Korea, and Vietnam—account for only 19% combined.

The often cited example of the iPhone—one of the biggest single contributors to the bilateral deficit statistics in the technology sector—is a good illustration. Most of the bill of materials for an iPhone consists of components from suppliers in the US, Japan, South Korea, the European Union, and other nations. While trade statistics count the full cost of the device as a US import from China, we estimate that the actual value that China adds to the average iPhone is somewhere between 4% and 20%. Measuring imports in terms of Chinese value added rather than the full value of the device would reduce the US"China deficit in computers, electronics, and electrical equipment by some 70%, according to a BCG analysis based on international trade data from the Organisation for Economic Co-operation and Development.

However, because the US has set its trade objectives based on the total value of devices imported from China, rather than on the value-added measurement, one option for reducing the size of the tech industry trade deficit is to reshore manufacturing back to the US. It will certainly be possible for US technology companies or their foreign manufacturing subcontractors to reshore *some*Chinese electronics assembly—particularly if high tariffs are imposed on Chinese-made products such as smartphones, personal computers, and televisions. As BCG's Manufacturing Cost Competitiveness Index has shown, the cost differentials between coastal China and advanced industrial economies have shrunk over the past decade, largely because Chinese labor costs have risen faster than productivity. Although manufacturers could partially compensate by shifting work deeper into China's lower-cost interior, the tariffs could make the manufacturing math favor the US in some cases.

But it's also important to keep in mind that for many products for which labor cost is an important factor and for which automation is difficult, it will be more economical for companies to shift production to *other* offshore locations, such as Southeast Asia or Mexico—effectively reducing the US trade deficit with China but increasing imports from the countries that replace China as manufacturing hubs. In the case of certain electronic devices that are associated with perceived cybersecurity risks, however, bypassing China in the supply chain may in itself be a reason for the US to push for re-sourcing—even if the net impact on the overall trade deficit is not material.

In any case, opportunities to cost-effectively reshore and re-source consumer electronics will be limited and would take years to implement. In some consumer electronics segments, there is a strong argument that China is at the center of complex global value chains and is therefore virtually irreplaceable. China's major regional suppliers, such as South Korea and Malaysia, have built their businesses around feeding China's manufacturing facilities. The *Wall Street Journal* has reported that some major global electronic manufacturing services companies have struggled to set up large factories in the US, suggesting that China's manufacturing advantages and scale make it difficult to replace as a major source of many consumer electronics devices.

The experience of some electronics goods targeted in the initial round of tariff hikes introduced in July 2018 supports the argument that higher tariffs will not meaningfully alter the bilateral flow of some products. For example, although US imports of Chinese printing machinery dropped marginally, Chinese shipments of electrical machinery increased by around 5%, to $154 billion, in 2018. At the same time, China's retaliatory tariffs likely contributed to the year-on-year drop in US exports to China. The current restrictions, due to intellectual property or security concerns, on US exports to China of some leading-edge technology products for which Chinese demand is booming, such as high-end computers and semiconductors, are likely to further inhibit deficit reduction.

US tariffs on Chinese products could also affect the ability of American technology companies to tap into the vast, burgeoning Chinese consumer market. Even though goods that US companies build in China for the domestic market do not appear in the bilateral trade balance, the Chinese government could regard their sales as US revenues—and use them as leverage to retaliate against US tariffs. In fact, during previous Chinese political or economic disputes with Japan and South Korea, Chinese consumers shunned brands associated with those nations.

THE POTENTIAL FOR IMPROVED TRADE IN DIGITAL SERVICES AND IP

Often obscured in the discussion of trade deficits is the role of revenues earned from intellectual property and digital services—particularly given that the levers to fundamentally change the bilateral flows in manufactured goods appear somewhat limited. Although the US had a $419 billion trade deficit in goods with

China in 2018, it registered a $40 billion surplus in services. And the US enjoyed a $51 billion worldwide balance of payments surplus in IP revenue in 2017, according to the International Monetary Fund—nearly double China's offshore earnings from IP.

Both IP and digital services such as cloud storage, content streaming, and e-commerce are sectors in which US companies could gain from better access to Chinese domestic markets, leading to a significant uplift in US exports and thereby contributing to an overall reduction in the trade deficit.

Intellectual Property. Ensuring that foreign companies can make market-based licensing agreements for their IP in China—and secure stronger protection of their patents—is a US objective. IP has been a source of tension, with disputes over licensing and antitrust practices that go to the heart of US"China technology competition.

The US has challenged China's technology-licensing practices through the World Trade Organization, alleging that they are imposing discriminatory obligations on US licensors in China and mandatory ownership of improvements by the Chinese licensee. A WTO panel is adjudicating the dispute.

In parallel, China has openly criticized the structure of the global technology industry, arguing that a small number of foreign companies generate high margins selling end-user devices at high premiums by leveraging their IP to block competition from emerging Chinese challengers through either high royalties or the threat of litigation. Over the past few years, China has been investigating alleged anticompetitive practices by some high-profile foreign technology companies doing business in China.

Cloud Services. Asia-Pacific is the fastest-growing cloud storage market, and China is the largest and fastest-growing market within that region. In its March 2019 National Trade Estimate, the Office of the United States Trade Representative (USTR) lists several digital trade barriers imposed by China that inhibit access by foreign cloud providers. China's Cybersecurity Law and a range of related implementing regulations, for example, restrict cross-border data flows and impose data localization requirements. China prohibits foreign companies from directly providing cloud-computing services to customers in China. Instead, it requires foreign providers "to partner with a Chinese company and to turn over to that partner their technology, know-how, and brands in order to enter the market," the USTR report states.

Although China continued to reduce formal restrictions on foreign investors in 2018 by removing foreign-equity caps and joint-venture requirements, the USTR alleges that the Chinese government still restricts access to the cloud market through administrative licensing and approval processes.

Streaming and E-commerce. China is the world's second-largest market for subscription video-streaming services, with $3.7 billion in revenue in 2018, according to Digital TV Research, and is set to grow rapidly. China already leads the world in e-commerce revenues. A growing number of Chinese internet-based companies, meanwhile, have attained the expertise and technological capabilities to successfully compete globally.

Access to China's domestic market in many of these sectors may be restricted, however. The USTR claims that China's "extensive blocking of legitimate websites" is "affecting billions of dollars in potential US business." China blocks 10 of the top 30 global sites and more than 10,000 domains, according to the USTR. Progress in achieving a more open trade environment for IP and digital services such as cloud storage, streaming, and e-commerce could contribute to a better balance of US"China trade. However, these levers alone will not make a big impact on related US objectives, such as bringing manufacturing jobs back to the US or minimizing perceived cybersecurity threats.

POTENTIAL SCENARIOS FOR A NEW TECH TRADE PARADIGM

"Fixing" the bilateral tech trade deficit and satisfactorily addressing mutual concerns on complex issues such as IP, market access, and cybersecurity will not be easy. Multiple outcomes, all of which encompass significant change and can affect sectors positively or negatively, are possible.

The new US"China technology trade relationship can be framed in terms of potential changes along two key dimensions: the scale and scope of bilateral tariff measures and the dynamics of technology competition, which may involve industrial policy or nontariff barriers, such as export and import restrictions in the name of national security. Tariff measures can range from narrow and targeted to broad and sweeping. The emerging bilateral relationship regarding technological competition can range from open trade to managed trade, under which specific technologies and even companies are singled out for trade restrictions. Based on this framework, we see four potential scenarios for the US"China tech trade relationship.

- True Reciprocal Access. Under this scenario, the US and China resolve key differences that inhibit technology trade. For example, they may refocus the measurement of the trade deficit in goods on value added, agree to improved terms on licensing US intellectual property to China, and open up most of their respective digital-services markets. They may also allow cross-border technology mergers and acquisitions. The US rolls back broad-based tariffs but may continue to impose tariffs or other barriers to market access on a narrow and targeted basis in response to industry petitions regarding dumping or subsidization, or in response to alleged IP, privacy, or security infringements. As a result, the US trade deficit is reduced moderately in the short run by a rise in US services. In the long run, the deficit could be reduced by market-based supply chain shifts, as Chinese costs rise and more electronics manufacturing companies invest in capacity in the US or in countries such as Vietnam, India, Brazil, and Mexico.
- Managed Trade. The two countries agree to a framework to manage trade and technology competition. Broad-based tariffs are rolled back in the context of a meaningful bilateral

trade agreement for tech and other sectors. The US places or maintains selective tariffs, export and investment restrictions, or market access barriers on only a few sectors and products that it considers strategically important or highly important to national security, such as supercomputers, 5G, and advanced semiconductors. At the same time, China maintains nontariff restrictions in order to build technological competitiveness. The bilateral trade gap changes little over the short to medium term under this scenario.

- Walls and Drawbridges. The US and China fail to resolve bilateral structural issues, leaving each side's policies regarding IP, investment, licensing, and other nontariff matters essentially unchanged. In the absence of agreed-upon solutions to these issues, the US deepens and selectively broadens its tariffs on Chinese imports, although these may stop short of hitting the most popular consumer electronics products, such as smartphones, laptops, and TVs. The bilateral trade balance could change moderately. Uncertainty remains high for technology companies, with no clearly established framework to manage friction in areas such as IP, cross-border M&A, antitrust, and cybersecurity. Instead, each individual dispute becomes a bargaining chip in the geopolitical conflict between the two countries.
- Technology Cold War. The US and China further escalate nontariff restrictions, including US bans on specific high-tech exports to China. China restricts exports of essential materials such as rare earths, takes antitrust measures against US tech companies, and accelerates indigenous technology development efforts. In response to concerns over IP protection and national security, the US broadens its tariffs or market access restrictions to cover all valuable electronics—including consumer electronics. In an extreme but not implausible case, cyberattacks—such as the one in October 2016 in which hackers gained access to websites by inserting malware into connected devices such as baby

monitors, web cameras, and routers—could cause every single networked electronic device imported from certain countries to be considered a potential threat and therefore banned. This would effectively halt the bulk of bilateral technology trade and prompt a massive redefinition of global technology supply chains. It would also lead to fragmentation of global technology standards in areas such as telecommunications, computing architectures, and operating systems.

The impact of each of these scenarios would vary widely by company, depending on its products, service offerings, supply chains, and manufacturing footprint. In fact, a company could have businesses, products, and services susceptible to different scenarios. For a company that sells semiconductors as well as electronic devices and digital services, for instance, the new trade relationship would affect different parts of its business in different ways.

BUILDING RESILIENCE WITHIN A NEW TRADE PARADIGM

As negotiations continue to start, stall, and stop—and as various enforcement mechanisms are engaged—each of the scenarios described above could materialize, and potentially even coexist, depending on the specific technology or company. Rather than try to predict which scenario is most likely, we recommend that companies analyze their business and products against each scenario. They can then take proactive steps to minimize risk, make their organizations more resilient to change, and gain competitive advantage.

In our experience with clients across sectors, we have found that companies that take the following actions can best maximize their opportunities in the new global environment, however it plays out.

Analyze exposure and develop playbooks. Building a fact base can help companies understand how their value chains are exposed to each scenario in terms of revenues, costs, and asset allocation. This will enable them to estimate the impact of potential tariffs and technology restrictions on their businesses.

Companies should then create a playbook of actions to take under each scenario. This will help them adapt quickly when actual change comes. For example, a company might identify alternative production sites and suppliers in other nations that can meet its needs and assess how those alternatives would affect production costs, quality, and speed to market.

Companies that are truly well prepared will have assessed the exposure not only of each of their own product lines, but also that of key competitors in each segment. Identifying relative differences in impact may reveal new competitive advantages and disadvantages.

Consider this powerful example of forward-looking planning amidst the current US"China trade friction. When the US first indicated that it would raise tariffs on products imported from China, the senior leadership of a durable-goods company began reviewing the implications of potential scenarios three months before the initial round of tariffs were to be levied. By the time the US raised tariffs from 10% to 25% on a broad set of imports, the company had already begun more than two dozen cross-functional mitigation projects with oversight from top management. Meanwhile, many of its competitors waited for the US and China to make a deal that would bring back the previous status quo. As a result, while its competitors were just beginning the process of analysis and adaptation, the company had gained a 9- to 12-month advantage.

Be proactive to build resilience. We recommend that companies identify a series of no-regrets moves, such as creating sourcing options by prequalifying new suppliers. They can also consider deploying automation and other advanced technologies that could change the economics of their supply chain. And beginning the shift toward more flexible, regional approaches to global manufacturing supply chains, a move BCG has long advocated on its own merits, will bring additional resilience in the current trade dynamic. Some major Chinese consumer electronics manufacturers, for example, have been expanding their manufacturing networks by adding capacity in nations such as India, Vietnam, Brazil, and Mexico to serve growing consumer demand in Southeast Asia and Latin America.

The apparel industry, which by the nature of its products requires highly flexible and responsive supply chains and is often subject to changes in trade rules and labor rates, is a good example of how to proactively build resilience. Some leading apparel players have designed their global industrial models around a series of trade agreements linking production facilities in countries with acceptable costs to markets for finished goods in North America and the European Union. This has allowed them to modulate production by product and market type in the event that any of these trade agreements is disrupted.

In addition, ensuring end-to-end transparency and integrity of the supply chain—such as through the Internet of Things or blockchain, which enables goods and digital products to be traced in real time—is likely to be increasingly critical to compliance with heightened scrutiny and could potentially serve as a competitive differentiator in a world with high cybersecurity concerns.

Shape policy. Finally, while there is still time, company leaders should consider seeking to influence the shaping of detailed policy to create relative advantage. Of course, determining which policies to advocate requires careful analysis. They might be broad and structural, or perhaps more technology specific. Companies should determine whether it is most effective to work in tandem with other companies through industry associations or to voice concerns specific to the company on their own. Different approaches will be required for authorities in China and the US, given the different political systems.

During the recent NAFTA renegotiations, several companies in the automotive sector—makers of cars, buses, and recreational vehicles, as well as tier one suppliers—conducted deep evaluations, such as those mentioned above, of how their supply chains would be affected by the proposed new rules. They also assessed how those rules would impact competitors, given their different product portfolios and global supply chain structures. These companies were able to identify where the proposed rules would have an asymmetrical impact on them compared with the rest of the sector and, potentially, create a relative competitive advantage. These companies then translated this information into robust, detailed materials for their discussions with policymakers.

Given the broad underlying geostrategic and technological dynamics, it is clear that US"China tensions surrounding trade in general, and technology trade in particular, will persist for years. This will present risks, to be sure. But change will also open opportunities for companies in both China and the US. For technology companies, we see no advantage in waiting: every day lost is another day of growing risk. A proactive and strategic approach will enable resilient technology companies to navigate through the uncertainty and thrive as the world's most important trade relationship is reset.

Bibliography

Ahmad, Imtiaz: *State and Foreign Policy: India's Role in USA*, New Delhi, Vikas, 1993.

Alam, Aftab : *US Policy Towards South Asia: Special Reference to Indo-Pak Relations*, Raj, Delhi, 1998.

Arend, A.: *International Law and the Use of Force*, London, Routledge, 1993.

Chandra, R.: *Judicial System in Mechanical Warfare*, Lucknow, Print House (India), 1992.

Chitkara, M.G. : *Indo-Pak Relations Challenges Before New Millennium*, APH, Delhi, 2001.

Dan Nabudere: *The Political Economy of Imperialism*, London, 1977.

Deepak, B R : *India and China : 1904-2004 : A Century of Peace and Conflict*, Manak, Delhi, 2005.

Feis, Herbert, *Foreign Aid and Foreign Policy*, NY, 1964.

Hollihan, Thomas A. : *Uncivil Wars, Political Campaigns in a Media Age*, Boston: St. Martins, Delhi, 2001.

Jain, U.C. and Jeevan Nair : *Encyclopaedia of Indian Government and Politics*, 2000.

Janowitz, M.: *The Professional Soldier: A Social and Political Portrait*, N.Y., The Free Press, 1960.

Jha, Prem Shankar : *India, America and China : The Battle Between Soft and Hard Power*, Penguin Books India, Delhi, 2010.

Kelly, John B.: *Britain and the Persian Gulf 1795-1880*, Oxford, Clarendon Press, 1968.

Kripalani, Krishna : *All Men are Brothers*, Navjivan Publishing House, 1937.

Kunju, N. : *Indo-Pak : Nuclear Cold War*, Reliance, Delhi, 2002.

Laquer, Walter: *Terrorism Attack from Computer Hacking*, Oxford: Oxford University Press, 1999.

Leo Tansky, *US and USSR Aid to Developing Countries: A Comparative Study of India, Turkey, and the UAR*, New York, 1967.

Mclean, I.: *Democracy and New Technology*, Cambridge, Polity Press, 1989.

Ottomar, H.: *Distribution of Stock of Money,* Effingham, London, 1892.

Paletz, David L. : *The Media in American Politics,* Addison-Wesley, New York, 2001.

Patnaik, Naveen: *A Second Paradise: Indian Courtly Life, 1590-1947*, Garden City, New Jersey, Doubleday, 1985.

Peter Kunstadter. : *Southeast Asian Tribes, Minorities and Nations.* Princeton: Princeton University Press, 1967.

Qureshi, A. Iqbal : *Islam and the Theory of Interest,* Kitab Bhavan, New Delhi, 1994.

Rhodes, Richard, *The Making of the Atomic Bomb*, New York: Simon and Schuster, 1988.

Rishiraj Singh: *Arms Control : The Politics of Disarmament*, Dominant, Delhi, 2004.

Saksena, N.S.: *India: Towards Anarchy, 1967-1992*, New Delhi, Abhinav, 1993.

Sarvepalli Gopal: *Jawaharlal Nehru: An Anthology,* Delhi, 1980.

Schroeer, Dietrich, *Science, Technology, and the Nuclear Arms Race*, Ontario: John Wiley & Sons, 1984.

Schudson, Michael : *Watergate in American Memory; How We Remember, Forget and Reconstruct the Past,* Basic Books, New York, 1992.

Seligman, E. R. A. : *Currency Inflation and Public Debts,* New York, 1922.

Stephen E. Ambrose and James Alden Barber: *The Military and American Society,* New York, 1972.

Sullivan, Ezra N.: *Bureaucrats and Policy Making*, New York, Holmes & Meier, 1984.

Sunil Sondhi : *International Relations : Search for Security and Development*, South Asian Pub, Delhi, 2007.

Trivedi, P.R. : *Concise Encyclopaedia of India,* Indian Pub., Delhi, 1998.

Whitakar, A. C. : *Foreign Exchange. Appleton,* New York, 1920.

White, J. R.: *Terrorism: An introduction: 2002 update,* Belmont, CA: Wadsworth, 2002.

Yasin, Mohammad : *Indian Politics : Processes, Issues and Trends,* New Delhi, Kanishka, 2004.

Index

❑❑❑